THE SIXTH:
AN ESSAY IN EDUCATION
& DEMOCRACY

THE SIXTH:
AN ESSAY IN EDUCATION
& DEMOCRACY

William Reid
(University of Birmingham)
& Jane Filby
(University of Aston)

The Falmer Press
A member of the Taylor & Francis Group

ISBN 0 905273 29 X

Jacket design by Leonard Williams

Printed and bound by Taylor & Francis (Printers) Ltd, Basingstoke, Hampshire for

The Falmer Press
Falmer House
Barcombe
Lewes BN8 5DL.

CONTENTS

LIST OF FIGURES AND TABLES

Acknowledgments

We are grateful to all those people and institutions who contributed to the writing of this book through their support, encouragement, suggestions, comments and criticisms.

Our initial engagement in the 'sixth form question' as an object of research was made possible by grants from the Schools Council for Curriculum and Examinations, and we were fortunate subsequently to enjoy the financial support of the Social Science Research Council and the Department of Education and Science. Our acknowledgment of their role in helping us to develop our ideas in no way implies that what we have to say in the book represents the policies of these bodies.

We thank all those teachers, heads of schools and colleges and sixth form students who at various times talked to us, answered our questions and allowed us to visit them and join in their activities.

Our historical researches were made easier by the helpful and efficient service provided by the Librarian and staff of the Faculty of Education Library, University of Birmingham. That they could assist us as much as they did is a tribute to their resolve in the face of savage cuts in resources suffered over the last two years.

We benefited from the comments of numerous colleagues who read drafts of the book. Especial thanks are due to Ted Brennan, Maurice Holt, Roy Lowe, Joseph Schwab, Julia Stanley, Philip Taylor, Janek Wankowski and Penelope Weston for their helpful suggestions.

Above all, we are indebted to Ian Westbury of the University of Illinois, Champaign-Urbana who at many points provided critical insights into our work and devoted many hours to helping us wrestle with the problems we encountered in our writing.

Finally, we are grateful to Malcolm Clarkson of the Falmer Press who has been a constant source of encouragement, and Anne Colston of the Management Centre, University of Aston, who has given freely of her time and expertise in preparing our work for publication.

Birmingham,   W.R.

16.4.82   J.F.

1 EDUCATION, DEMOCRACY AND THE SIXTH FORM

> Unless we know the roads not taken by our ancestors we cannot but believe that we walk down the only conceivable path. An engagement with the tradition is the only means of discovering that collective past which is active in our present.
> (Eva T.H. Brann, **Paradoxes of Education in a Republic**)

The scope of this book is wide and the issues it raises complex. This means that not every aspect of its subject matter can be treated in depth - the word 'essay' in the title is used advisedly. However, we would argue that there has been too great a tendency in writing on education to avoid wider issues through fear that their treatment may appear superficial; for to construe the study of education in such a way as to exclude broad themes is to divorce it from fruitful contact with currents of national political, cultural and social development with which the forms and functions of education interact in significant ways. Through understanding the story of the English sixth form we appreciate how the policy decisions to be made today on sixteen to nineteen education have both specific and general importance: specific in respect of what our choice of institutions and curricula implies for the experience of students of that age as members of our society; general in respect of what it also implies for our view of the nature of that society and how we would like it to develop in the future. If these decisions are to be wise ones, we must venture the journey into difficult questions of historical and sociological evolution, however discontent we may at times become with the limits that time and resources put on our investigations. For only in this way can we resist the press for educational decisions affecting the quality of our individual and collective existence to be taken on simplistic criteria, whether related to economically based notions of cost, supply and distribution, or to ideologically based assertions of unexamined dogma and unyielding principle.

The agenda we have set ourselves demands that at the outset we consider three basic questions: what is the sixth form? what is democracy? and what is education? We raise these not as questions to be answered but as ideas which need some preliminary examination before we try to illuminate them further through the subject matter of the book. We have also to consider two related issues; those of class and religion which are central to an understanding of English society and the forms of education which it supports.

The Sixth Form

The sixth form is the institution through which full time academic education was traditionally offered to students in England and Wales in the age range fifteen to nineteen. Today the level of enrolments in this group has risen to the point where the character of the sixth has become diffuse and hard to specify. Prior to that, its forms were relatively stable for a period of roughly seventy years, from the Education Act of 1902 which led to the establishment of state supported secondary schools to the raising of the school leaving age from fifteen to sixteen in 1973. Over that period the sixth form existed only as part of the secondary school, though it also presented many of the characteristics of a self-contained institution. These were inherited from the sixth forms of independent public schools and were developed over a span of fifty or so years from about 1830 to 1880. The public schools of the nineteenth century were boarding schools catering exclusively for boys and they lent qualities to the character of the sixth which it has retained ever since. Over the period of its early development it was an essentially masculine institution, serving a tiny minority of the age group and separated from the rest of the school by status and by curriculum. Status

2

separation arose because sixth formers began to be used as assistants to the school authorities in organizing and disciplining younger pupils. Curriculum separation came about because entry to the sixth was decided on grounds of academic achievement and sixth form teaching was undertaken by head teachers who were often outstanding scholars. Masculinity was emphasized by the disciplinary role of sixth formers, and later by their association with the cult of team games in the public school. By the time that sixth forms became established in state secondary schools, a clear link had grown up between sixth forms, public examinations and entry to universities, though by no means all sixth formers were aiming at higher education.

The early state schools reproduced many of the characteristics of the public schools. Most were single sex and pupils were almost invariably admitted as fee payers as well as through scholarships. The schools were encouraged to set up sixth forms for students wishing to stay to seventeen or eighteen, and especially for those aiming at university education. These students assumed authority over those in the lower forms and pursued specialized courses of scholarly study with senior members of staff. State schools, however, introduced new elements into the conception of sixth forms in that they were day schools and that some of them admitted both boys and girls.

Over the next seventy or so years, sixth forms in state and public schools pursued parallel though slightly differing paths. State sixth forms expanded at a faster rate and by 1950 accounted for more than two thirds of all sixth formers. From this point on, the general growth in enrolments became very rapid and the proportion of seventeen year olds in full time education trebled between 1950 and 1970. They were still, however, a minority group, with only one in five of the age cohort enrolled in sixth form education, and the number of university entrants lagging far behind that (for details of figures, see Statistical Appendix).

The curriculum of the sixth continued to be specialized, but by the 1930s had moved away from the dominantly classical character it had assumed in the nineteenth century public schools, though the final eclipse of Latin and Greek did not arrive until the 1960s. Today the most popular courses are in Science, Mathematics and Humanities (English and History). Social Sciences and Foreign Languages are also widely taught. Practical and aesthetic studies, however, are pursued only by a small minority.

Since the late 1960s the traditional character of the sixth has been eroded both in its curricular and institutional status. The definition of 'sixth former' is now being extended to include those who are not only not aiming at higher education, but not even sharing the curriculum of those who are. Also, full time academic courses for the sixth form age range are being offered through various types of colleges which are totally separated from the lower secondary school and the whole question of the usefulness of the sixth form as a conception is being challenged by pressures to enrol, in some form of education or training, those who would normally leave school at sixteen to take up employment but are no longer able to find jobs.

Thus, the institution with which we are dealing is one which initially went through a phase in which it grew towards stability and uniformity, which then achieved a fixed and durable character, and which finally experienced, and continues to experience, conditions of uncertainty as some of its key assumptions become increasingly out of tune with contemporary social and educational developments.

Democracy

The notion of democracy has, for two centuries, played a central role in the development of English political thought and structures, yet it remains an elusive conception, adaptable to many circumstances and purposes. Basically, it denotes a form of government in which rule is exercised by the **demos** or people, but this does not take us very far. The first difficulty is to define the **demos**. Even the United States, in many ways the most democratic of countries, was slow to extend the franchise to slaves and to native Americans. And when did England become a democracy? After the Reform Bill of 1832? Or after the later nineteenth century reform bills? Or only after all women were given the vote in 1928? But, beyond this, arises the question of how rule is to be made effective. It is often assumed that democracy exists when the people (however defined) are given the opportunity to choose, by a free vote, who the rulers shall be. This was the view taken by political theorists such as Edmund Burke who held that, while it was necessary that leaders should be subject to election, they were under no obligation to carry out the wishes of the electorate. Stronger definitions of democracy, however, demand that the people play a more active part in deliberating on and making political decisions, and deny that democratic principles have been satisfied when votes have been cast. Such conceptions of democracy extend it beyond a matter of how government is to be organized and into questions of the organization of society itself and of the relations between people within it. The democratic ideal comes to affect not only our view of what society as a whole should be like, but also how individuals should think about and conduct themselves. James Bryce in his **American Commonwealth** captured this sense of democratic life, as opposed to democratic forms, when he said that the American citizen 'has a sense of ownership in the government, and therewith a kind of independence of manner as well as of mind very different from the dimissness of the humbler classes of the Old World.'[1]

Structural and social conceptions of democracy imply different roles for education. If democracy is thought of mainly as a matter of how government is organized, with opportunities provided from time to time for views to be expressed and representatives elected, then the function of education, in so far

5

as it relates to democracy, is likely to be seen as, on one hand, equipping citizens with the competencies needed to perform a civic duty, and, on the other, with persuading them that the degree of 'demissness' required of them on other occasions is justified through the priority of some greater good. But if democracy is understood as requiring that the people be good and wise and vigilant to see that their ownership of government is not abused by the leaders, then there is a need to ensure that education systems are truly 'educational' in that they aim to engender capacities rather than teach competencies, and that they encourage in all people feelings of full membership in the commonwealth rather than show on what grounds membership is to be confined or limited.

A classic statement of this view of the nature and purpose of education and educational systems was already to be found in the preamble to Jefferson's **Bill for the More General Diffusion of Knowledge** of 1779:

> Whereas it appeareth that however certain forms of government are better calculated than others to protect individuals in the free exercise of their natural rights, and are at the same time themselves better guarded against degeneracy, yet experience hath shown, that even under the best forms, those entrusted with power have, in time, and by slow operations, perverted it into tyranny; and it is believed that the most effectual means of preventing this would be, to illuminate, as far as practicable, the minds of the people at large, and more especially to give them knowledge of those facts, which history exhibiteth, that, possessed thereby of the experience of other ages and countries, they may be enabled to know ambition under all its shapes, and prompt to exert their natural powers to defeat its purposes.[2]

6

Jefferson's conception of education was, however, elitist. He did not believe that everyone could be initiated into a full knowledge and experience of other ages and other countries. That extension was made by American liberal educators of a later age who saw practical evidence of the power of school systems to enrol students in post-compulsory education. R.M. Hutchins could declare, in 1954, 'Democracy requires liberal education for all. I believe this proposition to be true.'[3]

English understanding of the relation of democracy to education has, however, pursued a different path. In the English tradition social interpretations of democracy have tended to be separated from political ones. Democratically inspired policies have been concerned to promote an egalitarian distribution of goods arising from economic and cultural activity, rather than to emphasize the role of the individual as an active contributor to the common good, and have, in typically English fashion, focused more sharply on questions of social status than political status. At least, this has been true in recent times, but a study of the origins of sixth forms shows that, in their formative period in the public schools of the nineteenth century, they were very much linked with political understandings of the development of a democratic spirit, both as it affected the state and the individual. It is also the case that the story of how this initially democratic impulse became diverted into other channels provides an important key to the broader question of the past and current relationship between democracy and education in England. It is this issue of the relationship between democracy and education as expressed and exemplified in the development of sixth forms and of the idea of a sixth form which provides the central theme of this book.

We consider that the major function of an educational system in a country which aspires to democratic ideals is to provide a means of incorporating citizens into a public actively concerned for the furtherance of the common interest. Educational systems should also perform other necessary functions, such as conveying essential knowledge, or regulating the passage of students from schooling to employment but, where goals conflict, it is the mark of a system with an overriding concern for democratic ideals that the goal of incorporation takes precedence. We also assume that the ability of the educational system to pursue the goal of incorporation is largely determined by its ability to reflect, within its own structures, important educational roles and categories which are valued in society generally. The system must be a prime mover in the creation of such roles and categories, but if they are to become the marks of successful organizations within a system they must enter into general currency and capture the support of the public at large, or some major and significant section of that public. In terms of the realization of democratic ideals it is, of course, critical that such categories be as widely shared and supported as possible.

Education

Notions of what education is are both inspired and conditioned by conceptions of democracy. For some, education is to be construed as something that helps to make democracy work; for others it is something that helps create democratic forms and values by virtue of being itself a democratic institution. The former view takes education to be a means for the maintenance of a democratic polity, while the latter takes it to function as end as well as means (if the distinction has to be made) in relation to a democratic way of life. Where education tends to be thought of as a means to democratic ends, which we argue is the case in England, it is supposed that its job is, on the one hand to supply the necessary skills and knowledge to create and expand the social surplus and, on the other, to ensure that this surplus is equitably distributed. The trouble with this conception of the function of education systems, which, at the sixteen to nineteen level, is at present being heavily promoted through advocacy of universal 'job and life skills' training, is that there is no satisfactory historical evidence that educational curricula and enrolments have ever been significantly in step with economic growth or with changes in the occupational structure. Fritz Ringer, after a searching survey of the development of national systems of education in England, France and Germany and the United States, concludes: 'social conventions have at least as much to do with the demand for education as any supposedly objective requirements of the economy'.[4] His verdict is one that is shared by many who have seriously examined the question of the connection between education systems and the delivery of 'useful' skills. Robert Dreeben, for example, prefaces his analysis of stability and change in patterns of American schooling by declaring: 'To discover that what one has known all along to be true is at best partially true (or possibly not true at all) is a most unsettling experience; but I have had that experience examining the well-known proposition that schooling becomes more prevalent as the economy and occupational structure of a society become more industrialized.'[5] The idea that education does, or conceivably could stand in a planned relationship to the transmission of specific competencies, the social distribution of which is highly correlated to the activity of the system is almost certainly a myth.[6] There is equally little evidence that education systems can or do function to modify social class differences or level up career opportunities, and a good deal of research and analysis suggesting that, if anything, they tend to reinforce existing inequalities.[7] Much as one may regret the inadequacy of studies of these matters which measure inputs and outputs and neglect the intervening variable of curriculum, or deplore the blinkered dogma underlying some historical and sociological analyses, the fact remains that the weight of evidence is against the efficacy of education systems as engines of social democracy in ways in which this has conventionally been understood.

None of this, however should lead us to suppose that education systems do not have a function, that their function is peripheral, or that it can have no connection with democratic aspirations. Systems which attract vast investment, not only of money and resources, but also of personal commitment, ideological capital and political energy are not without significance for society; the question is, what is the nature of that significance? To assume that the significance is generated from within, by structures that educators determine and by strategies that move from organizational means to societal ends, may be to turn things on their head. Dreeben's failure to find the expected connections between schooling and the economy led him to look at others and to 'consider changes in the structure of school organization, the growth of citizenship, and the social conditions under which individuals learn the principle of universalism'[8] as possibly illuminating the problem of change in education systems. John Meyer has pressed this kind of analysis further and formalized it somewhat. Meyer considers that the most significant educational categories are not, in fact, those internal to organizations that provide schooling (classes, courses, etc.), but those which are understood and supported by external publics and to a greater or lesser degree **reflected** in the work and structure of particular schools and colleges (grade levels, disciplines, etc.). These he refers to as 'institutional categories', contrasting 'institution', in the sense of socially established custom or practice, with 'organization', thought of as a structure designed and set up for a particular purpose. He conveys the essence of his idea through his use of the words **'exo**skeletal' and **'exo**skeleton' to emphasise the notion that what gives shape and meaning to educational enterprises are things that come from society at large and therefore stand on the **outside** of the system. This is in sharp contrast to the more generally adopted way of conceptualizing education for purposes of research and analysis which assumes, explicitly or more often implicitly, that shape is given by what is **inside** the system; that the work of schooling, like the body of a mammal, is shaped by an **endo**skeleton.[9]

10

The sixth form is clearly an institutional category in Meyer's terminology. Its realization in particular contexts is varied and in some instances far removed from what the ideal account of the category would seem to demand. But it is valued and it is understood in the sense of being linked with current and future statuses and activities. Changes in the nature of sixth forms are, on this view, either attempts on the part of the system to modify the institutional category, as popularly comprehended, or attempts on the part of a public for which the category has meaning to have its realization through the system moved closer to a conception of its current or desired character. Our study of the development of sixth forms gives us the chance to raise questions which are not addressed by Meyer: how do institutional categories come into being, and how are they subsequently modified? How are institutional categories related to social and political developments in the wider community, and, especially, what are the implications of the nature and development of particular categories, such as the sixth form, for the growth of democratic forms and values?

We do not intend our work to provide a test, or detailed application of Meyer's idea. We draw attention to it, however, as affording a perspective which has had an important influence on how we have organized our account, and as providing an explanatory framework which sometimes visibly surfaces in our treatment of particular events or arguments.

Class and Religion

The history of the sixth form is part of the history of the development of educational forms and structures which proceeded through most of the nineteenth century with minimal state intervention. In this respect, England was unusual. Most continental countries had set up centrally administered state education systems well before the end of the century; by 1860, every state which then formed part of the United States had a superintendent of schools. Alone among the leading industrialized nations, England preferred the provision of education to be in the hands of extra-governmental agencies. This was largely because, while England had an established church, the non-conformist churches were powerful and popular enough to present a serious challenge to its supremacy. In fact, when a census of church attenders was taken in 1851, non-conformists outnumbered anglicans - but only just (forty-nine per cent of total compared to forty-seven per cent).[10] Herein lay the peculiarity of England's situation. The official church was not so strongly entrenched as to be able to claim that it could rightfully accept any advantage that state intervention in education might yield for it; but neither did the non-conformist churches outweigh it sufficiently for them to be able to insist on a form of state intervention which withheld any advantage from it. The stalemate could be only eroded, not resolved by an agreed formula - at least until the Education Act of 1902, and that provoked civil disobedience in non-conformist strongholds and was in real danger of being repealed by the incoming liberal government of 1905. Therefore, the provision of education throughout the nineteenth century was guided by sectional rather than national interest and principally the great interests which the society of the time recognized, and through which it recognized itself - those of religious and social class affiliation.

The public schools which nurtured the sixth form were, at the beginning of the century, an aristocratic institution. Later they came to reflect the conjoint interest of those elements of upper and middle classes which sought a common identity by defining themselves as 'gentlemen'. The emergence of such a group was made necessary by the processes of centralization of government and administration which accompanied Britain's economic transformation. This both created a need for a supply of suitably prepared men to take up positions in the central bureaucratic structures which were set up to assume new responsibilities or take them over from local areas, and also demanded that such men see their role in national and cosmopolitan, rather than sectional or parochial terms. Where other countries achieved this through the development of state supported education systems, England relied on the reform and extension of the existing privately endowed secondary schools. Commissions were appointed by the central government to assist this process. The Clarendon Commission, set up in 1861, investigated and made recommendations on the curriculum and organization of the major independent boarding schools: Winchester, Eton, Westminster, Charterhouse, Harrow, Rugby, Shrewsbury, St. Paul's and Merchant Taylors'. The brief of the Taunton Commission of 1864 was to review all other endowed and proprietary secondary schools. Later in the century, the Bryce Commission carried out a futher enquiry into the progress of secondary and technical education which led, eventually, to the creation of a state supported secondary sector through the Education Act of 1902.

Since the public school had aristocratic origins, its natural religious ties were with the Anglican Church. But the extension of the category to include middle class interests involved both a degree of ecumenicism on the part of the established schools and a willingness on the part of non-conformist and catholic schools to copy forms which might have seemed alien to their own traditions.[11] With the great expansion of public school enrolments around the middle of the century, the religious character of the schools changed. Though still much emphasized, the practice of religion became a formalized part of the institutional apparatus designed to produce the gentleman, rather than the core of a moral crusade it had been for the early reformers of the 1830s and 40s. These forms of religious observance and commitment, which eschewed dogma and emphasized the stoic virtues of courage, patriotism and endurance were able to live on in state secondary schools when these finally arrived on the scene after the Education Act of 1902. In alliance with a narrowly academic curriculum a stress on discipline and character formation and the encouragement of manly pursuits such as team games, they ensured that the new sixth forms would continue to embody and reflect the middle class interest which had given rise to their predecessors in the public schools. The breaking of the religious deadlock in national policy-making on education had come too late for radically new directions to be set to rapidly move its forms away from sectional ties. And though the institutional category of 'sixth form' was to be greatly extended from its original conception, the process of secularization and democratization was long drawn out. The controversies of the present day illustrate that it is still far from complete.

NOTES

1   Bryce, James, **The American Commonwealth,** New York, Macmillan and Co., 1910, Vol.2, p.369 (Original edition, 1894).

2   Quoted in Brann, Eva T.H., **Paradoxes of Education in a Republic,** Chicago, University of Chicago Press, 1979, p.40. Jefferson's Bill failed to pass the Virginia Legislature.

3   Hutchins, R.M., **Great Books: The Foundation of a Liberal Education,** New York, Simon and Schuster, 1954, p.7.

4   Ringer, Fritz K., **Education and Society in Modern Europe,** Bloomington, Indiana University Press, 1979, p.261. The book focuses on European systems and the USA is brought in for comparative purposes.

5   Dreeben, Robert, 'American schooling: Patterns and processes of stability and change', in Barber, Bernard and Inkeles, Alex (Eds), **Stability and Social Change,** Boston, Little Brown, 1971, p.83.

6   This is not to say that some **parts** of educational systems may not be well correlated with occupations. And it must be stressed that we are concerned here with systems performing an educational rather than a training function.

7   The most influential source here, both in England and the USA is Jencks, Christopher et al., **Inequality,** New York, Basic Books, 1972. Recent works emphasizing the function of education systems in reproducing societal inequalities are too numerous to cite. They include Bowles, S. and Gintis, H., **Schooling in Capitalist America,** London, Routledge, 1976 and Bourdieu, P. and Passeron, J-C., **La Reproduction: Elements pour une Theorie du Systeme d'Enseignement,** Paris, Editions du Minuit, 1970.

8   Dreeben, 1971 loc. cit.

9   See Meyer, John W., 'The structure of educational organizations', in Meyer, Marshall W. and Associates (Eds) **Environments and Organizations,** San Francisco, Jossey-Bass, 1978 and 'Levels of the educational system and schooling effects' in Bidwell, C.E. and Windham, D.M. (Eds), **The Analysis of Educational Productivity,** Vol.2, **Issues in Macroanalysis,** Cambridge Mass., Ballinger, 1980.

10 Best, Geoffrey, **Mid-Victorian Britain, 1851-70,** Fontana/Collins, 1979, p.199.

11 See, for example, Seaborne on the architecture of Mill Hill or Mangan on attitudes to team games at Stonyhurst (Seaborne, Malcolm, **The English School: Its Architecture and Organization** 1370-1870, London, Routledge, 1971, pp.165-6. Mangan, J.A., **Athleticism in the Victorian and Edwardian Public School,** Cambridge, Cambridge University Press, 1981, pp.65-6).

FIGURE 1

THE RUGBY SCHOOL SIXTH FORM IN 1861

UPPER SCHOOL SIXTH FORM, 42 BOYS

No	Age* Yrs Mths	Date of Entrance into Form or Division	Date of Admission into School	Form or Division of Form in which placed on his Admission into School.	Length of any protracted Absence since Admission into School	Set in which the Boy is placed in	
						Mathematics	Modern Languages or Natural Philosophy +
1	18 1	Feb 1860	Feb 1858	Upper Middle, 1st division	- - -	3	
2	17 5	Aug 1860	Aug 1858	5th Form - -	- - -	1	
‡3 F	18 0	Feb 1860	Aug 1857	Upper Middle, 1st division	- - -	1	Nat Phil
4	18 8	"	Feb 1858	5th Form, 2nd division -	- - -	1	"
5	18 1	"	Feb 1857	" " -	- - -	3	1
6	18 7	"	Oct 1856	Lower Middle, 1st division	- - -	2	1
7	18 4	Aug 1860	Feb 1857	§Lower Middle, 2nd division	Absent from Oct 1860 to April 1861	3	Nat Phil
8	18 1	"	Sep 1859	5th Form - -	- - -	4	2
9 F	17 11	Oct 1860	Feb 1860	" - -	- - -	2	1
10	17 10	Aug 1860	Sep 1859	" - -	- - -	3	1
11	16 11	Feb 1861	Feb 1856	Upper Remove - -	Absent from Aug 1857 to Feb 1859	4	1
12	16 6	Aug 1861	Oct 1858	Upper Middle, 1st division	- - -	1	1
13	17 2	Feb 1861	Aug 1858	5th Form, 2nd division -		4	2
14	17 5	Aug 1860	"	" "		2	1
15	18 11	"	Feb 1858	Upper Middle, 1st division	- - -	2	2
16 F	18 0	"	Sep 1859	5th Form - -	- - -	1	1
17	18 4	"	Aug 1857	Lower Middle, 2nd division	- - -	1	1
18	17 4	Oct 1860	Aug 1858	5th Form, 2nd division -	- - -	3	1
19	18 8	"	Feb 1857	Lower Middle, 2nd division	- - -	4	1
20	18 0	"	Oct 1857	Lower Middle, 1st division	- - -	2	2
21 F	18 1	"	Aug 1856	Lower Middle, 2nd division	- - -	3	1
22 F	18 5	"	Feb 1856	Upper Remove - -	- - -	3	2
23	16 9	Aug 1861	Oct 1858	Lower Middle, 1st division	- - -	1	Nat Phil
24	18 2	Feb 1861	Feb 1858	Lower Middle, 2nd division	- - -	3	"
25	16 10	"	Feb 1859	Upper Middle, 2nd division	- - -	3	1
26 F	16 8	Aug 1861	Aug 1858	5th Form, 2nd division -	- - -	1	Nat Phil
27	18 5	Feb 1861	"	Upper Middle, 2nd division	- - -	3	1
28	18 1	"	"	5th Form, 2nd division -	- - -	2	2
29	17 9	Aug 1861	Feb 1859	Upper Middle, 1st division	- - -	2	Nat Phil
30	18 3	"	Feb 1857	Upper Remove - -	- - -	4	"
31	17 3	Oct 1861	Aug 1858	Upper Middle, 2nd division	- - -	2	2
32	17 9	Aug 1861	Feb 1858	Upper Middle, 1st division	- - -	4	2
33	17 2	"	Oct 1858	Upper Middle, 2nd division	- - -	3	2
34	16 7	Oct 1861	Apr 1860	5th Form - -	- - -	2	2
35	18 1	"	Aug 1857	Lower Middle, 2nd division	- - -	4	2
36 F	16 3	"	Feb 1859	Upper Middle, 2nd division	- - -	2	2
37	16 6	"	Sep 1859	5th Form, 2nd division -	- - -	4	2
38	18 6	"	Oct 1857	Lower Middle, 2nd division	- - -	4	Nat Phil
39	17 3	"	Feb 1858	Upper Middle, 1st division	- - -	4	2
40	16 10	"	Sep 1858	Upper Middle, 2nd division	- - -	4	2
41	17 3	"	Aug 1853	3rd Form (lowest at that time)	- - -	4	2
42	19 4	"	Aug 1856	Upper Remove - -	- - -	2	2

* The age, in every case, is given to December 1861.

+ Wherever Nat Phil is put, it indicates that the boy learns Natural Philosophy; where a number, it indicates that the boy learns modern languages, and that he is placed in the set denoted by the number.

‡ The letter F denotes that the boy is a Foundationer.

§ In these tables, Lower Middle First Division corresponds to what is now called Upper Middle Third Division; and Lower Middle Second Division to what is now called Lower Middle. The names of these forms are often changed.

(Source: Report of the Clarendon Commission)

2 ORIGINS OF AN EDUCATIONAL IDEAL

The sixth form is a difficult conception for strangers to the English educational scene to grasp. On the face of things, it refers simply to a level of schooling which takes its place within a numerical sequence, just as 'sixth grade' does in the American high school. But the sixth represents much more: it has a character, a status, a flavour which mark it off as a self-contained category of educational experience, and this in spite of the fact that, until recently, it has always formed part of a larger organization - a secondary school overlapping or sequential to elementary provision. It is a 'school within a school'.

How was such an a 'school within a school' able to come into being? As we have pointed out, its origins date from a time when the institutional categories of education evolved in response to the needs of particular publics. We therefore have to ask what those needs were and how the sixth form responded to them. But first it is necessary to examine the broader category within which the sixth form developed - the English public school. Though the term 'public school', denoting a school open to fee payers and not restricted in its admission of pupils by the conditions of an endowment, was current in earlier days, it was not until the late eighteenth century that it came to have the sense of an institutional category reflected in the large boarding schools such as Eton, Winchester and Harrow which served an essentially aristocratic clientele.[1] The evolution of sixth forms as a distinctive category within such schools was bound up with the transformation of the public school itself, from the 1830s onwards, into an institution which served the needs both of the traditional clientele for an alliance with the rising middle class, and of a new clientele for a relatively inexpensive, but at the same time publicly recognized way of marking the entry of their family, or some members of it, into 'gentry' status.

This development was related to specific social, political

and economic changes in English society, the industrial revolution, coupled with the growth of centralized administrative structures, created complexities of government which the ruling landed aristocracy were equipped neither in numbers nor by inclination to handle. Simultaneously, the examples of the French and American revolutions heralded political pressures for moves towards greater democracy in the forms of government. And improvements in transport and communications led to a greater emphasis on the national rather than the local scene as a focus of action and ambition. The need was for an extended ruling and administrative class with a cosmopolitan rather than a local outlook, and the reformed public schools, together with new foundations patterned upon them, offered a way of defining and legitimating such a class. They provided an evolutionary means of bringing about social change which was congenial to the upper echelons of a nation which had, from the late seventeenth century chosen the path of developing a 'consensual elite' rather than allowing the prerogatives of government influence to be a matter of conflict between contending and ideologically opposed groups.[2]

But in order to fulfil this function, they had to rid themselves of certain characteristics which were acceptable to a traditional aristocracy but unattractive to the aspiring middle classes who, lacking the 'barbarian' confidence of the hereditary rulers, held a conception of education and educational institutions that was at once more cautious and more directive.[3] The development of the schools depended especially on ridding themselves of the reputation for anarchy and violence which had dogged them in the late eighteenth and early nineteenth centuries.[4] Families with an aristocratic adherence to hallowed custom and contempt for ease and comfort might be content to send their children to schools where flogging and bullying were prevalent, but those who had worked hard to achieve prosperity through their application to commerce and trade were more likely to demand a modicum of civilized conduct in the educational establishments they supported. The schools' solution was, in part, to co-opt senior pupils into control of younger ones by exchanging privilege for reponsibility. Whereas previously the divide had been between masters and boys, now a hierarchy was set up, each level of which drew its authority and concessions from the one above, so that each was meshed in a web of obligations and benefits and could be constrained to act, if with some harshness, within a framework of custom which was generally recognized and whose limits were known. The evolution of a 'non-commissioned officer' class of senior pupils was one of the processes which gave rise to the 'sixth form' tradition. The creation of this special class was a contribution both to the popularity and the stability of the schools.

The principal architect of this innovation was Thomas Arnold who became Headmaster of Rugby School in 1828. Arnold did not invent the sixth form, neither was his sixth the first to exercise strong authority over the lower school.[5] But he was the first to connect the authority of the sixth with the reform of the school that was needed to make it a fit instrument for the leavening of the old aristocracy, and also to identify the power of the sixth with the capacity of the school to be a moral and intellectual force in the nation. Stanley, his biographer, explains:

> . . . he determined to use, and to improve to the
> utmost, the existing machinery of the Sixth Form,
> and of fagging; understanding, by the Sixth Form,
> the thirty boys who composed the highest class -
> 'those who having risen to the highest form in the
> school, will probably be at once the oldest and
> the strongest, and the cleverest; and if the school
> be well ordered, the most respectable in
> application and general character': and by fagging,
> 'the power given by the supreme authorities of the
> school to the Sixth Form, to be exercised by them
> over the lower boys, for the sake of securing a

> regular government amongst the boys themselves,
> and avoiding the evils of anarchy . . .'
>
> The power . . . of personal chastisement vested in
> the Praeposters over those who resisted their
> authority, he firmly maintained as essential to the
> general support of the good order of the
> place . . .
>
> But the importance which he attached to it arose
> from his regarding it not only as an efficient
> engine of discipline, but as the chief means of
> creating a respect for moral and intellectual
> excellence, and of diffusing his own influence
> through the mass of the school.[6]

The aim of this policy, as Newsome puts it, was to put an end to 'the war between autocracy and republicanism' - meaning the autocracy of masters and the republicanism of boys.[7]

However, the Arnoldian reforms were not intended to put an end to freedom and individuality. The suppression of anarchy did not imply the imposition of detailed control. It was only later that the public schools began to regulate minutely the life of the schoolboy through fully integrated boarding houses, compulsory games, uniforms and the keeping of bounds. And though he strove, through placing authority in the hands of the sixth and through the expulsion of offenders ('the first, second, and third duty of a schoolmaster is to get rid of unpromising subjects' [8]), to keep the atmosphere of the school morally wholesome, Arnold did not believe, as some later heads did, that the school was a dependable and predictable instrument for the development of 'character'. The sixth itself might have character because it was a tried, tested and selected group. But, for the majority of boys, the school, like the great world outside, was a place of trial where some would summon up the moral fibre to succeed while others would be found wanting. The schools of the 1830s, 40s and 50s afforded not only **'noble** histories . . . of honour and success' but also **'awful**

20

histories . . . of hopes blighted and habits learned, of wasted talents and ruined lives'[9]. And the word 'awful' was intended to be understood in its root sense as 'worthy of (religious) awe'. The sins of adolescent boys (even sinful thoughts) were not negligible in the sight of God. But boys should not be protected from the temptation to sin: 'the innocence of mere ignorance is a poor thing . . . the true preparation for life is not to have been ignorant of evil, but to have known it and avoided it'.[10]

It was not long, however, before this rather fatalistic view of school life began to give way to one which built on the more positive aspects of the idea of a sixth form. As a function of the sixth, mere repression of anarchy was increasingly subordinated to leadership and the setting of examples, and the idea grew that it could become an instrument for the cultivation of desirable traits of character in younger boys. As Butler, headmaster of Harrow put it in his evidence to the Clarendon Commission in 1864:

> . . . the knowledge on the part of the school at large that a certain portion of their own body, of which they hope some day to become themselves members, is charged to maintain right and to put down wrong, must have a most powerful moral influence in forming manly characters[11]

Thus the sixth became associated not just with the idea of the christian gentleman, but with the forces needed to **produce** the christian gentleman and therefore with social, political and military leadership. Within the category of the public school which was identified with membership of the new ruling class, the sixth became identified with the shaping, directing and preserving of that class.

What were the desired attributes which class members were supposed to acquire? Arnold had put the aims of a public school education in the following order: '1st, religious and moral principles; 2ndly, gentlemanly conduct; 3rdly, intellectual ability'.[12] But, whatever order we choose to express them in, the qualities

21

of which the sixth was to be the special guardian had a high degree of mutual interdependence. The 'Sixth form', as an institutional category, has, from its origins, exhibited moral and social, as well as academic and propedeutic aspects. The fact that the public schools were, essentially, boarding schools enhanced the possibilities for the embodiment in them of a conception of educational role with this dual yet unified character: learning was to be pursued because of its association with virtue, and virtue was to be acquired through learning. Connections could be made with monastic and collegiate traditions in which isolation both gave the occasion for study and also meshed it in the daily activities and relationships of a closed community. Participants in such communities are 'role perfomers' in that they act out a particular conception of a valued existence - one which is delimited by a commitment to religious or ideological tenets and by restrictions arising from the forms and structures of a dominant organization. But the role is not just one of 'learner', or 'leader', or 'community member': it is one that has all these facets to it.[13] In the case of the sixth form, they were facets which could be seen as relevant to the incorporation of gentlemen or would-be gentlemen into a nation-wide class linked to the upper level of the cultural, political and social life of the country as well as to the academic world and the professions.

The sixth were initiated into this special role through their close relationship to the headmaster. Arnold's was a mimetic theory of learning. That is, he saw the process of becoming educated as one in which the learner copied the example, that of the master, which was set before him. Sixth forms were usually restricted in size to numbers that could be conveniently taught by one man. The Clarendon Report of 1864 gave the size of the Eton sixth as twenty, Westminster eighteen and Shrewsbury twenty-three, though Winchester mustered forty-one Rugby forty-two and Harrow as many as sixty-two.[14] Such close personal contact ensured on the one hand that individual sixth formers absorbed the gospel of godliness and good learning and on the other that the message spread rapidly among the schools as old pupils themselves became masters and headmasters.[15] In considering the question of the power of heads we should note that, in the Victorian public school, there was a vast gulf between the poorly paid assistant master and the headmaster whose earnings placed him squarely in the gentry class. Bamford calculates Arnold's income as in the region of £4,000 per annum, remarking that this 'put him into a unique class locally, high above the rest of the community, with a style of living superior to everyone else and generally inferior only to that of the aristocracy'.[16] Heads of the major public schools were well connected and could reckon through their church affiliations to have an excellent chance of moving on to a bishopric. Four of them reached the ultimate pinnacle of the See of Canterbury.[17]

The experience of the public school under Arnold's influence was celebrated and made known to a wide audience through an ex-Rugby pupil, Thomas Hughes, in his novel **Tom Brown's Schooldays**, published in 1858. This was sixteen years after Arnold's death and, in reading **Tom Brown**, we have to remember that its author was already projecting a public school image which had moved beyond that of the 1830s the period of Tom's attendance at Rugby. When he arrived there for the first time, he left behind the clannish world of the minor rural aristocracy and his games and expeditions with the boys of the village to be projected into a society imbued with 'large views and glorious humanity'. As the author puts it in his preface when contrasting the old life of the squirearchy with the new: 'We were Berkshire, or Gloucestershire, or Yorkshire boys; and you're young cosmopolites, belonging to all countries and no countries'.[18] But Tom left in a stage-coach. Not until his return to the Vale of the White Horse did he take the train, that final instrument of the transition of the upper classes from locals to cosmopolitans which the author of **Tom Brown's Schooldays** so deplores while at the same time lauding Arnold's Rugby which was the train's closest collaborator in the same process: 'Oh, young England! young England! You who are born into these racing railroad times, when there's a Great Exhibition, or some monster sight, every year; and you can get over a couple of thousand miles of ground for three pound ten, in a five weeks' holiday; why don't you know more of your own birthplaces?'[19]

Tom Brown not only stayed at Rugby to become a sixth former, but took his master's advice to go up to Oxford rather than enter a trade or profession. Not that he was a great scholar but his time at Rugby taught him respect for scholarship, and it came quite naturally to him to converse about Aristophanes, Herodotus and Cervantes while, as captain of the eleven, he watched the innings of the men from Marylebone. The 'grand old classical curriculum'[20] was the only one that public school boys knew at that time. Science at Rugby depended on occasional visits from a peripatetic teacher and, even a quarter of a century later, Thring of Uppingham could refer to studies such as chemistry, music or French as 'the extra subjects', meaning that they were outside the proper curriculum.[21] From a modern standpoint, or even in the view of some thinkers and commentators at the time, the possibilities offered by Latin and Greek might be thought limited and limiting but, like other features of the public school, the curriculum was functional rather than merely arbitrary or accidental. Unlike some of the endowed grammar schools, the public schools would have been free to change the curriculum if they had so wished.[22] But Latin and Greek had advantages: they dealt in knowledge which was not, in fact, arcane but, while appearing to outsiders to be so, provided insiders with material for discourse at a variety of levels (Tom's being a rather common-sense one); they were the means of initiating boys into the 'public school', and hence 'gentleman' role, and suitable for it because what was critical was not the possession of precise

24

knowledge, but familiarity and acquaintance with shared topics and terminology; they communicated the sense of rootedness in past culture which seems necessary to all elites; they provided boundless opportunities for the presentation of issues related to morals and character without risking the alienation of students through personal involvement or through the imposition of dogma. Finally, in the minds of educated people, they were intimately connected with established religion. As Gladstone said in his evidence to the Clarendon Commissioners:

> The materials of what we call classical training were prepared, and we have a right to say were advisedly and providentially prepared, in order that it might become, not a mere adjunct, but . . . the complement of Christianity in its application to the culture of the human being, as a being formed both for this world and for the world to come.[23]

Thus, the classical curriculum was admirably suited to the ethos and purposes of the reformed public school, just as it had been to its aristocratic predecessor. The success of the schools meant that, far from being compelled to change the knowledge base of their curriculum, they were able to project it on to outside institutions. When procedures for competitive entry to the army and civil service were introduced from the 1850s onwards, the subject matter of the examinations was that of the public school and university curriculum. Thus, far from opening up the corridors of power to all and sundry, the effect of the new measures was 'to stengthen and multiply the ties between the upper classes and the holders of administrative power . . . Jobbery was to go, and education was to become the test; but stratification was to remain'.[24] If anything, as time went on, the classical curriculum became more 'useful' while still presenting the strong advantage for the would-be gentleman of being decidedly not 'utilitarian'.

Tom's attitude to learning reflected that of his father:

25

'Shall I tell him to mind his work, and say he's sent to school to make himself a good scholar? Well, but he isn't sent to school for that - at any rate, not for that mainly . . . If he'll only turn out a brave, helpful, truth-telling Englishman, and a gentleman and a Christian, that's all I want.'[25] But what Squire Brown did not appreciate was that the definition of a gentleman was changing and that the classical curriculum was instrumental in expediting that change. The innovatory potential of a curriculum rests not only on novelty of subject-matter but also on the use that is made of it to connect subject-matter with social purposes. Tom did not reject the curriculum the better to concentrate on achieving the role of English gentleman; the curriculum was accepted by him, and was instrumental in confirming him in the 'reformed' gentry class, even though his academic achievement on any kind of objective test was probably quite low. And while Tom, as a member of the minor aristocracy, was being initiated into his social role at Rugby, the public schools generally were providing the means whereby the sons of middle or even lower class entrepreneurs could use the wealth generated by the Industrial Revolution to make the transition to gentry status. All over the country there had been examples of artisans and tradesmen moving up to become the proprietors of businesses and then exchanging the benefits of commerce for the social and cultural advantages of the park and the manor house - carefully placed out of sight of the mill. Often the progress of an individual can be charted through parish records of births marriages and deaths as on various occasions he is recorded first as a tradesman, then as 'mill owner' and finally as a 'gent'. But achieving gentry status by this route was an expensive matter, and by the middle of the century the supply of desirable estates was drying up:

> Then, in the fifties and sixties, it became clear
> that a way could be found round the
> difficulty . . . County gentlemen and urban
> 'gentlemen' need not after all assimilate to one

another, or even undergo the embarrassment of meeting. Their sons could do it for them. The urban 'gentleman' would retain undisturbed social ascendancy in his own social sphere and would seek no more of the reality of county life than the make-believe landownership of the suburban villa; his sons however would mix with the sons of the county on the common ground of a 'public school', and come out stamped as gentlemen together.

And by the 1880s doubts over the definition of the gentleman had been to a large extent resolved: 'anyone was a gentleman who had been to a public school or who successfully concealed that he hadn't'.[26] Social ambition was satisfied but, in the process, the chance of developing other models of learning and citizenship was lost. As T.C. Worsley points out:

> The middle-classes had to sacrifice . . . a new tradition of libertarian thinking . . . and a new tradition of intellectual enlightenment which might have rescued the Industrial Age from the worst of its follies and its miseries and its squalors. In exchange they received the doubtful privilege of having their sons educated alongside the gentry, and in due course being called gentlemen themselves.[27]

The mid-nineteenth century expansion of the gentry class was parallelled by a numerically much greater expansion in the size and importance of the middle class generally. This arose from industrialization and from the concomitant increase in the extent and complexity of public administration and services. The range of 'public schools' shaded off at its lower end into a variety of private institutions which were more local in their appeal, might or might not take boarders, and tended to offer the more

27

practical curriculum - English, maths and science - which attracted those for whom earning a commercial living was a serious consideration. Through the greater part of the nineteenth century there were no state schools to fulfil this function,though later some 'higher grade' or upper elementary schools were to do so. Students in the private 'non-public' schools tended to leave at sixteen or even fourteen rather than the eighteen or nineteen which was common in the more prestigious establishments. Though sixth forms had a tenuous hold in some of them, such schools had little influence over the creation of an image of what sixth forms should be. The idea of a 'school leaving age' did not yet exist: children enrolled in, and dropped out of elementary education as and when they could, while time spent in secondary school was related to the extent of the pressure on various social groups to take up paid employment, or help in family businesses. The Taunton Commission on the endowed schools, which reported in 1868, recognized three such social groups: those whose interest in education was mainly social and cultural, who could afford to keep their children at school to the age of eighteen, and who were, therefore, potential clients of the public schools or their imitators (the 'great' public schools were outside the Taunton remit, having been enquired into by the Clarendon Commission, 1861-4); a second group whose children were almost certain to leave school at sixteen, either because of the need to take up employment, or because that was the age at which their professional training would begin - here the demand was said to be for a curriculum which combined elements of the cultural and the practical; and finally a group whose children had to leave at fourteen to take paid employment, and who wanted them to have a practical 'clerkish' education to help them in the job market. Clearly, it was only the first group which could exert influence over the shape and character of sixth forms. If they had taken their stand on the need for a different style of sixth form education with a broader, more modern curriculum and less of a leaning towards social exclusiveness, a new educational category might have been created to rival that already in existence. And they would have found contemporary thinkers and education to support them. One has only to realise that Herbert Spencer's **Education: Intellectual, Moral and Physical** was published in the same year that the Clarendon Commission was set up to appreciate what breadth of view on education existed in England in the period under discussion.[28] Yet the public schools, it seemed, neither wished nor needed to take account of this. They were not under pressure from the source that mattered most - their own clientele - to change their newly developed conception of what a sixth form education should be, nor did the upper middle class lead the way in setting up alternative conceptions. As we have pointed out, and as Frank Musgrove has so convincingly argued,[29] the middle class was much more interested in assimilating itself to the gentry class than in setting the stamp of any vision of its own on schools and society. In doing so, they were providing their own, practical, answer to the large questions about society and politics - about democracy, culture and the state - which were exercising many thinkers and writers in the mid-nineteenth century.

One of the leaders among these was Matthew Arnold, son of Thomas and one of the first Inspectors of Schools. He was, on the one hand, poet, critic and essayist and, on the other, educator and administrator and, as such, a contributor to the deliberations of the royal commissions such as Clarendon and Taunton. Arnold was convinced that, socially and politically, English society was inevitably moving towards a condition of greater democracy. His notion of the nature of democracy was based partly on the events of the French Revolution (which was for him not much further back in the past than the Russian Revolution is for us) and, more particularly, on a knowledge of developments in the United States gained through writers such as Renan and Tocqueville.[30] On one level, he believed that, since democracy and democratization were unavoidable, the question of whether one was in favour of them did not really arise. In this respect he held a kind of functional view of political systems. But on another level, he conceived of good and bad versions of democracy (or aristocracy, or whatever system was in question). American democracy was definitely not to be emulated: there the handing over of power to the populace, without the existence of institutions which could impose on them 'a high standard of right reason', resulted in the economic and political self-seeking of factions. This might have been avoided if the proper relation of education to successful democracy had been recognized, but,

> The countries which, like the United States, have
> created a considerable popular instruction without
> any serious higher instruction, will long have to
> expiate the fault by their intellectual mediocrity,
> their vulgarity of manners, their superficial spirit,
> their lack of general intelligence.[31]

Even where attempts were made to set up facilities for 'higher instruction', Arnold was scathing about the results:

> the university of Mr Ezra Cornell, a really noble
> monument of his munificence, yet seems to rest
> on a misconception of what culture truly is, and
> to be calculated to produce miners, or engineers,
> or architects, not sweetness and light.[32]

At this point we should perhaps pause to consider what Arnold meant when he talked about 'sweetness and light'. The casual reader can easily make the mistake of thinking that the phrase foreshadows the kind of education celebrated a hundred years later in the Plowden Report, where images were presented of ideal primary classrooms in which children enjoyed harmonious and pleasurable relations with peers and teachers as, through experience and experiment, they discovered the wonders of the world. Nothing could be further from the truth. Arnold's phraseology is modelled on that of Swift whose satire **The Battle**

of the Books (dated about 1698) depicts a fight in the King's Library between the works of the 'ancients' (Homer, Euclid, Plato) and those of the 'moderns' (Milton, Descartes, Hobbes). A further metaphor casts the moderns as spiders 'producing nothing at all, but Fly-Bane and a Cobweb' and the ancients (of whom Swift approves) as bees 'which, by an universal Range, with long Search, much Study, true Judgment, and Distinction of things' bring home honey and wax - from which we obtain (or did in the seventeenth century) 'sweetness and light'. For Arnold, it is the ancients (as represented through the texts of the classical curriculum) who are to provide the enduring standards which should inform whatever kind of government the evolution of society produces. In order to acquire standards which enable us to make true judgements and proper distinctions we must make contact with classical authors and philosophers and be prepared to accept them as authoritative. Hence, while the advent of democracy was to mark the transfer of the source of political authority from the aristocracy to the people, or at least, to some section of the people (initially the middle class), the cultural sanction behind that authority was to remain the same. Arnold supported the aspirations of the middle class because he thought that, only by the incorporation of new elements into the political and administrative life of the nation, could anarchy be avoided. The new industrial society, unsettled by new ideologies, could not be controlled by the old aristocracy which had neither the taste nor the talent for bargaining, diplomacy (except overseas), or administration. On the other hand the middle class worried him because of its 'philistine' subscription to the mundane, the mediocre, the vulgar and the superficial. If this tendency could not be corrected, then English democracy would turn out to be no better than the American version - and that was intolerable. But even the old aristocracy, at least in its lower regions, could be touched by mediocre thoughts:

> 'I want to be at work in the world, and not
> dawdling three years away at Oxford.'

31

'What do you mean by "at work in the world"?' said the master, pausing, with his lips close to his saucerful of tea, and peering at Tom over it.

'Well, I mean real work; one's profession; whatever one will have really to do and make one's living by. I want to be doing some real good, feeling that I am not only at play in the world,' answered Tom, rather puzzled to find out himself what he really did mean.

'You are mixing up two very different things in your head, I think, Brown,' said the master, putting down the empty saucer, 'and you ought to get clear about them. You talk of "working to get your living," and "doing some real good in the world," in the same breath. Now, you may be getting a very good living in a profession, and yet doing no good at all in the world, but quite the contrary, at the same time. Keep the latter before you as your one cbject, and you will be right, whether you make a living or not; but if you dwell on the other, you'll very likely drop into mere money-making and let the world take care of itself for good or evil.'[33]

But Tom, as a good sixth former, was suitably impressed by his master's casuistry and sought sweetness and light at Oxford instead of committing the vulgarity of entering a profession. Arnold's problem was about how to touch those who did not have Tom's advantages of an aristocratic background and a career at one of the best public schools. He was convinced that the best hope for the future lay in the middle classes and that they needed to be weaned away from their narrow view of life and culture and put on the path of sweetness and light. Then they would exercise the rights and privileges of democracy by choosing as their representatives like-minded leaders who would ensure that the price for the avoidance of anarchy was not the loss of culture - Arnold's culture. Arnold held fast to Burke's notion of 'virtual representation'. Democratic representatives were not there to do the bidding of the electors; they were there to do what the electors would have done if they had had the same endowment of 'true judgment'. Only education could bring this about. Without it there was no escape from the problem that 'our whole scheme of government being representative, every one of our governors has all possible temptation, instead of setting up before the governed who elect him . . . a high standard of right reason, to accommodate himself as much as possible to their natural taste for the bathos.'[34]

This was a highly constrained version of democracy. The middle classes, perhaps even one day the populace itself, were to be co-opted into politics and government, but only on condition that they endorsed cultural values which, in spite of Arnold's claim, were not in any sense universal, but were the possession of a particular class, at a particular time and in a particular place. In fact, public schools and public school sixth forms were already achieving exactly what he wanted, not by convincing their clienteles rationally that this was the view they should take (which was probably a hopeless enterprise anyway), but by providing them with an environment in which the values in question were taken for granted, as was also the right of superiors to lead and the obligation on inferiors to follow, at all stages of the system. Tom accepted his 'good master's' advice without question or reflection, for behind the good master was the good Doctor (Arnold the elder himself) and the experience of the sixth had finally ensured that whatever the Doctor said or did would have Tom's full support: 'the Doctor's victory was complete from that moment over Tom Brown at any rate. He gave way at all points, and the enemy marched right over him . . . It had taken eight long years to do it, but now it was done thoroughly, and there wasn't a corner of him left which didn't believe in the

Doctor.'[35]

Not only did the public schools co-opt the Tom Browns of the world into the new view of democracy, they projected such an attractive image, that middle class status and achievement were measured not by how far they approximated to some ideal stemming from the middle classes themselves, but by how well they reflected the powerful categories that these schools proposed. What the new leaders gained from their education was not so much culture, or knowledge, as mystique; but it probably served the purposes of virtual representation even better. And they learned to create a good illusion of democracy by combining the ability to lead, but also to follow, with a concern for others that was genuine, even if appallingly narrow, and a real desire to be selfless and fair. They helped to create the form of democracy to which the younger Arnold's reasoning pointed, even if he might, in the event, have disowned it: one which preserves the notion that, though all may vote and have opinions there are some people who 'know what is best for you' and who, with your blessing, should be allowed to get on with bringing it about, so that you may wear your democratic status as an ornament, rather than have it burden you with actual choices and decisions.

The very success of the public school and its sixth form as institutions ensured that it was this kind of attitude towards democracy which eventually gained the upper hand. It is, however, by no means clear that it would have been subscribed to by the first founders of the sixth, such as Thomas Arnold, who seems to have been remarkably aware of the uncertain nature of social and political questions and the doubtful status of human authority. In 1840 he wrote that if 'one treats some great men as clearly wrong, yet other men no less great have justified us in doing so. Perhaps this consciousness of the actually disputed character of many points in theology and politics rendered it early impossible to my mind to acquiesce without enquiry in any one set of opinions; the choice was not left me to do so.' And his opposition to conservatism, which he described as ' the enemy of all good' was unrelenting.

> 'I cannot tell you,' he (wrote) in 1826, 'how the present state of the country occupies my mind, and what a restless desire I feel that it were in my power to do any good. My chief fear is that when the actual suffering is a little abated, people will go on as usual, and not probing to the bottom the deep disease which is to my mind ensuring no ordinary share of misery in the country . . .'[36]

By the mid-century the fear of revolution was past and public schools were prosperous and successful. Any thought that social and political issues were in need of continued 'probing' had receded. Far from engaging in a quest for new solutions which posed and confronted deep questions about the nature of society, the developing mystique was absolving the schools from engaging problems of national interest and at the same time shielding them from criticism. Mystique, which was far more in tune with Matthew Arnold's conception of 'sweetness and light' than with his father's distrust of conservatism, was built around the connection of the schools with other social, cultural and political groups which projected an aura of capability arising from private knowhow. The 'important ignorance' of the bourgeoisie was transparent (and ripe for Dickens' barbs); the blunderings of gentlemen scholars, cultivated administrators and well bred officers brought reverence in their lifetimes and elaborate memorials after their death. For the cult of the gentlemen rode upon the revival of chivalry which the eighteenth century had so nearly laid to rest. Burke could bemoan that '. . . the age of chivalry is gone. That of sophisters, economists, and calculators, has succeeded'. But his lamentation was premature. Qualities which the eighteenth century thought of as 'stupid rather than noble' were revived.[37] Inscriptions which stated baldly that someone's demise was due to blunders in military leadership cease to appear after the early years of the nineteenth century.

> (O)fficers were gentlemen, that is to say they possessed an effortless and uncontrived capacity for radiating self-assurance, good manners and a courteous if paternalistic mien towards those of inferior station. However mistaken they may have been in individual cases, the rank and file were able to look up to such men as being of a superior caste, omniscient, omnipotent, natural, preordained leaders . . .[38]

And the mystique which enfolded them was one shared by leaders in other spheres of social and political life who would make sure that cases of 'mistakenness' would be discretely covered up. It resulted from the schools' masterly, if not necessarily highly conscious exploitation of organizational boundaries.

The public school was a world apart. Most pupils were boarders and far removed from their homes. Schools founded on the general pattern of the Rugbys and Westminsters tended, unlike them, not to be in towns and cities but in remoter country areas. And, beyond this, the customs, curriculum and hierarchical structures of the schools ensured that to enter them involved passing through the fears and uncertainties of a period of intense initiation. But the growth of the sixth carried things a stage further. Reaching the status of sixth former depended on making a very special kind of transition, involving judgements of character, academic achievement and sporting prowess on the part of masters and peers, from the condition of ordinary citizen of the school to that of one having special rights and obligations. Often the status of sixth former contained within it further divisions into ranks of prefect or praeposter each with their own rituals of initiation and duties of office concerned with the organization or discipline of the school. But the structuring of statuses was not a private matter: it was publicly celebrated on regular occasions and open to the view of all, as Tom found on his very first day at Rugby when he attended the daily roll call:

> The master mounted into the high desk by the door, and one of the praeposters of the week stood by him on the steps, the other three marching up and down the middle of the school with their canes, calling out 'Silence, silence!' The sixth form stood by the door on the left, some thirty in number, mostly great big grown men, as Tom thought, surveying them from a distance with awe; the fifth form behind them, twice their number, and not quite so big. These on the left; and on the right the lower fifth, shell, and all the junior forms in order: while up the middle marched the three praeposters.[39]

This intensification of boundaries and the rituals associated with boundaries had three important effects: first, it produced in those who reached the status of sixth former a sense of shared, progressive experience intimately linked to particular places, people and events which ensured that a bond of sympathy between them lasted throughout their lives. The old prefects returned to their schools on visits for the sporting, social and academic events of the calendar, or to see their masters. In particular the successful ones returned, and current sixth formers could easily connect their present status with desired and attainable future statuses:

> the Old Boys in evening dress, openly twirling their moustaches, attended (prayers), and instead of standing with the masters, ranged themselves along the wall immediately before the prefects; and the Head called them over, too - majors, minors, and tertiuses, after their old names.[40]

37

But also the extent to which the boundary conditions were repeated from school to school, in imitation of the 'best', with slight variations on terminology and customs, broadened the sense of shared experience beyond the particular school to take in all who had been 'sixth formers'. The 'young cosmopolites' were not just detached from allegiance to particular unique backgrounds outside the school, but also inducted into a shared cosmopolitanism which could embrace the whole world when ex-public school boys met in the distant regions of the Empire. In both these ways, the institutional category of 'sixth former' gained meaning for those who were members of it: it was clearly linked to desired futures and it existed not only in relation to particulars, but also on an abstract plane which enabled those particulars to melt into an addictive mix of ideals, traditions and dreams. But the ideals, traditions and dreams were so focused and reified by the surrounding ritual and culture that the categories of public school and sixth became meaningful even to those on the outside of the boundary and without hope or ambition of ever being within it.

Just as a vast public who have never been near the Western States, heard a coyote or seen a saguaro can identify with cowboys, badmen and sheriffs through TV and films, so thousands of middle and working class children in England were captured, through reading, by the fascination of a similarly esoteric and improbable world peopled by Tom Brown, Flashman, the good Doctor and their descendants, whether serious, swaggering or comic. The full flowering of this phenomenon did not take place until the late nineteenth century and early twentieth century but, as Orwell points out in his essay **Boys' Weeklies**, the schools depicted in the **Gem** and the **Magnet** 'were much more like Tom Brown's Rugby than a modern public school. Neither . . . has an OTC for instance, games are not compulsory, and the boys are even allowed to wear what clothes they like.'[41] The psychology of the addiction to public school stories is only lightly sketched in by Orwell, and is a matter for speculation rather than informed judgement: what matters is that the categories of public school and sixth form were meaningful, though in different ways, to a variety of publics and not only the classes who actually patronized the major public schools. The whole process was a most remarkable one. The creation and institutionalization of public schools and the public school sixth form took place in a span of not more that thirty years from the 1830s to the 1860s. In that time the sixth achieved not only a real existence, it terms of organizational forms, but also an ideal one, in terms of its connections with the dreams and ambitions of a spectrum of publics. It could show its heros and chroniclers and, in Thomas Arnold, almost a martyr, following his early death in 1842. It assumed such an air of security and permanence that pupils entering the new or refounded public schools which sprang up in the 1840s, 50s, and 60s could already feel themselves heirs to a deep-rooted tradition, rather than pioneers in a new and experimental educational enterprise.

NOTES

1   Seaborne, Malcolm, **The English School: Its Architecture and Organization 1370-1870,** London, Routledge, 1971, p.79.

2   For the idea of a 'consensual elite', see Field, G. Lowell and Higley, John, **Elitism,** London, Routledge, 1980. The authors distinguish the elites which, as countries develop, take over the functions of a 'ruling class' into those that are disunified, those that are 'ideologically unified' and those that are 'consensually unified'. England is claimed as belonging to the last category after the settlement of 1688.

3   'Barbarian' is the term applied by Matthew Arnold to the aristocracy. The middle class he labels 'philistines'.

4   See, for example, Newsome, David, **Godliness and Good**

Learning: Four Studies on a Victorian Ideal, London, John Murray, 1961, pp.38-40.

5   'In many points he took the institution as he found it, and as he remembered it at Winchester' (Stanley, A.P., The Life and Correspondence of Thomas Arnold, D.D., 2 vols., London, Fellowes, 8th. Edn., 1858, Vol.I, p.98.)

6   Ibid., pp.98-9.

7   Newsome, 1961 op. cit. It has to be remembered that staffing ratios were very low. Rugby in 1842 had only ten masters for 375 boys.

8   Stanley, 1858 op. cit., Vol.I, p.103.

9   Farrar, F.W., Eric, or Little by Little: A Tale of Roslyn School, London, Hamish Hamilton, 1971 (Original edition, 1858), p.68.

10 Ibid., p.151.

11 Report of H.M. Commissioners appointed to inquire into the Revenues and Management of Certain Colleges and Schools, etc., 3 vols., 1864, Vol.2, p.281.

12 Stanley, 1858 op. cit., Vol.1, p.100.

13 'He (Arnold) certainly did teach us . . . that we could not cut our life into slices and say, "In this slice your actions are indifferent and you needn't trouble your heads about them one way or another; but in this slice mind what you are about, for they are important" - a pretty muddle we should have been in had he done so' (Hughes, Thomas, Tom Brown's Schooldays, London, Macmillan & Co., 6th edn., 1904 reprint, p.xiv).

14 Report, 1864 op. cit., Vol.2. The size of the whole school varied from 730 at Eton (upper school only) to 132 at Shrewsbury.

15 See especially, Newsome, 1961 op. cit.

16 Bamford, T.W., Thomas Arnold, London, Cresset Press, 1960, p.178.

17 Bamford, T.W., The Rise of the Public Schools, London,

Nelson, 1967, p.150.

18   Hughes, 1904 **op. cit.**, p.5.

19   **Ibid.**, p.4.

20   The phrase is due to Peterson (Peterson, A.D.C., **Arts and Science Sides in the Sixth Form,** Oxford University Department of Education, 1960).

21   Thring, Edward, **Education and Society,** Macmillan, Cambridge, 1864, p.35.

22   Until the Grammar School Act of 1840 the endowed schools had restrictions of curriculum placed upon them by statutes or the terms of legacies.

23   **Report,** 1864 **op. cit.**, Vol.2, p.43. Gladstone was MP for Oxford University at the time the Commission was sitting.

24   Briggs, Asa, **Victorian People**, Harmondsworth, Penguin, 1965, p.117.

25   Hughes, 1904 **op. cit.**, p.51.

26   Best, Geoffrey, **Mid-Victorian Britain 1851-70,** Fontana/Collins, 1979, pp. 276-7.

27   Worsley, T.C., **Barbarians and Philistines: Democracy and the Public Schools,** London, Robert Hale, n.d., (1940), pp.45-6.

28   Spencer, Herbert, **Education: Intellectual, Moral and Physical,** London, Williams and Norgate, 1861.

29   In 'Curriculum, culture and ideology', **Journal of Curriculum Studies,** 10, 2, 1978, pp. 99-111.

30   Tocqueville, Alexis de, **Democracy in America**, 1835. Renan, Ernest, **Questions Contemporaines**, 1868.

31   Dover Wilson, J. (Ed.), **Matthew Arnold, Culture and Anarchy,** Cambridge, CUP, 1954 (Original Edition, 1869), p.18 (This is a quotation from Renan).

32   **Ibid.**, p.22.

33   Hughes, 1904 **op. cit.**, pp. 256-7. Drinking tea out of a saucer would now be thought of as a lower class habit. Perhaps when George Orwell offended acquaintances by the

same behaviour he was betraying his Etonian education rather than showing solidarity with the working class as they supposed?

34   Dover, Wilson, 1954 **op. cit.**, p.114.

35   Hughes, 1904 **op. cit.**, p.259. This was a common theme of the time (note that this is Hughes' version of Arnold's relation to his students). Cf. 'He saw it all now . . . his impetuous pride, all the mischief he had caused . . . all the time he had wasted. Disgraced, degraded, despised . . . he now felt bowed down and conquered . . .' (Farrar, F.W., **St. Winifred's, or the World of School,** 1862, pp. 364-5). The boy has to repent of his own wilfulness. He cannot be coerced into virtue, in spite of the imagery of conquest (Eric, the hero of another Farrar school novel, was an example of a boy who sinned in spite of efforts to save him).

36   Stanley, 1858 **op. cit.**, Vol.2, pp.167 and 16 and Vol.1, p.39.

37   Girouard, 1981 **op. cit.**, p.19.

38   Dixon, Norman F., **On the Psychology of Military Incompetence,** London, Cape/Futura, 1979, p.223.

39   Hughes, 1904 **op. cit.**, p.69.

40   Kipling, Rudyard, **Stalky & Co.**, London, Macmillan and Co.,1908, p.175.

41   Orwell, George, 'Boys' 'Weeklies', in **Collected Essays, Journalism and** Vol.1., 1920-1940, Harmondsworth, Penguin, 1970, p.510. See also, Musgrove, 1978 **op. cit.**, where the connection is made with the Boy Scout movement ('It is **Scouting for Boys** which states the ideology which is crucial to an understanding of English education and society in the twentieth century' (p.107).).

FIGURE 2

Sixth Form Timetable, Rugby School, 1861

Monday	CL (1hr)	ML	CL (1hr)	CL (1½hr)	
Tuesday	CL	CL (1hr)	--	--	
Wednesday	CL	CL (1hr)	ML	M	CL (¾hr)
Thursday	CL	CL (1hr)	--	--	
Friday	CL	CL (1hr)	M	CL (¾hr)	
Saturday	CL	M	--	--	

CL = Classics, ML = Modern Language, M = Mathematics

Note (1) Classics also included elements of Divinity, Composition, History and Geography.

(2) It was also possible to take 2 hours of Physical Science.

(3) Books studied included: Cicero, Juvenal, Vergil, Lucretius, Aristophanes, Aeschylus, Homer, Herodotus, Thucydides, The Bible, Hughes' **Manual of Geography**, Robertson's **Charles V**, Euclid, Colenso's **Arithmetic**, Todhunter's **Algebra**, Goethe, Lessing, Voltaire and Madame do Stael.

(Source: Report of the Clarendon Commission)

3 SECONDARY EDUCATION AND THE MIDDLE CLASS

In England, as in the rest of Europe, the early to mid-nineteenth century was a period of social and political unrest. Expansion of population, industrialization and urbanization were transforming the face of society. In 1830, 10 million tons of coal were mined in the UK, the output of iron was 680 thousand tons and railways hardly existed. In 1850, a production of 49 million tons of coal and over 2 million tons of iron was being transported over a railway network of more than 7,000 miles. London expanded from a population of under a million in 1815 to almost $2\frac{1}{2}$ million in 1848, and Birmingham from 71 thousand to 232 thousand.[1] Structural and demographic change coincided with 'an intellectual revolution which seemed to threaten to cut traditional values and culture from their roots.'[2] Ruling classes everywhere in Europe felt threatened by the rush of economic development and the consequent growth of a potentially hostile urban proletariat. A feeling of 'loss of the stable state', according to Donald Schon, commonly provokes three kinds of response: the first is what he calls 'mindlessness' - a refusal to face up to the fact of change, but instead to seek for some kind of escape from reality; the second is 'revolt' - the search for a solution by rejecting the past and instituting, by revolutionary means, a new social order; the third is 'reaction' - an attempt to reimpose, perhaps by draconian measures, the state of affairs which existed, or was thought to exist, before instability set in.[3]

The problem for Victorian England was one of the waning of old power structures, coupled with the rise of demands for political recognition on the part of those who were excluded from government - the middle class and the urban proletariat. Discussion of what should be done to save the country from possible anarchy centred around the theme which the American and French revolutions had long since launched as an object of fear and wonder - that of 'democracy'. Matthew Arnold, in his essay with that title,[4] recognizes all three kinds of response. Some think that 'in England, things may probably never go very far; that it will be possible to keep much more of the past than speculators say'.[5] Arnold himself, almost against his better judgement, finds some justification for this view: 'democracy has been slow in developing itself, having met with much to withstand it, not only in the worth of the aristocracy, but also in the fine qualities of the common people. The aristocracy has been more in sympathy with the common people than perhaps any other aristocracy.'[6] (There is a fine parallel here with the idyllic picture painted by Thomas Hughes of Squire Brown's relations with his tenants and villagers, and a striking absence of discussion of the very different social conditions which existed in less favoured areas of rapid industrialization far to the North of the Vale of the White Horse.) The purveyors of revolution are not such as we would today regard as extremists; they are the likes of 'Mr. Cobden and Mr. Bright', admirers both of the 'old American Republic' who would connive at the ultimate disaster for the country - that it should become **'Americanized'**.[7] The third possibility (and one that Arnold contemptuously rejects) is the view that 'all democracy wants is vigorous putting-down; and that, with a good will and strong hand, it is perfectly possible to retain or restore the whole system of the Middle Ages.'

Mindlessness, revolt and reaction are all responses which fail because they do not address themselves to the discovery of the fundamental nature of the problem that has to be solved, or to the exercise of powers of imagination and invention in the search for solutions. However, Schon also recognizes what he calls 'constructive responses' which try to do these things; and it was the constructive response that Arnold and some other leaders of opinion in the educational world were seeking. On the side of the nature of the problem, he saw it as one that was common to most European countries. England was in many ways unique, but it could not escape the tide of change that was sweeping over the

46

whole Continent: 'Dissolvents of the old European system of dominant ideas we must be, all of us who have any power of working'.[8] But Arnold did not think that what would replace the old order would represent a kind of perfection. Like many leading historians, lawyers and constitutionalists of the day, like Buckle, Maine or Bagehot, he saw social and political life as a constant process of adaptation as society inevitably moved on from one set of fears and ambitions to another. There were no perfect solutions; only more or less adequate attempts to respect on the one hand the advent of the new and on the other the strengths and advantages of the old, which should not be heedlessly sacrificed. He claimed, and certainly with justice, that belief in the inevitability of change was widespread: 'At the present time, almost every one believes in the growth of democracy, almost every one talks of it . . .'[9] The difficulty was rather that many people, for a variety of reasons, failed to exercise their imagination about what might be done and took refuge in simplistic responses.

Arnold, like Mill, felt that the key to the question of how to handle the growth of democracy lay in education, and especially in the education of the 'middle class' (a concept they felt to be so well understood that it did not need definition). This was an innovatory idea at the time. Education had not usually been thought of in terms of how it might fulfill a political function. Arnold wanted to compound the innovation by securing 'middle class' schooling through state involvement in education. Mill disagreed: he felt that people were not inclined to see government as representing a 'public' interest, but rather one interest among many others to which it might run counter. More fundamentally he saw state provision as an interference with individual freedom: 'A general State education is a mere contrivance for moulding people to be exactly like one another; and . . . the mould in which it casts them is that which pleases the predominant power - whether this be a monarch, priesthood,

47

an aristocracy, or the majority of the existing generation.'[10] Mill's view, as against Arnold's, was widely supported. To the extent that they were entrepreneurs, the middle classes tended to be independently minded and opposed to interference on the part of government. This feeling was strengthened by their non-conformist connections. At the beginning of the century, dissenters still suffered from civil disabilities such as debarment from office holding and exclusion from taking degrees at Oxford and Cambridge. Such people were hardly likely to see state action as benign. On the other hand, nonconformism was enjoying a revival and dissenters could feel powerful enough to block any moves toward central direction which might favour the established church. This was a fact of political life which strongly constrained the possibilities for educational development.[11] If the need to educate the middle classes to assume more responsibility in government and administration was to be met, it had to be through the founding of independent schools, or the expansion of the existing ones.

And great energy was thrown into such enterprises. Public meetings were held, subscriptions raised and sermons preached. From the point of view of educating the middle class for the responsibilities and privileges of a democratic society this approach seemed to present several disadvantages. First, efforts left to individual initiative would pay little or no attention to the national pattern of need for provision. New foundations sprang up in the South and the West, but few in the North and the Midlands where the deficiency was greater. Second, schools that were directly paid for in fees by the middle class would, it was thought, reflect that class's narrow view of what education should be - commercial and instrumental. Thirdly, the haphazard growth of a system of private secondary education would allow for no proper preparation of the necessary teachers or control over the quality of instruction they provided - and it was plain that in some existing private schools it was of a very poor quality indeed.

But to put the objections in this way is to represent them as arising simply from a concern that the classes who would be exercising influence and power in the future should be generously and justly treated. Another way of looking at the matter would be to examine some of the underlying assumptions made by people such as Arnold when they put their schemes forward. These assumptions were essentially those of the conservative intelligentsia linked to the great public schools, and in opposition to those of the great middle class which grew more from the experience of trade and the market place. Notions that England should not just be a nation, but a great nation, that the best culture was that which strove for 'sweetness and light', and that cultural and patriotic ends were best achieved through emulation and competition were set against the bourgeois values of self-sufficiency, practicality and solidarity.

Now all of these characteristics can be seen as virtues or vices according to one's point of view. Yearning after perfection (even in the knowledge that it is unattainable) can be considered the greatest goal of mankind, that which marks off true life from mere existence, or it can be seen as the greatest affliction of the human race, that which substitutes dreams for realities and leads to conflict, suffering and privation.[12] A great concern with what is real and immediate can be thought of as the best safeguard of happiness and prosperity, or the occasion of small-mindedness, failure to see ahead and a narrow obsession with material benefits. One can argue for one or the other, one can discuss which kind of virtue best fits the politics of democracy or one can present the two kinds as complementary rather than necessarily conflicting. The dilemma was well captured by Orwell, a more modern explorer of the theme of democracy, when he drew on the analogy of the relationship between Don Quixote and Sancho Panza: 'noble folly and base wisdom . . . exist side by side in nearly every human being. If you look into your own mind, which are you, Don Quixote or Sancho Panza? Almost certainly you are both. There is one part of you that wishes to be a hero or a saint, but another part of you is a little fat man who sees very clearly the advantages of staying alive with a whole skin.'[13] Matthew Arnold spoke for the founders and builders of the public school tradition in calling anathema on all little fat men. They had no doubt that the only true virtues were those of high-mindedness and moral perfection; virtues of the other sort, a sense of the practical, the capacity for self-help and the enjoyment of basic pleasures were high on the list of those things to be beaten out of boys under the rubric of idleness, cheating and impurity - a philosophy which found its most classic expression in the saga of Billy Bunter whose world closely resembles that of the public school of the mid-nineteenth century.

Arnold, it has been said, 'offered a notion of cultivating the nation by nationalizing culture.' His defence of culture 'was, in political terms, the defence of an idea of a clerisy which had the capacity and the confidence and, most important of all, the legitimacy of traditionally derived right reason, to decide for society as a whole what is good and what is bad.'[14] This was a secularized and, in some ways, more authoritarian version of his father's prescription for treating deep seated social and political ills. It required for its realization a new image of the educated man who was also a responsible citizen. An important key to this was provided by the revival of chivalry. The concept of chivalry was able to tie together the qualities which defined the 'new model ruling class'[15] and give them point and focus for those who aspired to be members of it. The social and intellectual leaders of the early nineteenth century rediscovered and reinterpreted the Arthurian Legend and found in it a boundless quarry of images, virtues and sentiments through which to create and exemplify the character which they sought. Especially it provided them with a way of linking two apparently opposed commitments: uncritical subscription to a source of secular authority, and identification with the needs of the humble. The knightly qualities included loyalty, obedience and simple trust, but also compassion, honesty and generosity. An inherently unsympathetic attitude to democracy which was 'utterly opposed to all the principles of the ancient as well as of the Christian chivalry'[16] was thus cloaked by an ideology which portrayed the gentleman as untouched by moral, material or hereditary privilege and able to act for the good of all as though he were 'classless'. He could be of the elite without incurring the opprobrium of elite status because membership depended on virtue and virtue was something that anyone could, with effort, possess. The equation of knighthood with youth was also a great help: 'The young man of humble birth who combines natural nobility with ardour and great ability . . . can rise in society and be welcomed into the ranks of those who are gentlemen by birth.'[17] Key ideas here are 'service' and 'honour'. They look in two directions. 'Service' implies willingness to follow, but also willingness to make other people's problems one's own; 'honour' is indicative of uncritical acceptance of authority, but also of a commitment to high standards of trustworthiness. Such two-headed qualities, which take on a different aspect according to whether one responds to them in others, or cultivates them in one's self, became the regular currency of public school and, later, state school sixth forms. These, together with the public school of which they were part, were the new institutional categories through which Matthew Arnold's ideas could be translated into social reality:

> **Culture and Anarchy** was the prime social text of the new English ruling class of the later nineteenth century, for it provided more persuasively than anything else the intellectual basis upon which the aristocracy and bourgeoisie could adopt a common style.[18]

Thus the problem of accommodating to democratic impulses was construed as a problem of how to increase the number of those having a hand and voice in government while at the same time preserving conceptions of knowledge, virtue and action which, though presented as being disconnected from any particular form of political structure, were in fact closely woven into a kind of social order which was, if not properly aristocratic, at least legitimist and autocratic in its assumptions. The distinction is worth making. It is too easy to see the Arnolds, the Bensons and the Bradleys as aristocrats, or would-be aristocrats, working for the furtherance of the aristocratic cause by building schools in imitation of Eton. If Eton represented the aristocratic tradition, Rugby represented something new. Eton's sixth form was small in proportion to the size of the school and of relatively little significance. Through the period of the flowering of the public schools it maintained its own system of individual tutoring of boys by masters. Its head, on a matter of explicit principle, refused to follow Arnold's precedent, which was eagerly copied elsewhere, of combining the headship with the chaplaincy, explaining that 'boys are so easily influenced and so easily impressed with anything which is said from the pulpit' that a head should not presume to extend his already very great powers over them in this way, and adding an implied criticism of Rugby in noting the absence of 'mannerism and ostentation' in Etonians' practice of Christianity.[19] The Rugby tradition took it for granted that heads had the right and duty to impress their example and character on boys by all possible means, to 'march right over them' as Tom Brown was marched over. That, however, was not something one did to a true aristocrat. They came with a nature determined by their station: one did not have to create it for them. As has often been noted, the true aristocrat is as free of status consciousness as the true peasant or proletarian. Eton did not aim to emphasize gradations of rank, or differences of status, but Arnold's system inevitably went with a parade of effective and celebrated hierarchy. He was the general, the masters he appointed were his lieutenants, the sixth form he taught were his non-commissioned officers, and beyond were the ranks of the private soldiers who, by achievements and seniority, might one day show themselves sufficiently imbued with the requisite virtues to enter the sixth.

Most, however, would not. Any system which gears itself to an uncompromising pursuit of perfection will leave many of its population indifferent if not alienated or rebellious. The virtues which had to be embraced if one was to succeed were the ones already noted: dedication, application and a high moral tone. These were not exactly those favoured by the aristocracy. The antithesis is nicely put by Newsome in his account of an instance of 'immorality' at Wellington College in 1872:

> The . . . case concerned the sordid conduct of three foundationers who had misbehaved with a serving maid during one of the school holidays, the most interesting feature of which was the attitude of the intensely aristocratic Wellington governors who appeared to view with indifference - indeed amusement - the presence in the school of boys who had had carnal knowledge of a girl of fourteen: a nice indication that the oppressive moral code of the Victorian middle class had not penetrated the ranks of the aristocracy.[20]

It is also relevant to note that many of the complaints about the ignorance of public school leavers related to Eton, where application to book learning was somewhat less than at some of the other leading public schools. Indeed, Dr. Balston, the head, seemed genuinely puzzled by the insistence of the Clarendon commissioners on pressing him about provision for the teaching of something beyond a smattering of the classics:

> (Lord Clarendon) Would it not be considered necessary by the authorities of Eton to render obligatory a thing which they think ought to be part of an English gentleman's education?

- I should not.

You would not consider it necessary to devote any part of school time to its acquisition? - No, not a day.

You do not intend to do so? - No.

Do you not think that it is a matter which a boy should be required to learn? - He ought to learn French before he came to Eton, and we would take measures to keep it up as we keep up English.

What measures would you take to keep up French, and I may also add, what measures do you now take to keep up English at Eton? - There are none at present, except through the ancient languages.[21]

What was at issue was not just a question of how education should be developed to accommodate a move towards greater democracy, but what kind of assumptions educational provision should be based upon, and how these assumptions should be institutionalized. On the first point, there was widespread agreement that the immediate problem was how to bring the middle class within the compass of secondary education. The temper of English thinkers and administrators, as we have seen, leaned towards a gradualist philosophy. Extending power and responsibility meant extending it outwards from those classes which already possessed it to those most similar to them in station in the first instance, and only by degrees to those less similar. The gradualist philosophy had its eye on the next step rather than an ultimate goal. What was needed as a next step was 'middle class schools'. On the next point, there was less agreement. Mill and others argued that the setting up of schools and curricula should be left to private enterprise, and that citizens, while being laid under an obligation to educate their children should, beyond the elementary requirements of reading and writing, be allowed to choose what kinds of schools to send them to. More were inclined to follow Matthew Arnold and hold fast to the enduring values of what they saw as liberal education - an education based on notions of 'sweetness and light': a position which was reinforced by the way in which the classics had become identified with nurturance in the Christian faith. The actual content of such a curriculum was of less consequence than the general character which these sorts of assumptions gave to it. Arnold himself, for example, was in favour of a certain degree of curriculum reform. He thought that less time could be spent on classical texts and more on the study of English, History and Modern Languages. But the practical implementation of the 'sweetness and light' curriculum, as seen in the expanding public schools of the mid-nineteenth century, however adapted to circumstances, could hardly fail to reinforce social attitudes based on deference and exclusiveness. There was an awkward dissonance between Arnold's political pragmatism, directed to the preservation of wholeness and stability in society at large, and the uncompromising idealism he advocated in the small society of the public school, resulting in the potential alienation of many pupils. Not only were some clearly shown that they were of lesser account than those who were accepted into the charmed circle of the sixth and the personal tuition of the head master, but they were sent out into the world with little more than the wreckage of a failed attempt to induct them into a knowledge of the classics: 'Such boys . . . leave school at seventeen or eighteen years of age, very imperfectly educated . . . with stagnant and ill-formed minds.'[22] Democracy is left to struggle as best it can in the face of an education based on principles held to be inviolate whatever the political system within which it has to function.

It is perhaps some indication of Arnold's appreciation that his ideas could conflict with democratic aspirations, that he was not content that the institutionalization of the education he saw as desirable should be left to private enterprise. He wanted, and argued strongly for the State intervention to which Mill and others were vehemently opposed in order that what was created in the new schools should be modelled as closely as possible on the existing public schools:

> Thus the middle classes might, by the aid of the State, better their instruction, while still keeping its cost moderate. This in itself would be a gain; but this gain would be slight in comparison with that of acquiring the sense of belonging to great and honourable seats of learning, and of breathing in their youth the air of the best culture of their nation. This . . . would really augment their self-respect and moral force; it would truly fuse them with the class above, and tend to bring about for them the equality which they are entitled to desire.[23]

Democracy was, in a way, to be the gift of the aristocracy to the class that could show itself fit to be 'fused with them' through an educational initiation which parallelled the one which their own children experienced. But the condition for their elevation to a state of equality was that they passed through a process of selection, competition and promotion likely to encourage the adoption of values directly opposed to those characteristics of a truly democratic society. Those who entered the ranks of the governors would believe in their right to govern, while those whose role was to administer or to manage would not merely concede, but believe in the sanctity of that right. It is on these grounds that Arnold's proposal can be construed as legitimist and autocratic: it would tend to lay stress on criteria of 'fitness' for status and participation unrelated to a consideration of the rights, duties and knowledge associated with democratic citizenship, and would support the creation of cadres of politicians and bureaucrats who would only to a limited extent consider it necessary to accept the wishes of citizens as a restraint on their capacity for action.

However, Arnold was wrong to believe that this state of affairs, which he may or may not have fully intended, could be brought about only by central intervention. The founding or refounding of public schools aimed at a middle class clientele, which went on at a great pace in the 1850s and 60s, was marked by two outstanding characteristics. Firstly, the readiness of these schools to recognize and reproduce the institutional categories derived from the established schools (and especially Rugby) and, secondly, their success in giving to their practical realization of these categories, virtually overnight, the character of longstanding tradition. Cheltenham, Marlborough and Wellington were founded in 1841, 1843 and 1856 respectively, yet not only were they sufficiently esteemed by the early 1860s for an account of their organization and curriculum to appear in the Report of the Clarendon Commission, but the descriptions given convey an impression of solidity and permanence which belies their tender age. The case of Wellington is particularly striking. This was the most recently founded school, and was set up to commemorate the Duke of Wellington (of Waterloo fame) by providing for 'the gratuitous or nearly gratuitous education of Orphan children of Indigent and Meritorious Officers of the Army'.[24] Yet in the space of less than ten years Benson, the first head, had, from this unpromising beginning and against the opposition of the Prince Consort, who was the prime mover of the scheme, created a 'model' public school on Arnoldian lines, even to the extent of adding a gothic chapel to the originally innovative architecture of the school which has been described as 'of French-Italian design . . . with traces of the Jacobean manner.'[25]

Though the new schools like Wellington both reproduced and became a source of the stereotype of the public school and the sixth form, they were, in the terminology of the time 'middle class schools'. Often the declared intentions of the founders stated this, and, in any case, the point is made by examining the enrolment of boys in the established Clarendon schools and the new proprietary and endowed ones. Though the new schools vastly expanded the available places at a time when the old public schools were undersubscribed they nevertheless filled those places without undermining the custom of existing establishments.[26] Some of the founders were not content with launching single schools, but shared Arnold's vision of a nationwide network of middle class schools, provided, however, by private enterprise and not by the state. The outstanding case was Canon Woodard whose elaborate scheme for schools on three levels, corresponding approximately to the grades defined by the Taunton Commission (though about twenty years ahead of that body's report), came nowhere near to fruition but nevertheless was successful enough to create no fewer than seven foundations which achieved public school status.[27] Woodard's scheme was an energetic and overt attempt to enrol the middle class in a crusade to reinforce and revitalize the Anglican faith as a bulwark against revolutionary ideas: 'Somehow or other we must get possession of the Middle Classes, especially the lower section of them, and how can we so well do this as through Public Schools?' His efforts to reach the lower middle class without drawing on public money meant that his scheme envisaged education of a cheapness that did not meet with Arnold's approval. And he was clearer that the thrust of public school provision was towards the heading off of democracy rather than its planned extension, and that the Church should lead the forces of containment:

> Education without religion is, in itself, pure evil -
> nothing more nothing less - and engenders the
> opposite form of selfishness to that which is the
> curse of an evil aristocracy. Secular education
> makes Communists and Red Republicans . . .
> Unless the Church, therefore, gets possession of

this class at whatever cost, we shall reap the fruits, in some day of distress, of an universal deluge.[28]

Successful institutional categories must be capable of commanding widespread support by fulfilling different needs for different groups, and this, by the 1860s, the category of 'public school' was well fitted to do. It had its appeal to those who favoured an extension of democracy, as well as those who wanted to contain its spread, to those who sought incorporation into the gentry class as well as those whose goals were more intellectual than social, and to those who saw religion as central to education, as well as those who held more secular views of the nature and purposes of schooling. If all of these groups did not see exactly what they wanted in the public schools, they at least saw the possibility of its achievement and were not put off by any unpalatable features of the overall ideology of the schools. Moreover, successful categories have to be recognizable through well understood forms which can capture the public consciousness in ways which are striking but at the same time not so unambiguous that they give no play to the imagination. In this way too, the schools were effective. They owed their success to the fine feeling for form and symbolism which characterized the early Victorian intelligentsia and to the close networks of family and personal relationships within which its members lived and worked, and which meant that the transmission of form and feeling was based on personal contact and closely observed imitation, rather than on formal plans or schemes or on second hand sources of precept or exhortation. Several writers have traced the interrelated family trees of public school head masters of the nineteenth century, such as that of Butler of Harrow which included three other heads, and also the chains of head/assistant master or head/sixth former relationships such as that between Thomas Arnold and Benson via Prince Lee, head of King Edward's Birmingham.[29] Instinctively or by reason such men understood the force of symbolism connected to forms having at least the appearance of enduring character. They would have agreed with Bagehot that 'the mass of the English people yield a deference rather to something else than to their rulers. They defer to what we may call the **theatrical show** of society . . . Courts and aristocracies have the great quality which rules the multitude, though philosophers can see nothing in it -- visibility.'[30] They lived at a time when the past was being rediscovered and enthusiasm for romanticized accounts of the Middle Ages caused contemporary styles of architecture to be abandoned in favour of the gothic revival which showed itself in serious public buildings, such as Pugin's new Houses of Parliament, as well as in follies and over-elaborate country seats. As early as 1838 Barry's new design for King Edward's Birmingham 'resembled strikingly the chapel of King's College, Cambridge'.[31] Rugby had already reproduced the 'tudor-gothic' style of Eton in its rebuilding of 1809, though without altogether satisfying Thomas Arnold, who envied Winchester its antiquity and was 'anxious to do all that can be done to give us something of a venerable outside, if we have not the nobleness of old association to help us'.[32] When funds were available, the new foundations were more likely to revert to the older styles of architecture, however uncomfortable they may have been for practical purposes of living and teaching.

But the romanticism of tracery and cloister was curiously combined in the mind of the Victorian intelligentsia with the social and administrative rationalism of the age of commerce, industry and regulative government. Just as the gothic mansion concealed an elaborate machine for living which coordinated and differentiated the roles and functions of owners, relatives, guests and superiors and inferior servants, so the Victorian public school, beneath its ivied walls and pinnacled roofs hid an elaborately articulated social system geared to the induction of its middle class pupils into the bureaucratic structures needed by a country which could no longer be held together by the intermittent attentions of the old aristocracy. For, as Bagehot also noted, the deference of the people to the spectacle of power can, in the modern state, only be secured by the inconspicuous collaboration of the middle class in the role of day to day administrators and policy-makers. This was the condition on which the healthy survival of the state could be secured: that those classes which could enter into a social compact with the aristocracy by exchanging power for deference should do so, since 'if you once permit the ignorant class to begin to rule, you may bid farewell to deference for ever . . . A democracy will never, save after an awful catastrophe, return what has once been conceded to it.'[33]

The teachers in the public schools, old or new, were not aristocrats, but in the established schools, and especially Eton, Winchester and Harrow, they were admitted to a 'gentry' class which met aristocrats on their own ground and taught the children of aristocrats. These same forms of teaching were now conducted by people of the same type in the middle class schools privately founded and reproducing the public school stereotype. The schools served to determine which pupils should enter the 'aristocratic intelligentsia', and which should enter public careers of lower status, but rendered by their experience deferential to the wisdom of their betters, and hence unlikely to side with the 'ignorant class' in any aspiration to democratic power or revolutionary change which it might be infected by. The prime instrument for grooming candidates for the intelligentsia was the sixth form, personally taught by the head who was the chief representative of that social class in the school. Entry was on academic performance in the classics, and the whole of a boy's career up to that point was a continual sifting through 'taking places' in class, through mark lists and examinations.[34] Places in the sixth were usually limited, and arrival there spelled the end of place taking. From that point on, sponsorship was assured, short of some lapse in morality, and the way lay open to the universities, to government and to preferment in the church. The institutional role of 'sixth former' was thus clearly linked to present status and future career in a well-defined and understandable way. The expansion of opportunities for employment in the home and overseas civil service preserved and enhanced the firm career connection, and the limitation on numbers in sixth forms ensured that supply did not outrun demand. For example, at Marlborough in 1862, only 35 out of 315 boys were in the sixth and the head explained in a note to the Clarendon Commission that this was an exceptional and temporary measure. Only thirty would normally be accepted.[35] As long as the principle was held to that the sixth was taught by the head and that the teaching was on a personalized basis, this was about the highest number that could conveniently be accommodated in a single form. Of course, it was understood that being a sixth former entailed the learning of classics (what else could heads teach?) and where other studies were available, which was the case in some of the newer schools, either they did not lead to the sixth, or the pupils themselves failed to connect History or English or Mathematics or Modern Languages, taken as major subjects, with the status of sixth former (Benson noted of Wellington that 'there is on the whole an apparent decrease in zeal in work if those who join the mathematical divisions are compared with those remaining in others.'[36]). But the curriculum was really of much less importance (though often the issue raised by would-be reformers) than the manner of its implementation, which was the chief vehicle for making the sixth a vehicle for the rationalization of society through the incorporation of the middle classes into a class of cosmopolitan scholars and administrators.

The heads themselves were living proof of the connection in the Victorian mind between culture, scholarship and action. The intelligentsia was inclined towards an active rather than a contemplative or mystical romanticism, and those who went out from Oxford and Cambridge colleges into the public schools did so more as administrators, as realizers of visions, than as teachers in the narrow sense of the word. And when they were elevated from headships to bishoprics it was again their administrative qualities which were principally exercised. Entering the sixth meant accepting scholarly values, but it did not mean necessarily entering a cloistered way of life. It was a narrow way which led to wide opportunities.

Thus the great question of what should be done about the democratic impulses which were threatening to shake the foundations of society was settled, for the time being, in a way which was, on anything more than a local level, unplanned (excepting the half-formed schemes of Woodard) and which can be seen as either a vindication or a result of the kinds of pragmatic evolutionary conceptions of social change supported by English political and constitutional theorists of the time. Quietly, and without controversy outside certain limited circles, important new forms of education evolved, initially for a minority of the middle class, but with a potential for a much wider influence in the future.

The achievement of the great public schools was summed up by the Clarendon commissioners as follows:

> Among the services which they have rendered is undoubtedly the maintenance of classical literature as the staple of English Education, a service which far outweighs the error of having clung to these studies too exclusively. A second, and a greater still, is the creation of a system of government and discipline for boys, the excellence of which has been universally recognised, and which is admitted to have been most important in its effects on national character and social life. . . . These schools have been the chief nurseries of our statesmen; in them, and in schools modelled after them, men of all the various

classes that make up English society, destined for every profession and career, have been brought up on the footing of social equality, and have contracted the most enduring friendships, and some of the ruling habits of their lives; and they have had perhaps the largest share in moulding the character of an English Gentleman.[37]

NOTES

1   Talmon, J.L., **Romanticism and Revolt: Europe 1815-1848,** London, Thames and Hudson, 1967, pp.198-9.

2   Bowle, John, **Politics and Opinion in the 19th. Century,** London, Cape, 1954, p.213.

3   Schon, D.A., **Beyond the Stable State: Public and Private Learning in a Changing Society,** London, Temple Smith, 1971, pp.28-9.

4   Arnold, Matthew, 'Democracy' in Smith, Peter and Summerfield, Geoffrey (Eds), **Matthew Arnold and the Education of the New Order,** Cambridge, CUP, 1969.

5   **Ibid.,** pp.61-2.

6   **Ibid.,** p.53.

7   **Ibid.,** pp.148 and 57.

8   Smith and Summerfield, 1969 **op. cit.,** p.4.

9   **Ibid.,** p.61.

10   Mill, John Stuart, **On Liberty,** Harmondsworth, Penguin, 1974, p.177 (Original edition, 1859). He distinguished between state requirements that children be educated (of which he approved) and the actual provision of education by the state.

11   Kitson Clark, G., **The Making of Victorian England,** London, Methuen, 1962, pp.21-4 and 38-9.

12   For a Victorian representation of the clash of high-minded

idealism and earthly realism, see 'The Choice' by Sir Joseph Noel Paton, reproduced in Girouard, Mark, **The Return to Camelot: Chivalry and the English Gentleman,** New Haven, Yale University Press, 1981, p.157.

13 Orwell, Sonia and Angus, Ian (Eds), **Collected Essays, Journalism and Letters of George Orwell,** Vol.2., Harmondsworth, Penguin, 1970, p.192.

14 Shannon, Richard, **The Crisis of Imperialism 1865-1915,** London, Hart-Davis, MacGibbon, 1974, pp.33-4.

15 **Ibid.,** p.34.

16 Digby, Kenelm, **The Broad Stone of Honour,** quoted in Girouard, 1981 **op. cit.,** p.62.

17 Girouard, 1981 **op. cit.,** p.65.

18 Shannon, 1974 **op. cit.,** p.34.

19 Bamford points out that, whereas fifteen to twenty per cent of Rugby boys were sons of the clergy in the first half of the nineteenth century, the figure for Eton was five per cent or below (Bamford, T.W., **The Rise of the Public Schools,** London, Nelson, 1967).

20 Newsome, David, **Godliness and Good Learning: Four Studies on a Victorian Ideal,** London, John Murray, 1961, p.45.

21 **Report** of H.M. Commissioners appointed to inquire into the Revenues and Management of Certain Colleges and Schools, etc., 1864 (Clarendon), Vol.1, p.85.

22 **Ibid.,** Vol.2, p.314.

23 Smith and Summerfield, 1969 **op. cit.,** p.66.

24 Bamford, 1967 **op. cit.,** p.27.

25 Seaborne, Malcolm, **The English School: Its Architecture and Organization 1370-1870,** London, Routledge, 1971, p.255.

26 Bamford, 1967 **op. cit.,** p.17.

27 See Heeney, Brian, **Mission to the Middle Classes: The**

Woodard Schools, 1848-1891, London, SPCK, 1969.

28   Otter, J., **Nathaniel Woodard: A Memoir of His Life, 1925,** p.240, quoted in Bamford, 1967 **op. cit.,** p.30. Woodard felt that the admission of an uneducated lower middle class to political privilege would lead to 'corruption and bribery or a far worse mischief', but that this difficulty could be avoided if they were 'educated and trained in religious and conscientious habits' (Heeney, 1969 **op. cit.,** p.127). The passage quoted in the text dates from 1871 - after the publication of the Communist Manifesto.

29   See Bamford, 1967 **op. cit.,** p.149.

30   Bowle, 1954 **op. cit.,** p.259.

31   Newsome, 1961 **op. cit.,** p.101.

32   Stanley, A.P., **The Life and Correspondence of Thomas Arnold, D.D.,** London, Fellowes, 8th. Edn., 1858, Vol.1. p.128.

33   Bowle, 1954 **op. cit.,** p.259.

34   For a contemporary account of 'place taking', see Farrar, F.W., **Eric, or Little by Little: A Tale of Roslyn School,** London, Hamish Hamilton, 1971, pp. 27-9 (Original edition, 1858). For a description of practice in the leading public schools see **Report** of H.M. Commissioners, 1864 **op. cit.** At Marlborough, for example, 'At the close of the lesson the boys are marked according to the order in which they then sit' (Vol.2, p.528), this order having been determined by their success or failure in answering the teacher's questions.

35   **Report** of H.M. Commissioners, 1864 **op. cit,** Vol.2, p.509.

36   **Ibid.,** Vol.2, p.534.

37   **Ibid.,** Vol.1, p.56.

4 A NATIONAL INSTITUTION

Over the latter half of the nineteenth century, the sixth form moved from being a class supported institution to become one with national significance. This, however, did not happen through central intervention of any determined character. Nor did the sixth acquire the status of a national institution through widespread expansion of opportunities for participation in it. It achieved significance and meaning through its association with popularly understood and supported policies and values such as those associated with imperialism, and through the appeal to excluded outsiders, as well as initiates, of books and periodicals celebrating the culture and ethos of the public school. Of course, sixth form education, as part of secondary education, was also a formal national concern and this was recognized through the work of publicly appointed or controlled bodies, such as the various Royal Commissions which examined the provision of education in the period 1850-1870 and reported back to Parliament. The result of these exercises was generally the passing of acts which modified somewhat the legal framework within which private interests operated. After the Clarendon Commission on the major public schools had completed its work in 1864, a Commission with a much wider remit to examine the workings of secondary schools was launched under the title of **Schools Inquiry Commission.** It considered provision for girls as well as boys and exhaustively investigated all types of establishment. Its report, published in 1868 is generally known after the name of the Chairman of the Commission, Lord Taunton.

The Report produced a scheme for the development of secondary education which looked very like the earlier Woodard proposal. It recommended the establishment of three 'grades' of school. These were to be differentiated by the maximum age to which students would attend - eighteen or nineteen in the case of first grade schools, sixteen for the second grade and fourteen for the third. The question of who should go to what kind of school was to be decided, basically, by parental choice, though this choice would be very much circumscribed by income unless a state funded system was set up, as Arnold and others wanted. In the event, the working out of the system was left to the operations of the Charity Commission which, over the rest of the century, tackled the problem of rationalizing existing educational endowments, locality by locality, in order to ensure the efficient use of the available funds, which were considerable, and to try to transfer resources from areas which were well supplied to those where provision was minimal or non-existent. The pieces out of which a system had to be assembled were the endowed schools, the proprietary schools, and the private schools. The category of 'public school' cut right across these, since it was dependent on social and academic and not financial status.

   With the setting up of local school boards to administer elementary education after the Education Act of 1870, a further confounding category evolved. School boards in the large cities, such as London, Birmingham and Manchester extended the range of the elementary education for which they were now responsible upwards into 'higher grades', and eventually a category of 'higher grade school' was recognized which overlapped in the education it provided with the other types of school, though not with public schools, since these were exclusively of Taunton's first grade, while the higher elementary schools, with rare exceptions, did not reach beyond the definition of third grade. However, such schools did point up the possibility of secondary provision being achieved by a different route, and by the 1890s, two models were available for consideration: the existing one which saw the secondary problem as a problem about what to do about 'middle class education', and a new one which construed it as a question of how to build the work of the school boards upwards to cater for the teaching of subjects and crafts on a basis of elementary education. As Ackland and Smith put it in 1892: 'We may look upon secondary schools as mainly middle-class institutions, or as the crown of the edifice of primary education'[1]. And these really were alternatives and not possibilities which were compatible and capable of being merged into a unified system. They were kept apart by the great differences in curriculum between schools for the middle classes, which were drawn towards the subject matter of the grammar school, and elementary schools which, in spite of the efforts of the larger city school boards, were, for the most part, locked by the 'payment by results' scheme into the teaching of basic skills of reading, writing and arithmetic. Those who could pay the fees might be able to enrol their children in 'first' or 'second grade' schools whatever their level of knowledge, or, if that was not possible, they could pay to send them to private preparatory schools to give them a start in Latin and other grammar school subjects. The children of such parents would also have the advantage in competition for scholarships which would be based on tests for which elementary school pupils would be ill-equipped. If children from the elementary system did gain entry to first or second grade schools the going was tough for them, especially if the transfer took place at thirteen or fourteen as was often the case, and there was little time to make up for the advantage held by those who had followed a grammar type curriculum from an early age.

What happened in practice was that, generally speaking, the higher grade schools and private schools supplied the place defined by Taunton for third grade secondary schools (though hardly anyone used the word 'secondary' in speaking of them, and many resisted it strongly), while most of the reformed endowed schools occupied the second grade, and the first grade remained almost exclusively the preserve of the old and new public schools. A study of about 1890 surveyed forty-five endowed and proprietary schools for boys in London and found that 'the mass of the pupils are between the ages of eight and fifteen' and that only 'a few . . . stay beyond fifteen'.[2] A detailed review of three of the endowed schools produced percentages of sixteen for working class pupils, seventy-four for middle class and ten for professional. It would appear that the work of the Charity Commission did very little to change the character of secondary education, which remained essentially a middle class affair, and that the new or revived foundations were catering almost exclusively for the lower range who had no ambition to stay in school beyond the age of fifteen or sixteen.

The character of these developments in secondary education generally meant that the sixth form as an institution continued to be contained within the first grade schools, which were essentially the public schools, and that its evolution over the latter half of the nineteenth century was therefore conditioned almost exclusively by changes in these schools. These changes may be summed up under the broad headings of rationalization and secularization. By the mid-century, the rationalization of public schooling had progressed quite a long way in respect of organization for teaching and for discipline, the two being quite closely connected. The old school room was being abandoned in favour of class teaching, and systems of promotion were becoming age related. Specialist teachers in areas other than classics were beginning to make their appearance. Pupils started to be grouped by curriculum as well as by ability or by status - scholars or commoners. This was made possible by the popularity of the schools, enabling intakes to be regulated, which in turn reinforced the need for rationalization. The days of wildly fluctuating pupil numbers were left behind. The public school of the eighteenth and early nineteenth century would have had some difficulty in comprehending how a 'falling rolls' problem could exist. Rolls dropped like a stone, or rose dramatically just as Summer followed Winter. The entry to Harrow, for example, four times reached peaks of around a hundred between 1800 and 1850, on three occasions plunged to forty or even twenty, and, apart from a couple of interludes of stablility which lasted five years or so, was always on its way up or down.[3] From an organizational point of view, not much difficulty was caused. Endowments ensured that even without any students at all the school would survive, while extra pupils generated their own finance through fees. The schools were directly responsible for little more than the teaching, since boys were often lodged in private boarding houses and provided for their own recreation. Even the teaching effort was easily expanded or contracted. With classics as the staple of the curriculum, all teachers were more or less interchangeable, and there was in any case very little formal teaching. Boys learned their lessons and were periodically 'heard'. If the achievement suffered, no one was terribly worried because achievement was not all that important. However, the press for 'respectability', led by schools like Rugby which set out to attract middle class custom, began to change all that.

The move towards the rationalization of teaching at Rugby preceded the advent of Thomas Arnold and can be seen in the provision of classrooms in the rebuilding of 1809-16. Arnold's contribution was to work up the idea of the sixth as a controlling and civilizing influence and to extend the sphere within which the school regulated the life of pupils by elaborating and integrating the role of religion in their daily round (as we have seen, the more aristocratic schools were still resisting this in the 1860s). The creation of sixth forms as sources of control, authority and scholarship in the schools provided a focal point around which the rationalization of teaching and discipline steadily grew throughout the whole of the organization. By the time of the Clarendon investigations, all the major schools were operating elaborate systems of classifying, examining and promoting students, and had bureaucratic rules for the classification and chastisement of offenders (though both academic and disciplinary systems differed interestingly from place to place). Two major developments in the middle of the century gave added impetus to the process of rationalization. The first of these was the extension of examining

71

from something which operated within the schools to something which also involved outside agencies. This had begun in a small way with participation in university prize competitions, but the real expansion dates from about 1850 and proceeded on two fronts. First, and less important from the point of view of the public schools - though with great significance for the future development of sixth forms, outside bodies responded to the wish of schools that independent tests should be available to show how well they and their students were performing, and how appropriate their schemes of curriculum and teaching were. The College of Preceptors began to fulfill this function in 1851, and was later followed by the Universities of Cambridge and Oxford. Secondly, examinations began to become the avenue for entry to the professions. Examinations for the Army were instituted in 1849 and, though purchase of commissions was not finally abolished until 1871, at once affected what was taught in the public schools. The Indian Civil Service began recruitment by examination in 1853 and the Trevelyan-Northcote Report on the Home Civil Service recommended the introduction of examinations for that branch in 1854. By about 1870, most posts were being filled on the basis of examination results.[4] These reforms, too, exerted an important influence on public schools and public school sixth forms. The effect of the growth of examinations set by bodies outside the schools was twofold. First they served to reinforce and perpetuate the idea of fixed and universal 'standards' of achievement which marked off the successful from the unsuccessful student, and secondly they helped to turn public schools and public school sixth forms into institutions with national significance, that is, institutions with meaning for all sections of the population, and not just those on the inside of the schools.

The other main thrust towards rationalization came from the new proprietary schools which, on the one hand, had no endowments and had to plan their operations on the basis of a controlled and predictable throughput of students and, on the other, were under more pressure to respond to a public which wanted a more varied and flexible curriculum than the one traditionally offered in the older schools. New foundations like Cheltenham, developed 'modern sides' where subjects were taught which could cater for those who were not interested in classics, but which could be useful if offered for the new examinations which promised a route into the less academically or ecclesiastically oriented professions. The introduction of Civil Service and other examinations also helped advance the movement towards teacher professionalism. As the performance of those taught became more and more a criterion of success, as the variety of subject-matters which needed to be taught multiplied, and as, with the increase in size of schools, the aura associated with the character training aspects of the role came to be shifted from heads to assistant teachers, so teaching itself could lay claim to the status and rewards of a profession, and this in turn helped to change the schools from places of little organization to places of closely controlled and ritualized predictability.

By the mid-century, the process was already well advanced in matters of discipline and teaching. Over the next fifty years, the impetus was carried over into living arrangements and recreation. Studies and common rooms began to be provided for older students, and sometimes for younger ones as well. Boarding houses were brought firmly under the control of the school and house masters integrated into the overall administration:

> The houses ceased to be merely places where the 'foreigners' boarded and became integral parts of the organization of the school. Each house developed into a community with its place in the wider community of the school.[5]

Games became compulsory and were organized by teachers or under their direction, so that 'a civilized out-of-door life in the form of cricket, football and wholesome sports took the place of poaching, rat-hunting and poultry stealing'[6]. Five leading public schools, which in 1845 had mustered only twelve acres of games fields (owned or leased) between them, by 1900 had the use of over three hundred and Harrow alone laid claim to almost one hundred and fifty.[7] Systems of colours and uniforms - 'trappings of fealty and dominance: caps, badges, ties, belts, hatbands, stockings, scarves, tassels and shirts'[8] - were introduced and applied to teams, to prefects and to the rank and file of students at house and school level. Photographs, especially of sports teams, show a steady move away from the careless poses and individualistic costumes of the earlier period towards greater and greater uniformity and precision of dress and demeanour.[9] Not only did pupils become more like one another; schools did too. The creation of a public image, in terms of both ideals and forms for the realization of those ideals, reflected back on the schools, so that it could be said of the public schools towards the end of the century that, 'however considerable the differences between them in style or background, the resemblances seem even greater'.[10] This ironing out of differences was another factor in promoting the image of the schools as a national institution.

While on the one hand, this rationalization process helped schools to become stable, respectable, and economically successful, on the other it rendered useless any claim that they were not total institutions and did not have the automatic right to exact very precise conformity. By the end of the century the sixth form was not just a catalyst in the transformation of the school from a loose and unpredictable confederation of masters and boys to a tight and rule bound society; it was both the symbol of and the most active agent for the preservation of the new social order. From being a kind of last bastion of republicanism within the school, it became itself routinized, hierarchical and conformist. Systems of rotating duty rosters of a handful of praeposters or monitors were replaced by a permanent prefectorial organization with grades of seniority culminating in captains of schools. The captaincy motif was repeated across a range of sports and activities, and captains were expected to be paragons of virtue as defined by the school. The transformation was helped by the process of secularization which went hand in hand with rationalization.

Headmasters such as Arnold had been aggressively religious in a theological sense. They were concerned with doctrine, and therefore with the truth or falsehood of doctrine. They took sides in the basic religious controversies of the second quarter of the century. They saw the contest for boys' allegiance as a business of saving souls. In as much as they made an alliance between religion and the classics, it might be thought of as an alliance with Greek authors who saw questions of virtue and vice in contemplative terms. After 1850, the equation began to be more with a Roman conception of virtue associated with action, and especially military action. Teachers could still be religiously aggressive, but the aggression had more to do with an attitude towards life than a belief about doctrine. The struggle was not so much for souls, as for allegiance to an army of right-thinking and right and decisively acting patriots who could be of any religion or none (though C of E was usually preferred). Thus, as T.C. Worsley sums it up: 'What lessons does the chapel teach us now? The lessons of Christian Humility and the Sense of Sin? Certainly not, but to make vows of War before the Lord of Hosts - "To count the life of Battle good" '[11]. The Greek Testament had been a favourite text of some of the earlier heads such as Prince Lee: 'At a time when the highest honours of his university were falling to him over again through his pupils, he ever said that the study of the Greek Testament was that which he prized for them beyond every study and every honour'[12]. Such emphasis reflected a close concern with the central Christian message of sin and redemption. For the newer generation the parallel between the Old Testament and Caesar's **Gallic Wars** was more striking, and found its reflection in militant school hymns:

To set the cause above renown,

75

To love the game beyond the prize,

To honour while you strike him down,

The foe that comes with fearless eyes . . .[13]

The 'manliness' of Arnold's time, which was related to the assumption of christian moral responsibilities was gradually translated into the 'manliness' of the sports field - 'honour, loyalty, skill at games, and a certain stoical acceptance of pain, injustice and malign circumstances.'[14] As Worsley explains:

> The 'standardization' consisted in the self-conscious deification of the virtues which were merely latent in the wilder Public Schools, loyalty, courage and endurance, the Barbarian virtues, but without the Barbarian freedom; instead of the last, Philistine respectability was almost unconsciously elevated to the dais. The 'means' were athletics, and above all, team games.[15]

Not all headmasters rushed to embrace the new cult of games. At Rugby under Temple (1857-69), 'Athletes who neglected their work were obliged to sit in his study working while the important match for which they had been training was played within earshot; the "bloods" were never permitted to encroach upon the authority vested in the Sixth.'[16] On the other hand, Thring at Uppingham not only encouraged games, but joined in himself, marking the arrival of a new style of public school head which came to dominate the scene as the character of the older universities shifted. The rule of celibacy was relaxed from 1877 and there was no longer a need for young clerics who wished to marry to move out. Also, benefitting from their connections with the schools, the universities were in a period of rapid expansion and offered more scope for fellowships. An important factor in this expansion was the removal of the ban on admitting dissenters in the mid-1850s which was itself evidence that the universities too were becoming more secularized. Indeed by the 1880s Oxford could be described by Mark Pattison as a 'super public school with all its more unpleasing characteristics, its juvenilia, its newly-established-old traditions, its competitive games and competitive examinations, its lack of any real culture, its masculine Christianity'.[17]

This was the atmosphere in which the sixth form developed through the period immediately before it became clearly institutionalized in maintained grammar schools in the decade after the Education Act of 1902. As we have seen, there was, in the thirty or so years before that, very little expansion of the idea of the sixth into schools outside the circle of the public schools. With the beginnings of serious efforts to establish schools for girls, some examples of a rather more serious and less conformist type of upper school experience became available, and, though they never challenged the sixth on its own ground, the higher grade schools offered the possibility of a different model for education beyond the age of sixteen. But these influences were small compared to the tradition created and matured within the public boys schools. The strange thing was that, though this predominant image was so exclusive, class linked and foreign to the majority of the population, it became widely known and accepted as reflecting a right and inevitable way of educating older adolescents, and the object of a popular cult.

This popularization had begun as far back as the 1850s with the publication of **Tom Brown's Schooldays** which went through five editions in just over six months when it first appeared. This was the best known of the early school books, but it was far from alone in its class. Apart from the works of lesser known authors, Farrar's **Eric** was an almost exact contemporary of Tom Brown, and this, together with his later and less often quoted **St. Winifred's** had, by the end of the century, sold a total of about 100,000 copies. Obviously, in spite of the fact that it tended to be lengthy and expensive (**Tom Brown** cost 10/6d) the public school novel was reaching a market that went far beyond those who attended, or even had any direct connection with such places. The novels were followed by the boys' magazines. The most famous of these, the **Boys Own Paper** was launched in 1870, and featured school stories as a prominent part of its offering. These were inevitably set in imaginary public schools which exhibited the by then conventional trappings of fagging, bounds, team sports, sixth forms and prefects, all set in a context of ivy-covered walls, quads, cloisters and chapels (not that these figured very prominently in the stories which concentrated more on games fields and dormitories). Scholars such as E.C. Mack have speculated that these stories were already, in the last decades of the century, exerting an influence on the customs and organization of the reviving grammar schools and private day schools.[18] Such connections are very difficult to prove, but it is certain that the public school story was well established in the last quarter of the century in much the same way as the western and detective story later took hold of the popular imagination. It appeared in novel form, as a serial or short story in magazines, and in comic and comic strip form (fossilized and debased examples of which still survive). It appealed to a mass market which went far beyond the upper middle class, and must have included substantial numbers of elementary school children, and even their parents. But whereas the western deals with an alien setting, and the detective story concerns a profession with few members, the school story was about an institution in the home country of the readers, and offered roles which were, potentially, translatable into the experience of large numbers of people. There can be no doubt that it had a powerful effect in establishing the institutional category of the public school, and therefore the educational categories associated with it, across a broad spectrum of the English population. This process took place both the at the level of mystique and that of details of form. The mystique was actively promoted by parents and relations who gave copies of the canonical works to children as presents, and by schools, including elementary schools, which gave them as prizes. (My copy of **Tom**

Brown was a prize for 'writing and neatness' presented to my father in a London County Council elementary school in 1906). The children themselves would spend their tuppences or sixpences on the journals and comics which provided the specific details needed to associate the mystique with forms of organization, behaviour and dress. These ranged from the top of the market **Captain: a Magazine for Boys and 'Old Boys'**, launched in 1899, through the less specialized **Boys Own Paper,** to the later **Gem** and **Magnet** (1908), which carried the famous Frank Richards stories and gave Billy Bunter to the world. The details of public school life were conveyed through stories and illustrations, but also through answers to readers' queries and, especially in the case of the **Captain,** through factual accounts and features. Volume one gives prominence to photographs of school captains, commentaries on school magazines, how to play cricket (by C.B. Fry), and the present state of 'fags and fagging'. The connections with high status occupations are emphasized by lengthy articles on how to enter the civil service and on being a fresher at Cambridge. The mystical side is also taken care of by suitable quotations from the poets:

Go, lose or conquer as you can;

But if you fail, or if you rise,

Be each, pray God, a gentleman

and by historical articles on public schools. Public school mutinies is one topic and school ghosts another (even such a recent foundation as Marlborough is credited with one). The mystique also gains emphasis from the **en passant** commentary. The school captains' 'manliness' is noted: 'Nearly every one of these Captains has, you will observe, a strong mouth and jaw' - a phrase to be contrasted with the distrust of an earlier epoch for such traits: '. . . a glance at his countenance showed a self-sufficiency and arrogance which ill-became the refinement of his features'[19]. Reviews of school magazines reserve special scorn for those which accept advertisements from 'tradesmen'. The working classes get even shorter shrift. The lead story of the first issue concerns a public school which is under siege because the head has given shelter to a mill owner who is being chased by a howling mob of strikers. The vastly outnumbered boys defend the school bravely, smashing the rioting proletarians over the head with cricket bats and stumps. The advent of the school fire engine promises final victory, but the school captain falls into the hands of the strikers as a result of a rare and culpable lapse of concentration, and the gates are on the point of crumbling (being, naturally, very old). At this point the head, seeing 'the flower of his flock - the Captain of his school. . . fighting for his life amid that maddened mob' takes the decisive step of sending in the cadet corps with fixed bayonets. The strikers are routed and flee into the hands of police reinforcements marching up the road from the town. It is hard to believe that working class children were captivated by that kind of writing, but apparently they took to the **Magnet** eagerly enough though that too, in its way, is equally antipathetic to the working class whose members are almost invariably portrayed as evil or stupid (often both), and whose common pleasures - betting, drinking and smoking - are the subject of caning and flogging if they occur among the Greyfriars pupils. Yet this does not seem to have deterred working class children from spending their tuppences each week.

Boys magazines invariably coupled school stories with action-packed adventures set in a romantic past or in the modern far-flung Empire. In doing so they reflected the contents of the magazines produced by the schools themselves, which offered their readers contributions such as: 'With the Frontier Light Horse in Zululand', 'On life in Melanesia', 'A Kangaroo Drive', 'Pig-Sticking in Bombay', 'Elk Hunting in Ceylon', 'A Week among the Maoris', 'My first Shot at a Tiger', 'An Old Boy in the Bush', and 'On the Warpath in Manipur'.[20] The connection between public school, sixth form and prefects, on the one hand, and army, colonial service and the Empire is also made in the canonical novels such as

Kipling's **Stalky** or Vachell's **The Hill.** This intertwining of the themes of public school education and conquest and rule of Empire probably accounts as much as anything for the recognition by a wider public of what would appear to be upper middle class educational categories. It is also one of the aspects of the categories in their popularized form which is distinctively contemporary, and not part of a mystique which was already obsolescent. It is often forgotten that enthusiasm for Empire and attachment to the sentiments which went with it were a late Victorian invention. Before 1870 or so, the aristocracy were inclined to think of the colonies as an encumbrance, liberal reformers were opposed to imperialism on principle, and the lower orders, if their thoughts strayed overseas at all, turned to North America as a place of refuge from poverty in the home country rather than to Africa and India as scenarios for daring deeds. All that was changed by a combination of political opportunism on the part of conservatives such as Disraeli, and commercial self-interest on the part of liberals such as Chamberlain. The mood of the country responded to the new thrust of political thinking and imperialism was launched as a theme with appeal to all classes. Perhaps some kind of psychological transfer took place whereby the working class, by virtue of recognizing a stratum of poor, ignorant and uncivilized (though often fierce and aggressive) natives beneath themselves could displace class prejudice on to them, while they identified, in imagination at least, with Stalky and Co. on the North-West Frontier. The line of unquestioning trust which had been built from Arnold to the sixth and which resulted in the adherence to public school precept and example of boys (the majority) who would never be prefects, let alone captains, now seemed to be spreading into the world at large and producing a general population which would stomach all kinds of snobbish abuse in the belief that, behind the high priests and acolytes, lay an ineffable but secure and immutable wisdom. It is one of the anachronisms of public school stories of the later period, that, while masters tend to be depicted as narrow-minded fools (King and Prout in **Stalky and Co.**, Quelch and Prout in the Bunter stories - Richards denied that the latter name had been borrowed[21]), the head is remote but all-seeing and all-wise, and the wisdom rubs off on his intimates, the prefects and the sixth. Both Stalky and Bunter are 'outsiders' - never admitted to the mysteries and so always able to believe that somewhere behind the fiascos and the arbitrary beatings someone is in touch with the founts of wisdom and probably with God himself. Bunter might have made the sixth one day, though his credentials were unpromising. However, as thirty years of the **Magnet** never moved the saga beyond the confines of the Remove, we shall never know. Stalky, on the other hand, deliberately rejected the idea of collaborating with authority in favour of independence and the joys of a running battle with the rationalizers who wanted him to watch house matches and keep within bounds. Yet, in a curious anticipation of Willis's theory of how the school is bound to win[22], it is precisely through the conflicts with authority that Stalky learns all the tricks he needs to outwit the Malots and Khye-Kheens with his handful of Sikhs.

> Their eyes ceased to sparkle; their faces were
> blank; their hands hung beside them without a
> twitch. They were learning, at the expense of a
> fellow-countryman (the master), the lesson of their
> race, which is to put away all emotion and entrap
> the alien at the proper time.[23]

Whether you accept the curriculum or reject it, it gets you just the same. And even Stalky was totally taken in by a head whose only reaction whenever anyone was brought to him was to beat them. Somehow it was always an expression of profound and subtle wisdom. The Viceroy who admonished him in India was harder to excuse: 'if I thought that . . . two-anna basket hanger governed India, I'd swear I'd become a naturalized Muscovite tomorrow'.[24] Of course, he **did** govern India, but it was comforting to identify him with Prout and believe that he was just a front man for those who really **know best.**

In spite of rationalization and secularization, the 'know best' aspect of sixth forms was even stronger in 1900 than it had been in 1850. Doctrinal christians are given to self-doubt and those members of an organization who have to hold the line against anarchic and independently-minded boys roaming the countryside instead of playing supervised games have to have some kind of realistic conception of the nature of power and authority. But manly patriots who act as important cogs in an efficient machine are programmed for action and decision rather than reflection and insight. In this sense, the sixth form of 1900 represented a retreat from democratic promise. It was more of an oligarchy even than Arnold's sixth had been. What Worsley went so far as to call the **Fuehrerprinzip**[25] was celebrated in the worship of the captain and the publication of pictures of captains in sixpenny magazines sold off station bookstalls. Nor had the democratic potential of sixth forms been increased by an expansion of enrolments. After the upsurge of new proprietary schools in the 1850s and 60s, the development of secondary education had been a slow affair, dependent largely on the workings of the Charity Commissioners. Such expansion as had taken place had been linked to the growth of professions and the connection of entry to professions with the new examinations. The professions were keen to associate themselves with 'gentry' status. As Kitson-Clark puts it: 'some tests were needed which would extend the number of gentlemen, and which would rationalize and moralize the conception of a gentleman for a generation which the old . . . touchstones . . . would by no means suffice'.[26] Schooling and examining provided the social and academic grounds for limiting entry to professions (including the civil service) and, where it could be managed, the goal was a 'closed shop with an Act of Parliament to lock the door'.[27] After a time, the demand for professional men began to level off and there were calls to cut back on the expansion of first grade schools and universities as a result. 'There is a danger in England, as in Germany, of creating what Emperor William has called 'an academical proletariat' . . . (I)t is plain that nothing should be done to stimulate further the supply of such higher school education as is preparatory for professional life'.[28]

The goal of education in the middle class tradition had shifted away from any grand visions of a new order consonant with the inevitable onset of democracy, to one of supplying the new professionals and administrators who would organize society in the age of the steamship, the telegraph, the new boards and local councils (including the Board of Education and the school boards), and would administer the overseas territories. The more academic sixth formers would tend toward the former, the more sporting to the latter kind of occupation. Both would find their way back into independent, and later state secondary schools as teachers and head teachers. 'The most conspicuous result of this zeal for education (was) an addition to classical schools of the first rank, rather than any general progress in the promotion of middle class education.'[29] This was the state of sixth form education on the eve of the passing of the Education Act of 1902 which, for the first time, would provide public support for secondary schooling in England and Wales. Already, however, an institution was firmly in place which could claim to have pre-eminent and national significance as a vehicle for education at this level, and which, for schools which were in the process of establishing themselves, presented a tradition to be followed. It has been argued that, in spite of the often voiced complaints of the time that grant regulations were pushing secondary schools towards a practical and scientific curriculum, a 'national curriculum style' was already in existence which emphasized linguistic and textual studies and which defined desirable learning in terms of a content appropriate to sixth form scholars in the public school image.[30]

NOTES

1   Ackland, Arthur H.D. and Smith, H. Llewellyn (Eds), **Studies in Secondary Education,** London, Percival and Co., 1892, p.14.

2   **Ibid.,** p.161.

3   Bamford, T.W., **The Rise of the Public Schools,** London, Nelson, 1967, p.2.

4   Kitson-Clark, G., **The Making of Victorian England,** London, Methuen, 1962, p.266.

5   Laborde, E.D., **Harrow School: Yesterday and Today,** quoted in Mangan, J.A., **Athleticism in the Victorian and Edwardian Public School,** Cambridge, Cambridge University Press, 1981, p.150.

6   Cotton, Sophia A. (Ed) **Memoir of George Edward Lynch Cotton D.D.,** (headmaster of Marlborough, 1852-8), quoted in Mangan, 1981 **op. cit.,** p.24.

7   **Ibid.,** Table 1, p.71.

8   **Ibid.,** p.161.

9   See the photographs under the title 'Evolution of dress, Harrow Eleven 1863-1912' in **Ibid.,** pp.166-7.

10   Girouard, Mark, **The Return to Camelot: Chivalry and the English Gentleman,** New Haven, Yale University Press, 1981, p.176.

11   Worsley, T.C., **Barbarians and Philistines: Democracy and the Public Schools,** London, Robert Hale, n.d. (1940), p.90.

12   Newsome, David, **Godliness and Good Learning: Four Studies on a Victorian Ideal,** London, John Murray, 1961, p.109. The quotation is from the **Memorial Sermon** on the death of Prince Lee preached by E.W. Benson.

13   Worsley, 1940 **op. cit.,** p.89.

14   **Ibid.,** p.98. 'When Arnold exhorted his boys to be manly,

he meant that they were to put away childish things; but when Hughes portrayed Tom Brown as the paragon of manliness, he was expressing his admiration for the sort of boy "who's got nothing odd about him, and answers straightforward, and holds his head up . . . frank, hearty, and good-natured . . . chock full of life and spirits" ' (Newsome, 1961 op. cit., pp.197-8). Girouard says of Hughes that 'besides being a fine athlete he was a thoroughly nice, honourable, generous, open, uncomplicated man of whom the worst that could be said was that he never quite grew up' (Girouard, Mark, **The Return to Camelot: Chivalry and the English Gentleman,** New Haven, Yale University Press, 1981, p.144).

15   **Ibid.,** p.85.

16   Newsome, 1961 **op. cit.,** p.219.

17   **Ibid.,** p.227.

18   **Ibid.,** p.217. Other journals offering school stories were **Union Jack, Chums** and **Rover.**

19   Farrar, F.W., **Eric, or Little by Little: A Tale of Roslyn School,** London, Hamish Hamilton, 1971 (Original edition, 1858), p.153. Eric was not a prefect but aged sixteen and 'high in the fifth form' when this remark was made of him.

20   Mangan, 1981 **op. cit.,** p.137.

21   Richards, Frank, 'Frank Richards Replies to George Orwell', in Sonia Orwell and Ian Angus (Eds), **The Collected Essays, Journalism and Letters of George Orwell,** Volume 1, 1920-1940, pp.532-3.

22   Willis, Paul, **Learning to Labour: How Working Class Kids Get Working Class Jobs,** Lexington Books, Lexington, Mass., 1978.

23   Kipling, Rudyard, **Stalky and Co.,** London, Macmillan, 1908, p.26.

24   Ibid., p.270.

25   Worsley, n.d., **op. cit.,** p.13.

26   Kitson-Clark, 1962 **op. cit.,** p.255.

27   Reader, W.J., **Professional Men: The Rise of the Professional Classes in Nineteenth Century England,** London, Weidenfeld and Nicholson, 1966, p.68.

28   **Report of a Conference on Secondary Education in England** convened by the Vice-Chancellor of the University of Oxford, Oct. 10 and 11 1893, Oxford, Clarendon Press, p.24 (Remarks of the Rev. G.C. Bell, Headmaster of Marlborough).

29   Ackland and Smith, 1892 **op. cit.,** p.20. Their comment was directed towards the proprietary schools movement.

30   See Smith, M., 'The evaluation of curricular priorities in secondary schools: regulations, opinions and school practices in England, 1903-4', **British Journal of Sociology of Education,** 1,2, 1980, pp. 153-172.

5   A STATE RESPONSIBILITY

In 1902, the State at last assumed direct responsibility for financing and encouraging the growth of secondary education, though the actual provision and administration of it was left to local authorities. At this point, it is safe to say that there were many more sixth formers in public schools than in other types of secondary school. Taking in the new foundations and the day schools, the total population of the public schools was about 30,000 and, even using the historical ratio of sixth formers to overall numbers which can be deduced from the Clarendon figures on the 'nine', this would yield a sixth form figure in excess of 3,000. The Board of Education total for all students in 'forms above those taking the approved course', in maintained schools in 1904/5 is given as 2,742, and not all of these would have been classifiable as 'sixth formers'.* (However around half of them would have been girls, and this does mark the entry of a significant new factor in the development of sixth form education.) So, on the one hand, we can say that the public school and sixth form 'mystique' which had become public property around the turn of the century was founded upon institutions which involved very small numbers indeed - compared even to the total secondary school population which was itself small - and, on the other, we can judge that the developing sixth forms of the new or revived local grammar schools would be very much under the influence of the already established category as projected by the public schools. It was the first decade of the century that was the critical one in this respect: by the end of it, from the point of view of numbers, it was the state supported grammar schools that were dominant on the sixth form scene. In 1910 the over sixteen

---

*   For figures of sixth form enrolments and qualification for and entry to university courses, see the **Statistical Appendix** p.251.

population of maintained schools passed 12,000 and by the outbreak of war in 1914 it was approaching 24,000.[1] But over that first decade, the pattern of future development had been established through the direct influence of the products of public school sixth forms who served as heads and masters in the new schools, or contributed to debates on local and national educational policy, and through the indirect influence of such people who worked behind the scenes as framers and implementers of legislation, regulations and legal judgements.

At the time the Act was passed, however, it was not at all clear what its implications would be. The categorical status achieved by the public schools and transmitted to the endowed grammar schools over the previous fifty or so years gave their model of secondary education a clear advantage. Their supporters were quick to press it by projecting the alternative model of the higher grade school as linked with a more restricted range of social interests. On the other side of the question, state intervention was an unknown quantity which had long been feared. Some thought that the Act would empower other interests to secure political support for an interpretation of it which went against the public school lobby, resulting even in the disappearance of such schools.

The basic question to be decided was which of the two alternative patterns of secondary education should form the basis of the state supported system of secondary education which, though long delayed, was inevitably going to be implemented. Should it be the one which built upwards in order to 'crown the edifice of primary education' or should it be the one which grew out of the view that secondary education was 'middle class education' and offered a rationale for development in which what came below was a function of what happened at the top - in the sixth form? The idea that the pattern of the Higher Grade School should be refined and extended seemed to have practical advantages. It was almost inevitable that state supported secondary education would be provided through local bodies and the School Boards had by this time had a quarter of a century or more of experience of administering publicly supported education, in some cases well beyond the basic elementary level. Secondary education might have been expanded and revitalized through the encouragement of these initiatives. The severe problem of the correlation of elementary and secondary school curricula would have been simplified by building on the 'higher grade' initiatives. The growth of this type of secondary provision would have ensured that what was offered was relevant to the needs of local communities and appropriate to the character and resources of day schooling. The system could have grown organically in response to demand and could have been based on styles of organization which were flexible enough to accommodate a variety of curricula. By contrast the model of the public school seemed to offer only disadvantages. Apart from the limited Woodard-type schemes, the schools had always acted independently and very much according to the whim of powerful heads. In spite of the increasing uniformity of doctrine and practice which was visible over the latter part of the nineteenth century, they in no way constituted a formal system and had no experience of linking educational provision to complex cultural and social communities. Moreover, the model was centred around the sixth form as a fixed point to which other levels were subservient, so that correlation with existing elementary provision was difficult if not impossible. And the public school, as an institutional category, grew out of a context of boarding and of a middle to upper class clientele which was radically different from anything which could naturally be associated with a day school catering for the whole of a local community. Yet it was this unpromising pattern of development which prevailed.

The visible prime mover in the official initiatives towards the extension of the public school category into the maintained sector was Robert Morant, Secretary of the newly established

Board of Education who was educated at Winchester, one of the famous 'nine' schools. Morant's political skill was critical in ensuring that a number of important decisions went in the 'right' direction. But behind him lay a significant body of opinion and an established cadre of administrators who could make sure that nothing was lost at the point of implementation. The first move was against the higher grade schools and, indirectly, the school boards themselves. In 1900 a High Court judgement was obtained against the London School Board for illegally spending public funds on higher grade schools. This was not only a blow to the whole conception of the higher grade school, but also paved the way for disbanding school boards altogether through the Education Act of 1902 and giving the whole of primary and secondary education to the recently created local authorities. Secondly, Morant ensured that the Education Act was framed in such a way that there was no obstacle to setting up secondary schools on the pattern of existing public school practice, and thirdly the practical implementation of this possibility was enshrined, by him, in the Board of Education Regulations for Secondary Schools of 1904. These manoeuvres did not go unchallenged. Even after the passage of the Act, efforts were made to have it repealed under the Liberal administration which came into office in 1905. But by then the work of implementation was so far advanced that the attempt failed. Opposition within the Board of Education to the direction that policy was taking was also scotched, so that over the critical period when the 1902 Act was being put into practice, there was nothing in the way of administrative or regulatory discouragement to those who wanted the public school model to prevail.[2] On the other hand, a natural momentum, generated over the latter years of the nineteenth century, was pressing schools in that very direction.

Such obstacles as did exist were more likely to be put up by the LEAs themselves. On the curriculum front, however, their hands were tied by Morant's regulations. In the first place, these stipulated that 'The course of education must be complete' and that it could not be considered complete if it was not 'so planned as to carry on the scholars to such a point as they may reasonably be expected to reach at the age of sixteen'[3]. In other words, what was offered at any stage in the school was to be determined by what those who would leave at sixteen would achieve - and these, in the early days of maintained secondary schools were a small minority. Secondly, '(t)he instruction must be general; i.e. must be such as gives a reasonable degree of exercise and development to the whole of the faculties'. By standing square on the 'faculty theory' of education, the regulations could strike down any school which attempted to give instruction which was, in the language of the day, tainted with 'cheap utilitarianism'. The widely held view that only abstract or remote subject matter could truly exercise the faculties was reflected in the specific requirements for the teaching of subjects. Not less than four and a half hours a week were to be given to English, Geography and History and not less than seven and a half for science and mathematics, of which three must be for science. Three and a half hours were to be given to teaching a foreign language, or preferably six hours to two languages, in which case if 'Latin is not one of them, the Board will require to be satisfied that the omission of Latin is for the advantage of the schools' (how could it be?).

Regulations on this pattern continued to be issued yearly, but by 1908 there was enough confidence that the curriculum message had been instilled in both the schools and the authorities for the stipulations on teaching hours to be dropped, though there was correspondingly more emphasis on the need to provide courses up to the age of eighteen. The changes were accompanied by the comment that 'In carrying out the spirit of these rules the Board confidently look forward to the co-operation of Local Education Authorities and Governing Bodies, of Head Masters and Headmistresses, and of educated public opinion generally'[4].

By then the work of implantation had been well done by the proselytizers who, because of the way the regulations had advocated a strong role for heads and governors, had been enabled to carry the day on the fronts where the local authorities might have proved recalcitrant. The 1904 document had urged that 'the Head Master or Head Mistress should not be liable to any unnecessary interference in matters of school administration for which he or she is primarily responsible' and had stated clearly that '(t)he immediate relations of the Head . . . will be with the Governing Body; and the control of the Local Education Authority over the school . . . should be exercised through the Governing Body.'[5] This body was to have considerable discretion and should be composed of the 'best men and women available'. There was obviously a good chance that the 'right', public school educated people would find their way into positions of effective authority as heads and governors, since they had an undisputed claim to be the only ones who could put themselves forward as 'experts' on secondary education. The problem was to make sure that, where they were in conflict with LEAs, they would prevail. The keys to an effective strategy were the importation into the state system of the notion of the autonomy of the head and the apparatus of independent governing bodies. The propagandists of the doctrine of the public school model were insistent on this point.

One of the most prominent of these was Cyril Norwood, then headmaster of Bristol Grammar School and later to be head of Marlborough and Harrow. Of him it was said that 'more than any of his contemporaries, Norwood was in the tradition of the great Victorian headmasters'. Over the formative period of state secondary schools and right up to the passing of the 1944 Education Act, he was an unyielding advocate of the ideology of education represented by the public schools of the late nineteenth century. When he became head of a public boarding school he felt that he had 'passed into a different and better atmosphere'. In the early 1900s Norwood was not the significant figure he was later to become during his quarter of a century's tenure of the chairmanship of the Secondary Schools Examinations Council, a period crowned by the publication of the report which bears his name. But he was certainly representative of those who did wield influence. Norwood, in a 1909 publication, put forward the idea of the autonomy of headmasters in no uncertain terms:

> it will be the duty of the State to see that none
> but great and good men are given high command.
> If the monarchy is to be limited, it must still be
> a real monarchy, not a shadow of a legal fiction,
> since the little people of the realm are in the
> tribal stage which demands a chieftain to be
> followed, a living incarnation of strength and
> justice to be revered.

But the great and good man was to hold sway outside the school as well: he was to have 'full liberty to build up, within and without the walls, a school which shall reflect his ideals, and be, so far as he can make it, "himself writ large".'[6] On the character of governors, Norwood is more explicit than Morant's regulations could be. They are to be 'of educated and liberal mind' and preferably 'leisured men'. Their 'most critical and difficult duty' was to choose a headmaster and afterwards it was 'their business not to interfere unnecessarily'.[7] From 1907, it was laid down in the Regulations that the 'appointment and dismissal of the Head Master or Head Mistress of the School must be in the hands of a Governing Body . . .' (The constitution and functions of such bodies had, from the outset, been subject to the approval of the Board.)[8] Presumably a stage had now been reached when most governing bodies were composed of the 'best men and women available' and it was safe to make their authority over the appointment of heads universal. What the governors should do when faced with their 'most critical and difficult duty' is clearly stated by Norwood: they should 'try to introduce the public school tradition into a new element which badly needs it, by appointing for some time to come an old public-school man as headmaster when the post falls vacant, paying him liberally, and giving him a free hand, with teaching and leading, not clerking, as his function.'[9] 'Clerking' was a role which some unenlightened local authorities were trying to foist on heads. It went along with an excessive leaning towards the discredited 'higher grade' style of schooling which 'gave a utilitarian and showy type of lower secondary teaching at a nominal cost' and had thereby 'severely damaged the unaided and often poor' Grammar Schools and forced them into the undesirable expedient of earning special grants by teaching science. Freed from clerkish duties, heads would be able, with the support of their governors, to introduce all the apparatus of the public boarding school into local maintained grammar schools: houses, prefects, old boys associations, organized games and a cadet force. No thought is given either to whether such things have any intrinsic value for the new schools, or to the question of how, if they do, they can be adapted to the new situation. It is the duty of the new schools and their communities to adapt to what is self-evidently good. If the activity conflicts with what local people might want, that is simply proof that it is needed in order to repair the deficiencies of the native culture: 'the discipline of games is essential . . . for the boys . . . do not learn any sense of public spirit from their parents, nor can the inspiration of this spirit be expected of those whose daily life is spent amidst the methods of modern business and the processes of an individualist society.'[10]

What we see here is the persistence into the new century of Matthew Arnold's conception of that 'sweetness and light' which must remain the undisputed goal of education whatever the state of the country or the state of society. The 'best' is known and those who 'know best' must see that others do not worship false gods. Norwood's vision of the goal of education is the arrival of a Platonic society in which the lower orders 'contentedly accept the direction of those who know'.[11] Once the best is known, the problem is one of how to ensure that those who may be seduced in other directions (the Bunters of the public school, the day school victims of individualistic and utilitarian households) are got into line. The answer is summed up in the 'three great Imperatives': learn to obey, learn to exert yourself, and learn to deny yourself and overcome your desires.

> English . . . democracy is faced with a task such
> as never people had to bear before . . . (It) is
> called upon to show that a democracy can govern
> a mighty empire. It can only be done by
> self-discipline and self-sacrifice, and of these
> qualities little appears in any class in the country
> which has not been trained in its better Secondary
> Schools. If the lesson of unquestioning obedience
> to orders ceases to be taught there, to what
> quarter shall we cry for help?

And again: 'In every school it should be the primary maxim that boys must work, and, if they do not, must be made to work.'[12] The 'learn' of the imperatives is false: the message is that the lesson will be inculcated by whatever methods are to hand, pleasant if possible, unpleasant if need be. The end justifies the means.

This attempt to spread the gospel of the public school was aided, as we have seen, by the existence of the popular cult of 'manliness' which associated the schools with the call of the Empire. Even so, on any rational grounds, it seemed an improbable undertaking and Norwood himself had to admit that it raised serious practical difficulties. The 'trappings' did not fit very well: how was it possible to have 'houses' where there was no boarding? Prefects where there was no sixth form? Organized games without playing fields, coaches and equipment? But, more seriously, how was an enterprise whose doctrine grew, Platonically, from an ideal top downwards, to be implanted in schools which had a very poor retaining power for students? The proposal that things should be done this way round ensured that local grammar schools looked even more like artificial creations than the public schools on which they were modelled. Norwood's analysis of the Board of Education's statistics for 1906-7 showed that:

> about 2 boys out of every 62 in our Secondary Schools under the Board are doing really advanced work, are entering upon that specialized application of a sound general equipment which it is of the very essence of secondary education to encourage and secure; while, of the remaining 60, 18 are doing merely preparatory work, 17 will leave when they have taken a year's general training, 13 after two year's 'finishing', 8 will be allowed 3 years in which to learn something of the world's mysteries and achievements, while 4 will be lucky enough to complete an encyclopaedic course of instruction, but will not in any case be permitted to stay even a year longer in order to reap the fruit of this preliminary training.[13]

Thus, a kind of 'Catch-22' situation was created. Secondary schools were set up on a pattern which was totally foreign to the bulk of the prospective clientele, and then the customers were blamed for not appreciating what they were offered and sabotaging the system by not allowing and encouraging their children to stay into the sixth form which was practically the sole justification of the whole enterprise. But the patrons of the local grammar school were in a different category from the parents who sent their children to public schools. For a start, the fact that the latter could afford the fees was some guarantee that, however the career of the boy in the school developed, he would not lack opportunities for employment. The Stalkies and the Bunters might be failures in the sense that they never entered the sixth or saw the light or tasted the sweetness, but their role as foils to the 'palladium'[14] of the school did not leave them unequipped personally and educationally for the adult worlds they would enter. Their futures were secure whatever the rest of society might think about their fitness to enjoy a privileged existence. But children from poorer homes were not materially or psychologically ready to form a new generation of 'cosmopolites'. Employment, and the useful knowledge that could bring employment was an attractive prospect. A failed attempt to join, or even get close to the rarified world of the sixth held out nothing but disadvantage. A year or two of secondary education for a bright child who could get a scholarship, or whose parents could afford the subsidized fees was better than staying in an elementary school where there was no more to be learned, but the irrelevance of much of the curriculum, coupled with the atmosphere of intense competition in which those who had been in 'prep' schools or departments had a head start, was not conducive to a prolonged experience of schooling. However, the fact of early leaving, while deplored by the advocates of the public school model, could also be used as grounds for the argument about 'quality versus quantity' which began to be made at this time. By allowing their children to leave, the lower orders had shown that they were not worthy of what was being offered to them, and that 'the way would at length be clear for reform' only when they learned 'what a secondary education means'. Norwood quotes with approval a report on secondary education in Kent which says:

> The establishment of a a large number of low-grade Secondary Schools would probably be the most disastrous step that any authority could take . . . It would be a fatal policy to lower the level of the education given merely in order to catch pupils. The wiser plan is to keep the best system of school training before the eyes of the people, who will assuredly come sooner or later to appreciate it.[15]

These, he says, are 'words of infinite wisdom'. The argument, in

99

this form, had not been applied to the public schools, though some people had expressed concern that too great an expansion on that front might lead to an excess of aspirants to the professions. The argument in that case was not about the quality of the education, but about the connection of that education with high status occupations and the protection of these through maintenance of their exclusiveness. Now, however, the claim began to be heard that secondary education itself would suffer unless its expansion were controlled on the basis that only 'first grade' schools with sixth forms should be encouraged. Whereas in the public school the sixth form was an essential key to the organization of discipline and learning, in the new maintained schools, it was urged, the sixth should be seen as the essential justification of the school's existence. What went before was merely 'preliminary training'. This first version of the 'more means worse' argument was applied to schools rather than pupils. But the practical effect was the same. On the one hand, secondary education was billed as being for 'the few', and, on the other, the development of sixth forms became a priority for secondary school heads. The possession of a sixth form was taken as evidence of the quality of the education given by the school and thus the gulf between the work of the elementary and secondary schools was widened. Elementary education had its eyes fixed on the whole population and on the beginnings of learning. Secondary education focused on the sixth form and engineered a system of internal and external examination which operated to 'cool out' those who were not destined for high status.

The argument about quality was a strange one for the supporters of the public school style of education to make. If one thing was sure about the public schools, it was that the complaints about their poor teaching which had led to the setting up of the Clarendon Commission forty years earlier were still as justified as they had ever been. Norwood himself admits the justice of Rouse's critique of the results of the classical teaching which was the heart and soul of the curriculum: the better public schools do poorly by their best scholars who do not do as well as might be expected in winning university scholarships, while 'of the average boy it cannot be denied that he never understands Latin or Greek, can hardly write a sentence without a mistake, or read a book without a 'crib', and arrives at the University unable to write his own language with ease, and unwilling to work seriously at anything.'[16] When such issues were raised the usual answer was that the quality of teaching was being improved, and that, in any case, the justification of what was done was moral rather than purely academic - that the public school instilled the three great imperatives which were the prop of Empire: obedience, exertion and self-denial. But even if these effects were produced, and even if they were to be desired (both of which were dubious propositions), they were brought about by those features of the school which were related to its nature as a 'total institution' rather than to those parts of the curriculum which could readily be reproduced in the maintained grammar school.

Thus the effect of State intervention was curiously double-edged. The strong stimulus that it gave to the growth of secondary education is evidenced by the figures for the increase in numbers of grant-aided schools from 491 in 1904, to 1010 in 1913, and by the almost tenfold increase in enrolments beyond the age of sixteen over that period. But the expansion was from a very small base so that the essentially restrictive character of the new secondary education was masked, and the manner of the intervention was such that, initially, very little change took place in the nature of the sixth as an institutional category. The image of the sixth former was unchanged, ideas about the activities appropriate to the role were unaltered and the connections made between the role and future careers remained the same. Possibly some broadening of the image began around the essential centre focus of prefectorial and scholarly virtues. On one side, some of the earnestness that had faded since the time of Thomas Arnold was reinjected, as examinations took a tighter grip, and 'scholarship' boys who made it to the top brought single-mindedness to the endeavour. On the other, there was some softening of the image as the proportion of girls in sixth forms increased and as sixth forms developed in mixed schools. No doubt this was another front on which the upholders of the public school tradition would have liked to fight. Their stereotype of the female character was grossly at odds with the image of manliness with which they were so obsessed, and their prejudiced comments on co-education (often delivered obliquely through discussion of American high schools) were backed up by the popular school stories which, when they mention them at all, portray girls as weak, ignorant and generally 'soppy'. (Bunter, as well as being an embodiment of lower class vices, also exhibits equally undesirable girlish traits of giggling, snivelling and lack of enthusiasm for games). But, from a practical point of view, there was little they could do on that particular score. In many areas even mixed grammar schools were ridiculously small and it made no sense at all to have separate provison for boys and girls. In any case, the two aims - to secure a viable sixth form, and to keep the sexes separate - were incompatible. Something had to give, and it could not be the sixth. Thus the mixed school, with all its subversive implications had to be accepted. Girls schools were not so bad, because in the early days of education for women they fought their battles by showing that they could vie with men on their own ground. They strapped on their cricket pads, showed that they could command and lead with the best of men, and entered wholeheartedly into the competition for the chance of higher education in mathematics, classics and science. Nor were the mixed public schools a problem. They were set up in order to project a totally different image of what education could be like. Bedales never pretended to be working on the same ground as Clifton or Haileybury. But the mixed grammar school was a different proposition. It aspired to the conventional public school model, but brought boys and girls together in a context where they were as likely to assert their differences as their similarities.

In general, however, the new municipal grammar schools followed in the footsteps of those endowed schools which had been strengthened or revived following on the work of the Taunton Commission and which 'began to adopt the dress, manners, terminology and institutions of the public school'.[17] As Seaborne and Lowe note, even elementary schools had, before 1900, begun to reflect in their architecture some of the spirit of public school corporatism.[18] Though in retrospect the model of secondary education which was adopted for state schools may seem inappropriate, it is not clear, given the climate of opinion that existed, that a radically different one could have emerged. Probably state intervention came too late to disturb, other than in marginal ways, educational categories which had already imprinted themselves firmly on the national consciousness.

NOTES

1   Board of Education figures for grant-aided secondary schools. The numbers given are for students sixteen or over. Not all of these would have been in sixth forms. Problems are caused (a) by the fact that the definition of sixth form status was not clear or consistent, and (b) by the persistence at the secondary level of promotion by criteria other than age, leading to wide age-ranges within the classes of small schools, and faster and slower 'streams' in larger ones ('Brains, not age, must be the standard of promotion' (Norwood and Hope, 1909, p.306).). At a guess, the 'sixth form' figure was possibly about fifty per cent of the 'over sixteen' figure.

2   See, Lowe, Roy, 'The divided curriculum: Sadler, Morant and the English secondary school,' **Journal of Curriculum Studies,** 1976, 8, 2, pp.139-148.

3   Board of Education, **Regulations for Secondary Schools,** 1904-5, pp.7-8.

4   **Regulations for Secondary Schools,** 1908-9, p.xii.

5   **Regulations for Secondary Schools,** 1904-5, p.15.

6   Norwood, Cyril and Hope, Arthur H.(Eds), **The Higher Education of Boys in England,** London, John Murray, 1909, pp. 226 and 302 (At the time 'higher' was used synonymously with 'secondary').

7   **Ibid.,** pp.218-9.

8   **Regulations for Secondary Schools,** 1904-5, p.21.

9   Norwood and Hope, 1909 **op.cit,** p.185.

10   **Ibid.,** p.436. Norwood was much encouraged by the **Report of the Board of Education for the Year 1905-1906** which he referred to as the 'liber aureus' or golden book. This was notable for two things: first the deliberate choice, through administrative decision, of a model of secondary education which preserved its distinction from elementary, and secondly for the place it gives to the structural rather than curricular aspects of policy on secondary education. Like Norwood, the report sees the role of heads and governors as an essential key to the future development of the secondary sector. Governing bodies of municipal secondary schools, it says, lack power and responsibility which is centralized 'in the hands of an Education Authority far removed from the school'(p.55). Creation of strong governing bodies would enable staffing policies to be pursued and this would result in schools where 'thoroughness in intellectual work' was combined with 'a real and pervading sense of corporate life' (p.59). This was the style of education that the Board and its inspectors were anxious to preserve and develop. They recognised that by defining secondary schools as a 'kind' rather than a 'stage' of education they risked encouraging 'class education in compartments after the fashion of

Plato's **Republic**' which was 'contrary to the essence of democracy'. Nevertheless, they argued that it was necessary to have secondary schools which were different in kind from elementary and that the problem was 'how to alleviate the "break of gauge" for the majority' (p.61). The secondary school must 'correspond to its title, and must give an education higher in scope and character than that of an Elementary School'. Where they failed to do this, the Board would not 'lower standards' to allow them to be recognised (pp.63-4). All of this was very much in line with the public school ethos of education of which Norwood was such a strong supporter.

11 Norwood, Cyril, Harrow Lecture, quoted in Curtis, S.J. and Boultwood, M.E.A., **An Introductory History of English Education Since 1800,** London, University Tutorial Press, 1960, p.259.

12 Norwood and Hope, 1909 **op.cit,** pp.316 and 315.

13 **Op.cit.,** pp.55-6.

14 'The Sixth . . . is the palladium of all public schools' (Kipling, Rudyard, **Stalky and Co.,** London, Macmillan, 1908, p.65.) This is a misquotation from **Eric, or Little by Little,** where it is the monitorial (i.e. prefectoral) system which is referred to as 'a Palladium . . . of happiness and morality'.

15 **Op.cit.,** p.67.

16 **Ibid.,** p.344.

17 Newsome, David, **Godliness and Good Learning: Four Studies on a Victorian Ideal,** London, John Murray, 1961, p.217.

18 Seaborne, Malcolm and Lowe, Roy, **The English School: Its Architecture and Organisation,** Vol.2, 1870-1970, London, Routledge, 1977, p.96.

TABLE ONE

Enrolments in Grant-Aided Secondary Schools, 1920-1938

Year	Number of Schools	Total Enrolment	Average School Life (yrs-mths)	Pupils 16+ as % of total
1920	1141	308,266	3-1*	12.8
1925	1284	352,605	3-8	16.4
1930	1354	394,105	4-8	16.8
1935	1380	456,783	4-11	14.3
1938**	1398	470,003	4-11	15.7

*   1921

**   No figures available, 1939-46.

(Source: Board of Education Reports)

6 THE GRAMMAR SCHOOL TRADITION

The War years and the years immediately following saw a rapid expansion in the provision of secondary school places. Between 1914 and 1920, the number of ten to twelve year old pupils doubled, while the increase in the sixteen plus group was over fifty per cent. Lacey's chart showing the 'Hightown' figures against those for south-west Hertfordshire and Middlesborough, illustrates this growth.[1] The retention rate, however, still presented a problem. According to the Labour Party statement of 1922 'Secondary Education for All', which has become a classic document in the history of English education, while over five per cent of the age cohort of thirteen to fourteen year olds were in grant-aided secondary schools, the figure dropped to less than two per cent for sixteen to seventeen year olds and less than one per cent for seventeen to eighteen year olds, and the average length of time spent in the secondary school was just under three years.[2] The lack of correlation between the elementary school and the secondary school also persisted. The attempt to bridge the gap which had been made through the introduction in the 1907 **Regulations** of a requirement that schools must offer a quarter of their places to 'scholarship' entrants was described in the Labour Party policy statement as 'an empirical compromise between the traditional conception of "elementary" education as the education of a class and the new demand that opportunities of full-time secondary education should be given to some of the more intelligent of the children attending the primary schools.'[3] What in fact happened was that 'The existing assumptions and organization of "elementary" education were retained intact. But, by means of scholarships, free places, and maintenance allowances, bridges were thrown . . . between it and the newly-organized system of public secondary education.'[4] The duality of the education system was by now firmly entrenched and, with rising demand, the 'bridges' or the 'ladder', as it was more commonly known, looked increasingly slender. Other new initiatives, such as the introduction of a Higher Certificate examination for sixth formers by the universities, and the provision from 1917 of grants in respect of sixth formers on courses 'so planned as to lead up to a standard required for entering upon an honours course at a university'[5], had, if anything, the effect of sharpening the focus on the top end of the secondary school, and widening the primary/secondary gap. However, what was most striking about the development of the secondary system was the disparity in the provision between various parts of the country which, according to figures given in the 1922 Labour Party report, varied by a factor of as much as four between Rochdale with 27.3 secondary children for every 1,000 in public elementary schools, and Essex with 112.4. This was the easy and obvious target to attack. It seemed that the expansion that had been launched was likely to continue, but, at the same time, the base from which the expansion was taking place was so small that apparently quite radical calls for it to be regularized and encouraged did not look expensive. It was not as clear as it might have been in a period when emphasis on capacity was plainly an expensive option, that the real target for a radical reform movement was being allowed to escape unchallenged.

The most remarkable thing about the 1922 proposals is the extent to which they conceded the Arnoldian view of secondary education by default. Even the language of the report is borrowed from the 'conservative' intelligentsia of the nineteenth century:

> The demand of Labour for the democratizing of
> secondary education implies no wish to sacrifice
> the peculiar excellence of particular institutions to
> a pedantic State-imposed uniformity, still less to
> forego the amenities of culture for the sake of a
> utilitarian efficiency . . . Its desire is that what
> is weak in the higher (sc. secondary) education of
> the country should be strengthened, and that what

is already excellent should be made accessible to all.[6]

Matthew Arnold himself would have been pleased with that, believing as he did that one of the virtues of State intervention was precisely that it could be made to work against the uniformity to which schools tended when left to their own devices. And their position on the length of the school course would have met with Morant's approval: 'However much value may be attached to even a short period spent in the environment of a good secondary school, it will be generally agreed that, up, at least, to sixteen, each successive year gives a more than proportionate return.'[7] These statements, emanating as they do from the newly risen party of the working class left, show that what had been an institutional category for private education had now become firmly established in the public sector.

Once again, the education system was showing its talent for creating traditions overnight. The Grammar Schools, which had so recently been moribund, were well launched on the path that was to make of them an immovable part of the English heritage, complete with their houses and their captains, their prefects and their sixth forms. 'Secondary education for all' meant 'secondary schools for all' and these were not all to be Grammar Schools. Technical education was to be expanded, but the majority of ex-elementary pupils were to be transferred to 'modern schools'. In this way, the Labour Party thought, the invidious discrimination between secondary education for the few and elementary education for the many could be done away with. The problem was to see how a new category of 'modern school' could be created which did not assimilate itself to the already existing and well-established categories of 'grammar school' on the one hand or 'elementary school' on the other. Buildings can help to create an image, but they are not of the essence of it. The best hope was that the new philosophy of primary education expressed in the Hadow Report of 1931 might be extended upwards.[8] This philosophy represented a reaction from the previously popular 'faculty' psychology, and wanted the curriculum to be thought of 'in terms of activity and experience rather than of knowledge to be acquired and facts to be stored.' It was, however, severely in conflict with the grammar school curriculum which, throughout the interwar period, became increasingly routinized and standardized. The Labour Party made no claim that all children should get a 'grammar type' education, but neither did they suggest that the 'grammar' curriculum should be radically changed. However, any hope that schools could arise which offered a variety of curriculum emphases, but at the same time were all equal in terms of resources and esteem, was vain in the absence of some attack on established secondary schools whose whole curriculum ethos was built around the cultivation of a strong sixth form.

The development of sixth forms through the 1920s and 30s was more a story of routinization and entrenchment than of evolution and expansion. Though the secondary school population grew from about 300,000 in 1925 to almost 400,000 in 1937, the number of students aged sixteen and over increased only marginally from 37,500 to 46,000 and actually declined slightly as a percentage of the eleven to sixteen age group.[9] Little movement had taken place towards the democratizing of the sixth by opening it to a wider population, but it was over this period that the 'grammar' sixth achieved a stable character, closely related to, but also different from that of the public school sixth. The same causes which the Spens Report of 1938 noted as 'tending to produce uniformity' in the lower school curriculum were also operating, if anything more strongly, at the sixth form level. These were 'Firstly . . . the traditional prestige of the Public Schools and the Grammar Schools which has tended to assimilate the newer types of secondary school . . . to the grammar school type.' That is to say, the category of 'sixth form' as projected in the popular and professional imagination by the old established schools was so firmly rooted that, short of a serious and concerted effort to undermine it, the organization and activities of all sixth forms tended to be guided by it, without the formation of any clear intention that they should be. Secondly, the Report notes the enduring effect of the 1904 Regulations, and finally it points to the School Certificate Examinations as having 'undoubtedly had the effect of strengthening and intensifying the tendency towards uniformity.'[10] What was happening was that the criterion for entry to a maintained school sixth form was becoming routinely academic. Examination work was something the school could understand, and it fitted in with the whole system of scholarships and the 'ladder'. And, though the process was slow to gather momentum, it was something that could be 'sold' to parents who were doubtful about keeping their children at school. By 1921, the average 'life' of a boy in a secondary school which in 1913 had been under three years, had passed that mark. By 1928, it was past four years and by 1932 it was very close to five, where it remained until 1938 when the reporting of statistics was suspended for the war period. In 1939, the entry for the higher certificate examination, normally taken at the age of seventeen or eighteen, had risen to a figure of over 13,000 from a level of under 6,000 in the mid-'20s. By the 1930s quite a close relationship had developed between the examination entry and the numbers of seventeen, eighteen and nineteen year olds in maintained schools. For 1934, this figure was just under 20,000 and the higher certificate entry was just under 10,000. Allowing for certificates taken in independent schools, it would seem that it was almost the norm for those staying beyond the age of sixteen to be entered for the examination, and that the intention to take it was what marked a senior pupil as a 'sixth former'. On the other hand, the number of places available in universities remained fairly constant, and entrants from maintained schools who had numbered about 3,600 in 1926 were still around the same figure in 1938. Thus, given a pass rate of seventy per cent, possession of a higher certificate was by no means linked to undergraduate status. In fact, through the whole period, just under half the boys who left grant-aided secondary schools entered 'professional, commercial or clerical occupations.'[11] Many of these would have been holders of higher certificates. What we see is the development of a 'second layer' of bureaucratic, semi-professional work to match the top layer which had been the target of public schools in the nineteenth century. Then the routes had been examination based, but diverse, through civil service and army tests. Now, a common route was emerging through the school certificate examinations. In so far as the university was the goal it tended to be the 'redbrick' foundations - Leeds, Manchester, Birmingham - rather than Oxford or Cambridge (London was 'middleground') and was reached via science courses in the sixth rather than the old classical 'side'. The 'modern' studies (History, Geography and English) were also popular. Though the numbers of girls staying on were about the same as for boys, many were aiming at careers in teaching or nursing, and they created a demand for less conventionally academic courses. Thus, while the grammar school sixth kept many of the trappings of its counterpart in the public schools, and was supported by a common ideology, it was more local in its orientation, with many ex-students taking employment in the community, or going on to courses in universities with a regional or local bias in loyalty and intake.

The grammar school sixth was more likely, especially in single-sex schools, to be controlled in terms of entry and curriculum and teaching by public examinations, and this bias towards the routine preparation of examinations was accentuated by the commitment generated among 'scholarship' boys and girls. The usual sixth was smaller than its public school counterpart, and its connections with higher education more tenuous. The rare occasions on which pupils won entry to Oxford or Cambridge were marked by public rejoicing and a day's holiday. But more often than not, the achievement was an isolated one rather than a precedent for the building of a tradition. In practice, there was a strong tendency for the orientation of the sixth to be pulled towards science courses for boys leading to a course at a local university, and practical courses for girls without academic ambitions.

This persistence of the tension which had been noted as long ago as the 1890s between setting up a 'middle class institution' and 'crowning the edifice of primary education' is evident in the Spens **Report on Secondary Education** of 1938. It flirts with the idea of encouraging 'multilateral' schools which would combine the functions of 'grammar' and 'modern'. It echoes the Hadow Report's concern that 'it is useless, if not harmful, to try to inculcate ideas, however valuable they may be at a later stage of growth, which have at the time no bearing on a child's natural activities of mind and body, and do nothing to guide his experience'.[12] It takes seriously the problems of the challenges posed to democracy in the 1930s and wants a curriculum that will contribute better to an understanding of the modern world. It quotes at length the Bryce Report of 1895 on the folly of artificially separating 'technical and classical' instruction in terms of a conflict between the 'liberal' and the 'utilitarian', and it speaks sympathetically of the higher grade school and deplores the fact that their work was ignored in the 1904 Regulations.[13] But it finds an impassable obstacle confronting its endeavours to reform secondary education in the way these comments would indicate as desirable. And that obstacle was the sixth form. Multilateral schools are rejected because their sixth forms would represent too small a proportion of the whole school: 'Even where geographical and other conditions admit of relatively large schools there is much to be said for their being wholly of the grammar school type. This is so, in view of the importance of having large Sixth Forms which render economically possible a considerable variety of Sixth Form courses.'[14] What can be done about the curriculum is limited by the need to ensure that the organization and curriculum of the school should continue to cater for 'all those who are capable of making proper use of a university education'. The comment on this point is accompanied by an extravagant encomium of the sixth, which is described as: 'the most characteristic and most valuable feature in a Grammar School in the training of character and a sense of responsibility, and on its existence depends all that is best in the grammar school tradition'.[15] This shows firstly that, however much actual grammar school sixths might have developed towards practicality, reward based on measured ability, and a 'local' and domestic view of the world, the categorical status of the sixth as a moral, ideal and cosmopolitan institution was not under any immediate threat. And secondly it points up the sixth as the one feature of the secondary system which must be regarded as a premise when all other decisions have to be made. The work of the founders had been well done. The message about the sixth form had been implanted in the place where it was most influential and from which it was least likely to be dislodged - the minds of the teachers and head teachers. The writers of the Report were able to quote the strongly urged views of associations of teachers and head teachers in support of their position.[16] By now, of course, many secondary teachers had themselves been pupils in the grant-aided system and had had personal experience of sixth form status. 'State' sixth forms had become self-perpetuating just as public school sixth forms had in an earlier period.

Thus the Spens Committee found itself impaled on the horns of the classic dilemma which the political manoeuverings of the public school lobby around the turn of the century has set up for all who followed. They wanted reform, but the sixth was an overriding priority. As had become the habit by then, the proposed resolution consisted of reaffirmation of the need to preserve the 'sixth form tradition', coupled with anodyne plans for the encouragement of parallel developments in curriculum or organization which stood little chance of success because they were either in competition with established sixth form categories inside the school (more 'relevant' or 'practical' courses for those not aiming at the university), or, on the outside, had to meet the whole superior weight of the 'grammar' tradition crowned by its sixth (secondary modern schools). In the public school the sixth had become the fixed point around which the organization of the school revolved; in the state system, the whole provision of secondary schooling was beginning to be dictated by it.

The Spens Committee met at a time of stability in the history of education. Over the decade 1930-39, in spite of the pressures for the setting up of modern schools as well as for the expansion of grammar provision, the total population of secondary schools grew by only about two per cent per annum on average. Thus, while seeming to adopt a liberal policy about the provision of places, and about the equalization of the very disparate opportunities for post-primary education over the country (a situation which had improved not at all since the Labour Party Report of 1922), it could confidently put forward a figure of eighteen per cent as the proportion of the age group for which such provision should be made. As long as the public mood was not especially favourable to education, and the image of schools dominated by their sixth forms (however small these often were in practice) acted as much as a deterrent as an inducement to lower class, and even some middle class children and parents, much play could be made with figures of fifteen per cent, or eighteen per cent, or even twenty-five per cent without much, other than the reputations of educational theorists, hanging on the outcome of the rather sterile pseudo-psychological debate which this entailed. Whatever policy was decided on, the sixth could still be the lynchpin of an oligarchical system of education because the numbers involved were far too small to raise serious issues of democratization. The Spens Report can combine hints of radical sympathies in curriculum matters, and liberality over questions of the supply of places with injunctions about discipline, prefects,

esprit de corps, houses, games, and even the school chapel, all of which Cyril Norwood no doubt found wholly admirable. And the sixth naturally has pride of place:

> It is the English tradition to . . . delegate considerable responsibility for the good order and well-being of the school to a body of school prefects. We attach value in this form of self-government to the placing of authority in the hands of senior boys or girls selected from those who have most intellectual ability (a system associated with the name of Dr Arnold) and we welcome the fact that this is normally the case in day schools owing to the constitution of their Sixth Forms.[17]

The assertions about the necessary connection of such practices with the English liberal tradition are as confident as they were at the turn of the century. Nowhere it seemed, unless it was among the disaffected products of the public schools themselves - George Orwell, Cyril Connolly, T C Worsley, was a radical challenge being made which went to the heart of the matter. The depoliticization of educational debate reached its high water mark in the 1930s, but lingered for another thirty years in society at large, and even longer in the schools themselves. It was marked by the rise of organizations like the Association for Education in Citizenship,[18] and their accompanying ideologies which combined ethnocentric views about the nature of government with roseate visions of the virtues of being a sixth former and a prefect - a kind of pale pink Commonwealth version of the Empire conquered by rugby forwards and ruled by house captains. Nothing, it seemed was controversial. Though they were being suitably modest about it, the English knew how to run the world, and were public spirited enough to be willing to pass their knowledge on to others. As for education, there were a few technical problems to be sorted out, but Mr Burt and his fellow psychologists were making good progress on them, and soon there would be a plan for secondary education for all, except that those who could do Mr Burt's puzzles would be allowed to join the sixth, while the mechanics could be sent to the technical schools which still obstinately refused to lie down, and the rest would go to the modern school and . . . well something could be found for them to do.

Such a 'cool' and 'objective' way of appraising educational needs fitted surprisingly well with the authoritative pronouncement made in his 1929 publication **The English Tradition of Education** by the arch-priest of that tradition, Dr Norwood:

> The rule of discipline is then that you must do your duty, or pay the penalty; authority comes from above, but all share in the delegated powers for the purpose of living together a common life. This is supposed to be contrary to the modern democractic spirit in which authority such as it is is delegated from below. **Vox populi, vox dei.** Attempts have been made to graft these modern conceptions on to the old stock and traditions of the schools - such as forms of self-government and various types of school democracies. . . I can only say that these seem to me mere idle wasting of time. The business of a school is to work, and to get on with its life without bothering about whys and wherefores and abstract justice and the democratic principle. . .[19]

NOTES

1   Lacey, C., **Hightown Grammar: The School As a Social**

System, Manchester University Press, 1970, p.4. See also, R.H. Tawney (Ed), **Secondary Education for All: A Policy for Labour,** London, Allen and Unwin, n.d. (1922), p.51. (It is generally considered that this document was almost entirely Tawney's work).

2 Tawney, 1922 **op.cit.,** pp.51-2.

3 **Ibid.,** p.61.

4 **Ibid.,** p.62.

5 Edwards, A.D., **The Changing Sixth Form in the Twentieth Century,** London, Routledge, 1970, p.12.

6 Tawney, 1922 **op.cit.,** p.30.

7 **Ibid.,** p.50.

8 Consultative Committee of the Board of Education, **The Primary School,** London, HMSO, 1931.

9 **Report of the Consultative Committee on Secondary Education,** with special reference to Grammar Schools and Technical High Schools (Spens), London, HMSO, 1938, p.96. This was the period over which a huge gap opened up between the level of senior enrolments in the English secondary school and that in the American high school, where the percentage of the seventeen year-old age cohort graduating increased from 16.8 in 1920 to 50.8 in 1940 (Dreeben, R., 'American schooling: patterns and processes of stability and change', in Barber, B. and Inkeles, A. (Eds), **Stability and Social Change,** Boston, Little, Brown, 1971, p.84).

10 **Ibid.,** p.81.

11 **Ibid.,** p.102.

12 **Ibid.,** p.xxiii.

13 **Ibid.,** pp.66-7.

14 **Ibid.,** p.xxi.

15 **Ibid.,** p.166.

16 **Ibid.,** pp.333-4.

17 **Ibid.,** p.200.

18   Whitmarsh, G., 'The politics of political education: an episode', **Journal of Curriculum Studies**, 6, 2, 1974, pp.133-142.

19   Norwood, Cyril, **The English Tradition of Education**, London, John Murray, 1929, p.75.

7 THE CATEGORY EXPANDS

On two occasions in this century, wartime conditions have been associated with expansion in educational enrolments, especially at the upper level. This development was contrary to what an economic view of education might have predicted. As arms production and recruitment to the forces were stepped up in the late 1930s and the early war years, opportunities for employment, which had for a long time been very restricted began to increase, and schools and sixth forms might have become relatively unattractive alternatives. Yet secondary grammar enrolments went up from 470,000 in 1938 to 580,000 in 1947 (figures were not published over the war period), and, in the same year, entries for the higher certificate, which stood at 13,255 in 1939, reached 26,322. And this time postwar growth, which on the last occasion had been checked after only three years, was to go on at a fast pace for a quarter of a century. Expansion reflected both a new confidence in the value of education, and in social welfare programmes generally, which was expressed in the Education Act of 1944, and the start of a prolonged period of steady economic growth. A political consensus had been achieved on the direction that policy on secondary education should take. The promise of secondary education for all, finally conceded by the 1944 Act, pleased the Labour Party, while for conservatives, the ideological threat which this might have contained was nullified by the general agreement that the curriculum and ethos of the grammar school was to be preserved through the provision of secondary education on a 'tripartite' basis. Selective tests for a grammar school entry of about twenty per cent were to be retained and the majority of children were to transfer at age eleven from primary schools to secondary modern schools with a few going to technical schools. The classical statement of this policy is contained, not in the Education Act, but in the 1941 Report of a Committee set up 'To consider suggested changes in the Secondary

School curriculum and the question of School Examinations in relation thereto'. Its Chairman was Sir Cyril Norwood, President of St. John's College, Oxford, formerly Headmaster of Bristol Grammar School and Harrow, and author of **The English Tradition of Education** and (with A.H. Hope) of **The Higher Education of Boys in England** which thirty years earlier had argued for the implantation in the maintained schools of the public school tradition, and against the tradition of the higher grade school.

The Norwood Report begins by asserting the necessity for three types of secondary curriculum:

> First, there would be a curriculum of which the most characteristic feature is that it treats the various fields of knowledge as suitable for coherent and systematic study for their own sake apart from immediate considerations of occupation, though at a later stage grasp of the matter and experience of the methods belonging to those fields may determine the area of choice of employment and may contribute to success in the employment chosen.

> The second type of curriculum would be closely, though not wholly, directed to the special data and skills associated with a particular kind of occupation; its outlook and its methods would always be bounded by a near horizon clearly envisaged. It would thus be closely related to industry, trades and commerce in all their diversity.

> In the third type of curriculum a balanced training of mind and body and a correlated approach to humanities, Natural Science and the arts would provide an equipment varied enough to enable pupils to take up the work of life: its

purpose would not be to prepare for a particular job or profession and its treatment would make a direct appeal to interests, which it would awaken by practical touch with affairs.[1]

This is a most interesting passage on which to linger. Norwood must have been very clearly aware of how it reproduces the narrow 'liberal education' ideology of the nineteenth-century public schools. Yet the message is not immediately striking. If the prescriptions are read in reverse order, then one might take 'the balanced training of mind and body . . .' as a good statement of the liberal curriculum. But for one thing. The significant occurrence of the word 'training' with its echo of Matthew Arnold's barbed comment on 'skills of slavish utility', thrown at the unfortunate Ezra Cornell.[2] Liberal education was for leaders, governors and captains, not for slaves. The second type of curriculum too, seems as though it might provide the basis for a liberating 'polytechnic' education but, given Norwood's prejudices, the mention of 'industry, trades and commerce' marks it as clearly inferior. It is preferable to **general** training since it aims at 'a particular kind of occupation' which implies specialism and out of the ordinary skill, but 'trade', which had given rise to the 'utilitarian and showy' curriculum of the higher grade school (Norwood's expression of 1909), was a stigmatized activity.[3] What is it, then, which distinguishes the first style of curriculum as the most prestigious? One key phrase: 'for their own sake'. It is, in Norwood's view, the only **moral** curriculum. People who do things because they are useful, or because they lead directly to paid employment, however much they may enjoy or profit from what they do, are basely motivated. Only those who learn, for example, latin declensions for no known or discernible practical purpose can be said to have reached success through an effort of the moral will. This, for Norwood, was of the essence of the only liberal education worth having.

The second notable thing about the passage is the way in

which it presents the three types of curricula as concretely realizable. There is no suggestion that translating the words into classroom activities, curriculum materials, schedules, assessments, and so on would present any problem. It is as if they already existed and merely had to be put into service. This may have been true of the Grammar school curriculum in a reverse sense - that the ideology expressed in the description had been grafted on to an existing set of activities, and it is also likely that the teaching of specifically occupational skills through technical education was quite well understood. But what was this curriculum which was 'balanced', 'correlated', which **would** 'make a direct appeal to interests' and which **would** awaken them 'by practical touch with affairs'? What is here presented as totally and unquestionably within the professional competence of teachers was, in fact, highly problematic. It was rhetoric, not reality that was being offered.[4] Yet, for the future of secondary education, this was the key problem. If the first kind of curriculum was for the leaders, then it could only be on offer to about one in five. The demand for specialist mechanical and commercial skills was limited, so the third type of curriculum was, in fact, to be the curriculum of the majority.

Finally, the assumptions of the existence of definite and unassailable resources of educational skill and judgment within the teaching profession and those closely associated with it, extends beyond the assertion that certain kinds of curriculum are teachable to a claim that they are the only ones that **should** be taught. This claim is based on a theory of 'variety of capacity' which is presented, in the Report, as educational knowledge, backed by the testimony of teachers and educational organizations. In this way, the democratic implications of a proposal for secondary education for all were totally sidestepped, as they were also in the 1944 Act which contented itself with saying that education should be suited to the age and aptitude of the child - thus representing enrolment in a curriculum as a purely technical question. (In so far as the Act was 'political', it was mainly in relation to the settlement of the role of religious interests in education). The success of the public school curriculum lobby lay not just in the injection of its ideology into the maintained grammar schools and in sustaining it through the power of heads and governors, but also in its ability to project heads and teachers in grammar schools as educational experts for whom the content and delivery of a curriculum was a technical, not a political problem. The question of the balance between types of curricula, or the way they were related to actual school buildings might be politicized, but the heart of the matter - what was actually to be taught - was not. Even the Labour Party subscribed to this view. They argued that the disparity in the provision of grammar school places was unfair, that the system allowed too many mistakes in allocation, and there should be 'multilateral' schools which combined grammar and modern provision, or grammar and technical, or sometimes all three. But the basis of this last demand was not a rejection of the idea of allocation to different curricula, but rather the belief that 'mistakes' could be more easily rectified.[5] Talk about 'mistakes' implies acceptance of the legitimacy of the allocation process.

Thus, on one front, the integrity of the sixth as the lynchpin of the grammar school was preserved. The Norwood Report states that 'The full Grammar School course should be regarded as continuing to the age of 18+' and argues that the proportion of students staying to that age should increase.[6] The moral character of the sixth is celebrated in the section on Religious Education, where support is given to the 'tradition that there can be inspiration in the dwelling together of the teachers and the taught, that the Head and the staff, the Sixth Form and the main body of the pupils can and often do find a common life which has a spiritual basis . . .' There is even mention of the public school chapel: 'a place in which spiritual truths can be naturally and explicitly set forth'.[7] On another front, however,

125

that of numbers, the influence of the Act and the reports and pamphlets which preceded and accompanied its implementation would make the integrity of the sixth increasingly hard to maintain. The success of the grammar school and its sixth forms was dependent, to a degree which the report writers did not suspect, on its not becoming too successful. The grammar school had been strengthened by the steady increase in the staying on rate over the period of the 1920s and by the rise through the 1930s of entries for the higher certificate. As was perpetually argued, the grammar school depended on having an adequate sixth form. But what was adequate? And what would happen if numbers were to increase unchecked? Could the connection of liberal education, exclusivity and leadership be preserved?

Initially, it seemed that the innovations of the 1944 Act were working in favour of existing tradition. It introduced a further strengthening element into the sixth forms of schools by abolishing fees and linking entry to grammar schools exclusively to the 'scholarship route'. (Schools which did not want to take this step had to abandon maintained status and opt for independence or something intermediate such as becoming 'direct grant' which placed financial burdens upon them.) It had for some time been the case that 'scholarship pupils' were more likely to achieve good academic results and prolong their school life than fee payers were, so this was a step that was likely to increase sixth form numbers. The proposal for raising the school leaving age to fifteen from 1947 might be another factor encouraging entry to sixth forms and, generally, the support given to education, and to the idea that education was a personal and public benefit to be actively pursued also pointed the same way. However, the policies initiated in the postwar period also had potential for undermining the sixth form as an institutional category. First of all, the creation of parallel types of school, all recognized as 'secondary', would eventually raise the question of fairness of allocation at age eleven in a very sharp form. Acceptance of the idea that there should be allocation, which was part of the apolitical consensus, had, before the implementation of the Act, been largely a theoretical matter in that, in many areas, the old elementary/secondary dichotomy still existed in more or less the form it had been set up in 1902. In so far as it was not theoretical, experience of its implications arose in local areas where the issue tended to be complicated by the persistence of fee-paying, the lack of a firm, age-related, primary/secondary articulation, and the absence of any nationally sanctioned press for parity of esteem between types of school. But from 1944 onwards, more and more areas set up secondary systems enrolling all children, the eleven-plus transfer was standardized, and 'parity' became a declared policy objective. Moreover, some authorities, through choice, or force of local conditions, opted for multilateral forms of secondary organization. All these circumstances translated the question of allocation from the realm of the theoretic to that of the practical. And the practical problems and consequences were highlighted and documented. The effect on sixth forms was far from immediate, but it was bound to follow. A more immediate problem would be that posed by rising enrolments. On the face of it, these were entirely beneficial. But, given the curricular ideology of the grammar school and its sixth form, a point would inevitably be reached where problems would be created if the impetus to growth became self-sustaining. In 1944, this would not have seemed a likely outcome. Periods of expansion had, in the past, always been brief transitions between plateaus of stability.

To understand the potential for sustained growth becoming a problem, we have to look again at the educational ideology handed down by the Arnolds, moulded in the public schools, and translated to the State sector by Morant, Norwood, and others. Its main characteristic was its focus on a vision of perfection. Matthew Arnold had called it 'sweetness and light'. Norwood says: 'We believe that education cannot stop short of recognizing the ideals of truth and beauty and goodness as final and binding for all times and in all places, as ultimate values.'[8] Just as for Arnold, this conception of 'truth, beauty and goodness' was closely related to the subject-matter of the classical curriculum.

> We are not led by mere conservatism to wish to preserve for the future the study of the Classics because their study is traditional in the Grammar Schools of the past; rather we would say that it is traditional, not from accidental reasons, but from a sincere conviction, however variously expressed, that, unless a culture attains to and preserves self-knowledge, its continuity is not assured; failure in self-knowledge is a sympton of threatening decay.[9]

Now, visions are important to educational practice. The important question to ask is, how does the vision function to control and direct practice? Two related issues arise: first the nature of the vision itself, and secondly the possibilities that exist for connecting aspects of the vision with aspects of practice. Arnold's vision and Norwood's vision are unattainable: but they are not to be criticized for that. It is of the essence of visions that they are unattainable. We do not reach them, we pursue them. But we can ask what the vision has to say about the nature of the pursuit. Does it, intrinsically, have anything to say about who should pursue it? Or about the virtuousness or otherwise of degrees of success in the pursuit? Does it imply anything about how success is to be measured? What possibilities does it exhibit for making connections with practical human activities, such as education?

The first point to make about the Arnold/Norwood vision is that it contains within it strong, though not always overt, implications of exclusiveness. The basic reason for this, is the insistence that the elements of the vision are **unchanging**. What is immutable can have no dialogue with other viewpoints. Though it speaks of 'goodness' it is really more concerned with 'rightness'

- the rightness of those to whom the vision has been vouchsafed. This can be clearly seen in Arnold's approval of Renan's views on the United States which presented a different and contrasting pattern to the prevailing English system: 'countries which . . . have created a considerable popular instruction without any serious higher instruction, will long have to expiate the fault by their intellectual mediocrity, their vulgarity of manners, their superficial spirit, their lack of general intelligence.'[10] Such an assertion is necessarily connected with Arnold's attitude towards democracy: 'our whole scheme of government being representative, every one of our governors has all possible temptation, instead of setting up before the governed who elect him . . . a high standard of right reason, to accommodate himself as much as possible to their natural taste for the bathos'.[11]

How people relate to the vision, then, is controlled not by what is good for the people but by what is good for the vision. For Arnold, the middle class should be involved in government, not because this is a step towards a more desirable (visionary) style of politics, but to reduce the harm that might be done to the vision of sweetness and light if forces hostile to it went unchecked. There is a hidden premise that the vision is not available to all and that, indeed, its fundamental character would be destroyed if it were. There is no sense that the quest for the vision might in some way result in its reconstruction. The justification for the quest is precisely that the vision should be preserved intact, for the vision is self-justifying. It needs no external verification or explanation. It must be shown to people, and it is then up to them whether they enter into a moral engagement with it. It is this central aspect of the traditional ideology which gives force to the preoccupation of a succession of nineteenth century headmasters with Persius' verse: 'Virtutem videant intabescantque relicta.' 'Let them see the good. But let them rot if they pass it by,' which Prince Lee thought to be 'the finest single line in Latin literature' and Pollock, at Wellington, would murmur 'sighing to himself, sighing sometimes with the words 'and all the dreary round of sin'.[12] The message was that people's natures were more or less fixed and that, beyond hope and prayer, there was not much to be done about it. Fundamentally, the sentiment was pessimistic, and ill-assorted, one might have thought, with the growth of the idea that schools and headmasters were repositories of definite knowledge and expertise about how education should be carried out. But these ideas were no more ill-assorted than the conjunction of extravagant claims about the efficacy of the classical curriculum with the pathetically poor knowledge and skills demonstrated by most of those who experienced it - as evidenced by every objective enquiry into the matter made in the nineteenth century. Visions can sustain themselves either by making connections with reality or by denying it. Given its intrinsic character, it is hardly surprising that the vision of 'sweetness and light' took the latter course. Headmaster power and public school mystique prevented it from ever needing to explicate itself, or to show how arguments could be built out from it which could mediate between the vision and what was done in its name. Consequently, a divorce took place between the ideal and the actuality. The ideal became an ideology - a frozen rhetoric, incapable of directing educational development in any coherent or responsive way. Its basically antidemocratic and oligarchical tendencies and assumptions were protected from challenge.

Such a doctrine, therefore, did not merely imply exclusiveness when used as a justification for a form of education: it depended for its existence on exclusiveness. Some hint of this can be caught in the gradual shift of ground on the matter of when the grammar school course was to be regarded as complete. The 1904 Regulations, with a touch of realism in view of contemporary conditions, had suggested that the course of education could be 'complete' only if 'so planned as to carry on the scholars to such a point as they may reasonably be expected to reach at the age of sixteen plus'. By the 1940s it was becoming normal for grammar school pupils to stay until sixteen, and the goal was pushed further into the future. Norwood's suggestion of a course extending to the age of eighteen was taken up and embodied in the revised School Certificate examinations which were launched in 1951 as 'GCE'. Examinations were still to be available for sixteen year olds, but the intention was that grammar school courses should be designed on the basis that pupils would stay to eighteen and at that point take 'A-levels' in subjects they were still studying, having taken 'O-level' only in subjects they had dropped.

The Ministry of Education's 1951 Pamphlet **The Road to the Sixth Form** is about the grammar school curriculum and its title expresses the Ministry view of what the lower school curriculum was. It was thought to be correct to see it in this light, even for the early leavers:

> It is simply not possible for an academic education to reach any great measure of completeness by the age of sixteen, and to pretend otherwise would be doing no service to the many who do leave at that age. They are likely to get far more profit from travelling for some distance along an exacting but generous course of work which points at the future, than from a course which provides the illusion of a completed education.[13]

As the retention rate increased, so the definition of 'completeness' was shifted. Those who left at sixteen had not **really** had a grammar school education after all. In terms of a situation in which rhetoric and reality had taken leave of one another, this made sense. Systems sustained by false or irrelevant rhetoric can maintain their existence only by ensuring that what they purport to deliver has a scarcity value. If they have to cope with large intakes, then scarcity can be secured only by operating a kind of 'pyramid-selling in reverse'. In pyramid-selling, the number of participants must be maximized in order that those who initiate the process can derive the greatest benefit. However, as numbers increase, the gap between rhetoric and reality rises steeply and causes the whole operation to collapse. In the reverse process, one begins with large numbers, but on the premise that the rhetoric will match reality for only a few. Those who do not succeed can be led to believe that the mismatch is due to defective vision, while, for the few, the value of keeping up the pretence (or actually believing the rhetoric) outweighs the disadvantages of rejecting or subverting the system. (We may note here that all institutional categories surround themselves with protective rhetorics, which may stress either exclusion or inclusion. The issue is not about the existence of rhetorics, but about the use that is made of them and how this affects the experience of those within the categories and the connection of the category with social and political forces in society generally).

If this analysis has any force, then, for an institution like the sixth, given its historical origins, the numbers question was critical. The schools, in fact, very soon responded to the new GCE system with policies which were contrary to its central intentions. Against all official persuasion they continued to enter most of their students for public examination at sixteen as a matter of course, and fought bitterly against the regulations which banned entries from the under-sixteens. These were soon relaxed and, except for using a little of the latitude given by the acceptance of single subject entries in place of the 'group' scheme of school certificate, the grammar schools operated the new exam in the same way that they had used the old one. Thus, they kept up and further institutionalized an entry qualification to the sixth form - often based on passing five 'O-levels' - and made little or no effort to design a curriculum which gave any reality to the rhetoric of the continuous course to eighteen. In fact, if the character of the sixth was to be preserved, there was a hard balancing act to be managed between, on the one hand, asserting

132

its value as the true goal of a grammar school education, to which the curriculum of the early years was merely 'a road', and, on the other, maintaining the boundary between the sixth and the rest of the school in order to regulate entry to it, maintain its separate identity and prevent erosion of its privileged status. This, the schools were, for a period of almost twenty years, successful in doing. From 1950 to 1970, sixth form numbers in all types of schools went up from around the 100,000 mark to about 250,000. The number of students passing two or more 'A-levels' (roughly the equivalent of a pass in the old Higher School Certificate), increased from 34,000 to 77,000, and university admissions from 15,000 to 53,000. The forces for expansion had indeed got the upper hand. But it was taking place from a base that was still very small. In 1951, for the country as a whole, the percentage of seventeen year olds enrolled in secondary education was only just over six. Thus the sixth flourished, yet retained its institutional identity, its moral as well as its academic qualities, and its place as the key element in the educational system, around which most other organizational decisions were made. As a mark of the way in which traditional forms persisted, we might note that the peak year for A-level passes in Latin was not reached until 1965, when 6,012 candidates were successful. O-level Latin entries had by then passed their high point but were still eighty per cent above the figure for School Certificate twenty years before.

This, if one is to designate such a period, was the 'golden age' of the 'sixth': golden in that the institution brought off a difficult reconciliation between apparently incompatible aspects of its inherited character. On the other hand, its rhetoric was taken more or less seriously by increasing numbers of students so that it was, in terms of sustained and growing popularity, a success and a vindication of all that had been said about the value of grammar school education, and of a course prolonged to eighteen. On the other hand, it achieved all of this without in any serious sense democratizing itself and thus betraying the vision of the founders.

NOTES

1   Committee of the Secondary Schools Examinations Council, **Curriculum and Examinations in Secondary Schools** (Norwood), London, HMSO, 1941, p.4.

2   Dover Wilson, J. (Ed), **Matthew Arnold, Culture and Anarchy,** Cambridge, CUP, 1954, p.22.

3   On the stigmatization of trade in the public school ideology, see Worsley's comments on Vachell's **The Hill** (Worsley, T.C., **Barbarians and Philistines:** democracy and the public schools, London, Robert Hale, n.d., (1940) p.93).

4   Specific comment on the secondary modern school is limited to about half a page of very general remarks (Norwood, 1941, pp.20-21. See Note 1).

5   Max Morris, for example, advocated provision of secondary education for all by '(a) transformation of senior and central schools into modern schools equal in status, staffing and amenities to existing secondary schools. (b) Extension of secondary and technical schools. (c) Establishment of experimental multi-lateral schools' in order to 'transform our class-biased school system into a free democratic system'. In the multi-lateral school 'at the age of thirteen or fourteen, the children would be classified into streams according to their bent: some would proceed on a technical course, others on a commercial course, others would have a more academic training' (Morris, M., **The People's Schools,** the New People's Library, Vol.XX, London, Gollancz, 1939, pp. 94-5 and p.51).

6   Norwood, 1941, p.21 (See Note 1). The school leaving age was raised from fourteen to fifteen in 1947.

7   **Ibid.,** pp.86-7.

8   **Ibid.,** p.viii.

9   **Ibid.,** p.119.

10   Dover Wilson, 1954 **op.cit.,** p.18.

11   **Ibid.,** p.114.

12   Newsome, David, **Godliness and Good Learning: Four Studies on a Victorian Ideal,** London, John Murray, 1961, p.146.

13   Ministry of Education, Pamphlet No.19, **The Road to the Sixth Form,** London, HMSO, 1951.

8 THE GOLDEN AGE

The flourishing of the sixth in the 1950s and 1960s was part of a wider phenomenon of educational growth which embraced institutions at all levels of the system, and which was made possible by the agreement of all political parties that the expansion of education should be a major object of policy. What sustained and gave character to this period of growth, in its ideological as well as its material aspects, is hard to define but three factors were clearly of importance. One was the questioning of basic social assumptions which was stimulated during the war years: the rhetoric of the defence of democracy, the role of the armed forces as educational institutions, the mobility of populations (evacuation of children has been pointed to by a number of commentators as a key influence on social thinking), and the spirit of co-operation in adversity engendered by a long period of danger and privation all contributed to this: things could never be the same again and clear notice of this was given by the Labour victory in the 1945 general election. A second factor was the growth of a new middle class. If the proprietary schools of the mid-nineteenth century can be linked to the emergence of an upper level of middle class employment in the civil service and the professions, and the maintained grammar schools of the early twentieth century to a rapid growth in lower level middle class occupations in commerce and retailing, then perhaps the expansion of grammar schools and grammar school sixth forms in the post 1944 era can be seen as a reflection of a further shift in the pattern of connections between occupations seen as 'middle class' and the provision of high status extended education. The nature of this shift is a matter of controversy.[1] To some extent it was probably generated by the education service itself as more and more people entered teaching and as the status of the primary teacher was enhanced. At the same time the growth in social services created other 'caring' professions. But alongside these developments, there was also an increase in industrial, non-manual occupations which engendered a 'middle class' attitude towards the functions of education in those who took them up. A third and crucial factor was the steadily rising prosperity of the country over the 1950-70 period. This not only released funds for investment in education, but also created an atmosphere of optimism, in which implicit or explicit equations were made linking the phenomenon of economic advancement with government policy in general - a belief that 'Keynsianism' worked - and, more specifically, education itself - the conviction that schooling and progress were intimately linked.

The consensus on education was projected as 'apolitical' - and in a deeper sense than that which had supported the objective of 'secondary education for all' beginning in the 1920s. At that time, the argument had been about the provision of a definite and restricted form of secondary education clearly differentiated in status and objectives from the elementary system. The level of enrolment in secondary schools was very low, and thus progressive opinion could comfortably unite around the question of access, while putting on one side the deeper questions of content and purpose relevant to a secondary curriculum aimed at the majority of the population. In the post-war period, however, decisions about secondary schooling were taken against the background of the 1944 Education Act which had made its provision an agreed goal for **all** children up to the age of fifteen and, ultimately sixteen. Thus the consensus had now moved to a position where it was apparently about the purposes of secondary education for everyone, and how these purposes related to the political and social institutions which were to ensure progress towards the creation of a more prosperous, caring and democratic society. However, there was a fundamental conflict between those groups and individuals who saw education as the engine of progress towards democratic ideals - the legacy of the upheavals of the war years - and those who saw it basically in economic terms, as an investment in future national prosperity, or as a route towards enhanced status and rewards for their children. For the former, the connection of schooling with democratic citizenship was problematic. The structure of secondary education, its curriculum and its relations to higher education and the job market were things that needed to be rethought from first principles. For the latter, education tended to be a technical matter which could be left to the educational establishment - teachers, LEAs and Ministry of Education - or a question of status links between schools, higher education and employment. This economic viewpoint glossed over deep issues of content or purpose, though concern with the superficial 'modernism' of the curriculum might be expressed.

Both kinds of forces were at work in the debates over the expanding sixth form. **Sixth Form Citizens,** which was produced for the Association for Education in Citizenship in 1950[2] on the one hand argues that a lot of fundamental questions about the nature of the sixth form need to be addressed, and, on the other, produces evidence from a factual survey to show how, and to what extent, schools were responding to them. The agenda of questions was mostly to do with the sixth form as an agency of social and political educations:

> Is the experience offered by the Sixth Form right for the young people not only as specialists in training but also as persons and as future leading citizens? Is the content of the curriculum what it should be in view of the pressure of change in the modern world? Do the years in the Sixth Form promote the right skills for competence in the participant democracy which is slowly struggling into being as the new framework for national life? Does Sixth-Form experience bring to young people a grasp of the worth of those moral and aesthetic values upon whose guiding influence within society the maintenance of liberal democratic culture

depends? What precisely is the social function of the Sixth Form in the new age now struggling to be born?[3]

The last question was the most important and the most fundamental. It suggests that what had been taken for granted for so long could no longer be taken for granted. That it was time to take a hard look at the long tradition of 'sweetness and light', of 'ideals of truth and beauty and goodness' which had directed the course of the sixth form since the nineteenth century. Of course, to raise such a possibility was to undermine not only the grammar school ethos, but also that of the public schools from which it had sprung. But these too were under attack. Ten years earlier, T C Worsley had written:

> . . . the main problem which faces democracy may be expressed as the problem of achieving social cohesion. And the core of the indictment against Public Schools and the whole theory of education which they represent, is just that they prevent any chance of achieving this. . . What it requires . . . is that the body of the nation, however different as individuals in gifts and in abilities, shares a basis of a common cultural heritage, where the word 'cultural' would have a wider connotation than it bears at present. Social cohesion in this sense . . . could only be achieved **democratically** by a reorganization of the educational system.'[4]

But the forces of conservatism were equally vocal and forthright. They too appear within the pages of **Sixth Form Citizens**. The Chairman of the Schools Committee of AEC either did not read what his research officer had written or, more likely, disagreed with it and took the opportunity to say so in his introduction. His theme, which was one which was to be often repeated in future years in reports on sixth form education, was to lament that all these worthy things that people would like to do by way of introducing new ideas into sixth forms were very problematic because of the utter impossibility of interfering with what sixth forms were already doing:

> There would be less difficulty, of course, if we did not believe in the enduring value of the more traditional parts of the Sixth-Form curriculum. If we believed that the standard subjects of the curriculum, at any rate in their present form, have outlived their usefulness; if we believed that the curriculum as a whole was out of touch with the real needs of its pupils; if we thought it was too 'academic' - using the word 'academic', as it has occasionally been used, as a term of abuse! - then, indeed, the problem would be less intractable. We could make room for the New by the simple process of throwing out the Old.[5]

In other words, not only does he not want to try to answer the question: 'What precisely **is** the social function of the Sixth Form in the new age now struggling to be born?'. He does not see that it needs to be asked.

The survey found that a substantial majority of heads shared this view. Only about a quarter of the schools surveyed could be said to be making a reasonable effort to provide a course of study which attended to the citizenship needs of sixth forms. Admittedly, as the report points out, schools were under severe pressure to concentrate on a narrowly academic curriculum. The influences which the Spens Report had noted as 'tending to produce uniformity' were even more powerful than they had been in the pre-war years. But, in many instances, the support for the **status quo** was, as much as anything, ideological. A reluctance to change the traditional curriculum was linked with acceptance of an ethos of competition rather than co-operation, of 'loyalty' rather than questioning, and of authority rather than democracy. As one head said of his prefects: 'It is good for them to learn to give orders.' On the other hand, there were schools and heads that were posing the fundamental question and looking for answers to it. Often these developments were taking place in girls schools:

> . . . in the Sixth Form a thorough survey of the present is made. America and the Soviet Union are studied. . . When any opportunity for a valuable experience offers, the Headmistress believes in taking it, even if teaching time has to be sacrificed. . . There is a Pupils' Council with advisory powers . . . the citizen attitudes of the senior students do not leave one for a moment in doubt. The school seems completely free from absorption with examinations.[6]

Invariably, curriculum change went with ideological change. Whatever in the outside world - examinations, competition for places in higher education or the professions - was tending to nail the curriculum in place, the fact remained that, in terms of the view many schools and teachers held of the nature of sixth forms, it was a highly functional curriculum, just as it had been in the public schools of the nineteenth century. What the founders had provided was an ideology and a curriculum (using that word in its broadest sense) which were not terribly well connected with one another on any rational criteria, but were united by the air of immutability which they both projected. A few head teachers were prepared to cast off some features of the old fixed curriculum together with the notion of fixed truths and standards which jibed with it: more often, innovation was construed as **adding something** to what should not be basically interfered with. The existence of that something new then became problematic because of the pressures on time, energy and organization exerted by the traditional academic curriculum. Teachers found the effort to 'add

142

on' innovations too much, and students were impatient with what they saw as 'frills' on the essential core activity of sixth form work.

However, as sixth forms grew in number and in size, and as the whole character of secondary education changed with the implementation of the provisions of the 1944 Act, it did seem that the logic of that development would strengthen the case of those who were looking for substantial reforms. The Report of the Crowther Committee which had been set up in 1956 to advise the Minister of Education 'on the education of girls and boys between the ages of fifteen and eighteen' was therefore eagerly awaited. Would it determine that the whole trend of the education system was rendering the sixth form as it currently existed an anachronism, and tackle at the root the forces which were tending to inhibit change? Or would it confirm the view of those who felt that the only change which was acceptable was that which left intact the assumptions which had undergirded the sixth for more than a hundred years? Would it, in fact, say that the time had come for the possibilities of the sixth as a democratizing category to be exploited? Or would it, in spite of the growth of numbers and evolution in the character of English society, insist that the category be preserved as one based on exclusion rather than inclusion, on the politics of legitimacy rather than the politics of universal participation?

In some ways the Crowther Report,[7] which was published in 1959, reflected the temper of the times. It spoke of the need to implement the second stage of the raising of the leaving age to bring it to sixteen; it spoke of the need to 'tap talent' and produced figures which purported to show how far the system fell short of what might be achieved in this respect; it supported the provision of compulsory part-time education through 'county colleges' for all sixteen and seventeen year-olds not in full-time education - something foreshadowed in the 1944 Act; it advocated 'a great advance' in technical studies and pointed to the need for 'a coherent national system of practical education'. It looked forward to a time around 1980 when fifty per cent of boys and girls would remain in full-time education to the age of eighteen, involving a 'four-fold expansion' of the provision. Thus, the Report shared in the assumptions commonly held among politicians and opinion leaders of the time, that expansion was both inevitable and desirable, that it was linked with economic prosperity, and that there was no need to fear that limits would be placed on it because of lack of young people with the necessary ability to profit from education (from being an argument for restraint, the notion of 'ability to profit' was, around this time, transformed into the image of a 'pool of untapped talent' and urged as a justification for higher enrolments). Inevitably Crowther reiterated all the well-known drawbacks of the sixth form in its current state: it was a cause of premature specialization in the lower school, which was to be regretted; its backwash effect crowded out practical and aesthetic subjects in the secondary curriculum; it created problems of teacher supply to man a specialist curriculum which was twice as costly to staff as the curriculum of lower forms (certainly an underestimate). The Report pointed out that, as expansion took small sixth forms up to a more economic size, it would also create new small and uneconomic ones. It had to admit that academic sixth form courses were overburdened with content, often not very coherent, and an obstacle to the provision of a curriculum which was generally educational. All of this seemed to add up to a substantial indictment of the structure and curriculum of sixth forms, and one which would gain in force as enrolments expanded along the lines which Crowther both anticipated and wanted to encourage.

If the Report writers had used these findings as a cue to project their thinking forward to a situation in 1980 in which all children were enrolled in school to the age of sixteen, and fifty per cent remained in full time education to the age of eighteen, they must have been forced to the conclusion that sixth form education twenty years ahead would be qualitatively different, and that the right policy would be to ease the transition from the old to the new. However, it was characteristic of the expansionist thinking of the 1950s, and even beyond, to construe the empirical and intellectual work of expansionist theory as being simply to oppose arguments that 'more meant worse' by showing that 'more meant better' - typically in terms of discussions of 'pools of talent'. Investigations premised on the idea that more would mean **different,** and attempts to show how far and in what ways more would be different were seldom encountered. Possibly this tendency was due to the fact that the framing and justification of social policy was seen as essentially the work of economists and demographers. These were the people who were accorded 'expert' status, wrote the books, planned education courses and influenced the civil servants in the Ministry of Education who set the long term agendas around which committees and advisory councils worked.[8] However, it was also a stance which fitted in well with the still prevalent 'sweetness and light' tradition. If one accepted that basic purposes were more or less fixed, then there was no incentive to investigate alternative scenarios. In the case of the Crowther Report it would seem that these sorts of ideological considerations were important, for not only did it endorse almost without reservation the traditional pattern of sixth form education, it also provided elaborate pseudo-psychological justifications for the existence of this pattern which are rather out of character with the generally neutral statistical tone of much of the rest of the Report.

Before entering on its psychological theorizing, the Report set out what it thought to be the distinctively important features, or 'marks' of a sixth form. The key passage reads:

> (A) close link with the university is, in our opinion, one of the essential marks of a Sixth Form. . . The good and keen Sixth Former . . . has looked forward to being a science specialist, or a

classic, or a historian: his mind has been set that way by inclination. . . Whatever hinders specialization is to him, at first, a waste of time . . . specialization is a mark of the Sixth Form, and "subject-mindedness" of the Sixth Former. The third mark of the Sixth Form is independent work. . . Independent work by a pupil, as we understand it, implies a considerable amount of time to devote to a subject, time enough anyhow to make his own discoveries . . . The fourth mark is the initimate relation between pupil and teacher which is characteristic of a good Sixth Form. There is no commonly accepted phrase to describe the situation - perhaps "intellectual discipleship" comes as near as any. . . There is a fifth mark of the Sixth Form, or rather of the Sixth Former, which ought not to be passed over - social responsibility. . . Two things make it possible. The first is the mere fact of age, and the maturity which comes with it. The second is the thoughtfulness which comes from the intellectual life developed by Sixth Form work.[9]

What is set out here, as the Report frankly recognizes, is an ideal. Historically and empirically most of the statements just don't stand up. A few leading public schools apart, the relation between sixth forms and universities had never been clear cut. Through the 1920s and 30s university entrants had represented only around fifty per cent of the population of grammar school sixth forms and the post-war expansion had reduced even this figure. When Crowther reported, around 24,000 students were entering university courses, while over 40,000 were obtaining two or more A-level passes, and others were leaving sixth forms with lower qualifications, or having taken non-A-level courses.

And what of the future? Did the Crowther Committee really envisage that a four-fold expansion of full-time education in the sixth form age-group could go along with a substantial increase in the **proportion** of sixth formers admitted to university courses? And the implication that the only good sixth former is one whose sole ambition is to be a specialist scholar contains an odd value judgement which is supported only by a claim that, whether we like it or not, the prevalence of the specialist is a fact. However the basis of this assertion is a speculative theory (to which we will return) and not an empirical investigation. Those who later looked for empirical verification failed to find it.[10] The status of 'independent work' in sixth forms was also uncertain. Public boarding schools were in a good position to cultivate it, but the situation in most grammar schools was very different. There, the press to coach students for A-levels resulted in crowded timetables which allowed little time in school for independent study - probably about ten per cent is a realistic estimate[11]- and in didactic teaching methods which yielded highly directed homework assignments. The virtues of 'general reading' and 'organizing one's own work' were widely preached, but fell on deaf ears since students were already overburdened with scheduled tasks.[12] 'Intellectual discipleship' clearly marks a restatement of the 'mimetic' ethos of the sixth forms of Arnold, Prince Lee and other nineteenth century heads who reserved the teaching of the sixth to themselves and saw it as an extension of their own power and authority in the school. As a central experience for sixth form students, emphasizing as it did exclusiveness, sponsorship and dependency, it was ill-assorted with progressive, democratic values and, though it obviously had the sanction of history, was something for which a very high price would have to be paid if it were to be reflected in the quality and quantity of staff needed for a much expanded sixth. Finally, of course, the issue of 'social responsibility' was one with which **Sixth Form Citizens** had been much concerned, though the author of the document probably put a somewhat different construction on the phrase from the writers of the Crowther Report. The former quotes approvingly a headmaster who contrasts 'participant democracy, requiring a much-heightened social consciousness and general awareness' with what was appropriate to an earlier time 'when the national system was a combination of individualistic competition and formal democracy.'[13]

One suspects that the Crowther image of social responsibility harks back to an earlier, though post-Arnoldian, phase of public school education when Christian Socialist beliefs found expression in missions to the poor at home and assumption of the white man's burden overseas, and Christian English gentlemen played the part of 'a knight-errantry fit to keep the marches of an empire, and to purge the land nearer home of wrong, violence, lust'.[14] Certainly, such an interpretation is in keeping with the attitude the Report adopts towards 'juvenile delinquency'. The reluctance of teenagers 'to take very much on authority' is seen as a cause of their exploitation by unscrupulous tradesmen with 'goods or entertainment to sell'.[15] The more able who are better educated and therefore armed against such temptations (and who have more money to pay for them, though that is not mentioned) have a duty to rescue their less well equipped brethren. It was a scenario of which Charles Kingsley would have approved, and illustrates a recurrent theme in the arguments for maintaining the elite status of sixth forms and grammar schools.

Elites achieve their status by cutting themselves off from the rest of society. This engenders an ignorance of the nature of other social strata, and a concomitant fear that they are about to undermine the fabric of the nation which sustains the elite group. The way to ease these fears, and at the same time reassert the importance of keeping the barriers in place, is to represent the 'ideals' and 'standards' supported by the elite as a kind of beacon light which must be preserved because it is the only means of turning the eyes of the masses away from the bad examples set by fomentors of discord and subversion. This scenario demands that the masses be represented as idle, shiftless and a prey to sinful impulses - characteristics from which potential members of the elite have to be weaned away, and which must be countered in the general population by the setting of 'good examples'. As was said of the Church Lads Brigade in 1910: 'The cadets learn the duty and dignity of obedience; they get a sense of corporate life and of civic duty; they learn to honour the power of endurance and effort . . . and they come in contact with manly and devoted officers. . . These ideals are marked contrast with the listless self-indulgence, the pert self-assertion and selfishness and want of reverence, which are so characteristic of life in a low district.'[16] Norwood, at the same time, was approvingly quoting Stanley Hall's indictment of the 'lessening sense for both duty and discipline; the haste to know and do all befitting man's estate before its time; the mad rush for sudden wealth and the reckless fashion set by . . . gilded youth.'[17] These sentiments did not require the prosperity of the Crowther era to make their appearance in the pages of the sixth form ideologues. Their persistence into it was certainly not conducive to any sane discussion of the democratizing tendencies implicit in an expanding sixth form.

The status of the sixth form ideal in terms of past history and current practice was undeniably shaky. But, more important, was its dubious connection with any imaginable future. In fact, the Report never makes such a connection. The virtues of the sixth form are simply asserted and some palliatives for the ills it was currently causing, particularly in terms of defective general education of sixth formers and constraints on the lower school curriculum, suggested. The alleged virtues are clearly those of the traditional public school sixth form and one can only suppose that the Crowther Committee was packed with ex-public school boys and masters or by others who had been indoctrinated by them.

The Committee did, however, feel obliged to provide some justification for its central claim that a specialized academic curriculum was right for sixth forms and should be maintained. The form which the justification took was an admission that the Committee's stance on the sixth form issue was ideological - in contrast to the empiricism of its treatment of some other questions - and, at the same time, an indication of how weak its case really was. It had to face the awkward fact that nothing like the sixth form curriculum existed anywhere else in the world. This was doubly unfortunate because many of the arguments for educational expansion were posited on the experience of other advanced industrial societies such as the USA, France and Germany.

Before setting out to defend this difficult position, the writers of the Report admit to the defects of the curriculum as it is currently implemented: 'If . . . we had to rest content with some of the practices that are to be observed in English schools at the present time, we might well reverse our view.'[18] Again, it is to be the ideal that is to dictate policy, and without any serious consideration of the potential of the ideal for being directive of it. It is also stated that the position will be defended on grounds of liberal education, rather than in respect of the efficiency of the curriculum in conveying skills and knowledge - though it is not clear what difference this makes to the argument unless the assumption was that no other country aspires to provide a liberal curriculum.[19] Then the psychological arguments are put forward: 'The first step in the argument for specialization is that able boys and girls are ready and eager by the time they are sixteen - the ablest by fifteen - to get down to the serious study of some one aspect of human knowledge'. No evidence is given to support this assertion. 'The second step in the argument is that concentration on a limited field leads naturally to study in depth'.[20] The point of this step is to show how 'independent study' comes into the picture. Depth leads to mastery and thus to self-guided learning. 'The third step . . . is that, through this discipline, a boy can be introduced into one or two areas which throw light on the achievement of man and the nature of the world in which he lives'.[21] Step three is important because it sets the ground for step four, which is that 'given the right teaching, a boy will by the end of his school days begin to come out on the further side of "subject-mindedness" '. Since the curriculum of the sixth is non-vocational and can be seen as paradigmatic of broad areas of human thought, it can be a key to the broad exploration which will follow on the commitment to narrow enthusiasm. Finally, it is argued that the only way this desirable state of affairs can be secured is through the allocation of large blocks of time to specialist study in an atmosphere of 'intellectual discipleship' - a restatement of the mimetic theory of learning which can be traced back to the days when the great Victorian headmasters assumed personal responsibility for the teaching of the sixth.

The whole idea is so strangely baroque that it is hard to know where to begin to comment on it. It is even less credible than the 'transfer of training' argument which was used by Norwood and others to bolster the grammar school curriculum introduced by the 1904 regulations. Much along the lines of justifications for selective and restricted secondary education in the 1930s, it presupposes the existence of a group of students who are qualitatively different from all others. It suggests that they should be exposed to a curriculum which is also qualitatively different from that which other students of the same age will experience - and to such an extent that the scope for finding common curricular ground between the groups is virtually non-existent. It then devises a psychological account of the need for this special curriculum which can claim no basis in fact, and which seems to be contradicted by the experience of all other countries. Viewed as an attempt at a retrospective justification for what already existed, of course, the 'theory' makes much more sense. All the hallowed features of the traditional sixth are reflected in it, including even the 'express' streams which led the more able to enter it at age fifteen rather than sixteen. The point of the Report, however, was to produce justifications for what should exist in the future, not what had existed in the past. And that future, as the Report writers themselves insisted, was to be different from what had gone before at least in a **quantitative** sense. But the **qualitative** aspect of change which would seem to have been implied in their remit 'to consider, in relation to the changing social and industrial needs of our society . . . the education of boys and girls between fifteen and eighteen'[22] appears not to have impinged on the Committee's deliberations: in common with many other exponents of educational expansion in the 1950s and 60s, they failed to grasp the crucial point that the question of whether more was better or more was worse was irrelevant. The issue to be confronted was how and in what ways more would be different. But just as the Committee had not looked at qualitative change in sixth forms in any serious way, it also failed to ask any deep questions about the significance of the development of the comprehensive school in the evolution of the secondary curriculum. Comprehensive schools were regarded as 'experimental' (a term often used at the time to avoid serious discussion of them). They could provide an administrative solution to problems of educational provision in certain special and limited kinds of area such as 'thinly populated country districts', but, even then, they would not provide a challenge to accepted conventions: 'As far as we can foresee development, what is true of Sixth Forms in grammar schools will be true of the comprehensive schools, and the views we hold about the one, we should expect to hold also of the other'.[23] One connection was, however, firmly made between the sixth form question and the comprehensive schools. Just as the Spens Report in 1938 had used sixth form numbers as a criterion for doubting the feasibility of multilateral schools - the precursors of the comprehensives - so Crowther determined that to produce a viable sixth form a comprehensive school would need to be 'somewhere between 1,200 and 2,000 strong'.[24] Once again, preconceptions about the nature of the sixth form were being used as decisive arguments in the shaping of secondary education as a whole.

It has to be said, of course, that few comprehensive schools existed in the late 1950s; that the general pattern of secondary and sixth form provision had been relatively stable for a long time; that economic projections were more powerful in public policy-making than arguments about the relation of public institutions to societal goals of a cultural or humanistic character. Nevertheless, the inability to see very far was certainly connected with a feeling that it was not necessary to see very far, which, in its turn, was based on strongly, if covertly held beliefs that educational purposes do not change, and that the institutions we have are necessarily and tightly linked to the achievement of those purposes. The message of 'sweetness and light', like the tablets from the mountain, was a final one: there was no provision for supplements, revisions or adaptations. 'In England', we are told, 'the secondary school is traditionally concerned with educating an elite, an intellectual aristocracy on whom the most stringent academic demands can be made and in whom there can be awakened a real love of learning. It treats them as adults capable of a reverence for knowledge, beginners in a lifelong quest for truth, which they can share with those who teach them'.[25] The vocabulary mirrors the religious and chivalrous ideology of the nineteenth century public school. It is not surprising that the discussion of 'subject-mindedness' focuses quite unashamedly on 'boys', or that the 'new sixth formers' are identified with girls:

> If they expect, and are expected, to get the same
> number, and the same sort of combination of
> subjects as more academic pupils, their education
> will go seriously astray. But there are Advanced

level syllabuses in art and music; in domestic subjects as well as in Latin, physics and history. Provided that this new type of Sixth Former is not expected to get a particular number or combination of subjects, and provided that **she** has two years to give to Sixth Form work, there is no reason why a suitable course should not be devised for **her** which would include in many instances some Advanced level work.[26]

Given such underlying assumptions, it is easy to see why the efforts of the girls schools to get to grips with innovation in sixth form curriculum failed to make an impact on the imagination of policy-makers: the core values of the sixth were linked to the teaching of subjects which could be fit material for 'quests' - Latin, physics, history - not those concerned with slavish accomplishments such as art, music, cooking or sewing. Crowther's message was that this still remained true: it was a message that many were still willing and eager to hear.

NOTES

1   See Centre for Contemporary Cultural Studies, **Unpopular Education: Schooling and Social Democracy in England Since 1944,** London, Hutchinson, 1981, p.113 for some comments and references on the 'new' middle class in the post-war period.

2   Association for Education in Citzenship, **Sixth Form Citizens,** London, Oxford University Press, 1950.

3   **Ibid.,** p.3.

4   Worsley, T.C., **Barbarians and Philistines: Democracy and the Public Schools,** London, Robert Hale, n.d., p.281.

5   Association for Education in Citizenship, 1950 **op. cit.,** p.viii.

6   **Ibid.,** pp.94-5. The AEC survey of forty girls' schools

showed above average allocations of time 'outside the examination specialisms' (p.65). Girls' schools were also more likely to lay on 'general' courses for sixth form students not following A-level courses (Central Advisory Council for Education (England), **15 to 18** (Crowther Report), London, HMSO, 1959, p.255).

7   See note 6.

8   See, Centre for Contemporary Cultural Studies, 1981 p.74ff.

9   Crowther, pp.223-225.

10   Peterson's research which was almost contemporary with the work of the Central Advisory Council concluded that 'If the number of subjects were limited to three and all external pressures removed the largest single group of English Sixth Formers (39.9 per cent) would choose to present at A-level some combination which included both Arts and Science subjects' (Peterson, A.D.C., **Arts and Science Sides in the Sixth Form,** Oxford University Department of Education, 1960, p.25.) His finding was later confirmed by a survey commissioned by the Schools Council (Schools Council, **Schools Council Sixth Form Survey,** Vol.1, **Sixth Form Pupils and Teachers,** Councils and Education Press for Books for Schools, London, 1970, p.162).

11   See, Taylor, P.H. et al., **The English Sixth Form,** London, Routledge and Kegan Paul, 1974, p.23.

12   For some empirical evidence on the nature of sixth form teaching methods, see Wankowski, J.A., 'Teaching method and academic success in sixth form and university', **Journal of Curriculum Studies,** 6, 1, 1974, pp.50-60. My own experience as a sixth form tutor around the period of the Crowther Report gave a clear impression of the extent to which the time of A-level students was preempted by assigned tasks. Teachers who adopted more flexible working

methods were rare.

13   Association for Education in Citizenship, 1950 **op. cit.,** p.10.

14   J.H. Skrine, 'The romance of school', **Contemporary Review,** LXXIII, 1898, p.438, quoted in Girouard, Mark, **The Return to Camelot: Chivalry and the English Gentleman,** New Haven, Yale University Press, 1981, p.222.

15   **Crowther Report,** pp.42-44.

16   A remark attributed to Sir Henry Newbolt and quoted in Girouard, 1981 **op. cit.,** p.253.

17   Norwood, Cyril and Hope, Arthur H. (Eds), **The Higher Education of Boys in England,** London, John Murray, 1909, p.546.

18   **Ibid.,** p.261.

19   The falsity of this position is demonstrated by the publication of the **Harvard Report** which must have been known to at least some members of the Advisory Council (Harvard Committee Report **General Education in a Free Society,** Cambridge, Mass., Harvard University Press, 1945).

20   **Crowther Report,** p.262.

21   **Ibid.,** p.263.

22   **Ibid.,** p.xxvii.

23   **Ibid.,** pp.425 and 200.

24   **Ibid.,** p.418.

25   **Ibid.,** p.259.

26   **Ibid.,** p.303. (Our italics).

TABLE TWO

Numbers of secondary schools of various types - 1950 and 1970

	1950	1970
Comprehensive	10	1250
Grammar	1192	1038
Technical	301	82
Modern	3227	2691

(Source: Seaborne and Lowe, p.158 (See note 18 to Ch.5))

TABLE THREE

16+ Enrolments in secondary schools 1957 and 1977

	1957		1977	
Grammar	101,000	(60%)	55,000	(15%)
Comprehensive	-		225,000	(63%)
Other Maintained	17,000	(10%)	14,000	(4%)
Direct Grant	17,000	(10%)	24,000	(7%)
Independent	34,000	(20%)	37,000	(10%)
Totals	169,000	(100%)	355,000	(99%)

(Source: Ministry of Education and DES Statistics)

9   THE FORCES OF CHANGE

The period around the publication of the Crowther Report marked a high point in the thrust to move sixth form education into new channels. Had the Report given official backing to reformist ideas, as the Plowden Report was to do for primary education nine years later, it is possible that the lobby supporting change would have grown in strength and created initiatives sufficient to overcome the well known inertia in the curriculum which every report since Spens had commented on. As it was, the Crowther message that nothing much needed to be changed as far as the sixth form was concerned pleased those heads and teachers who wanted nothing better than to run and manage a system of familiar structure and comfortable ritual, and gave renewed vigour to those for whom the defence of existing theory and practice was an ideological crusade. The late fifties and early sixties saw the publication of a number of volumes which, while advocating some adaptation to new social, economic and political circumstances, celebrated the traditional values of the sixth within a defence of the Norwood image of the grammar school. Frances Stevens in **The Living Tradition** (1960) posed the question 'Why cannot all be initiated' and answered it confidently, asserting first of all that grammar school education is 'only for the intelligent', secondly that 'although many in all classes of society would like the material or social advantages of "a good education", few are anxious to be fully awakened or to court the pains of thought' and thirdly that the segregated institution of the grammar school is needed as a bridge between the privileged bastions of the independent public schools and the secondary moderns and that in this role it makes for social equality.[1] A little later a similar message was conveyed by Harry Davies in **Culture and the Grammar School** (1965). Davies quotes Matthew Arnold's definition of culture as 'a pursuit of our total perfection by means of getting to know . . . the best which has been thought and said' and, though he is less certain of

159

his conclusions than Frances Stevens, also sees the grammar school as fulfilling a bridging function, this time 'at the meeting point of the elite and the popular cultures'. He argues that it 'not only will but should survive' to play its part in 'the civilizing of mass society'.[2] On the other side of the question of whether an institution founded on a principle of exclusion can play a democratizing role was Young's **Rise of the Meritocracy** (1958) which couched its warning of the dire, if long delayed, results of separatism in the form of an Orwellian parable.[3] In so far as the grammar school was concerned, its injunction can be said to have been heeded, at the level of institution if not curriculum, through the growth in the 1960s of comprehensive secondary education. But the form and structure as well as the curriculum of the sixth form were to remain impervious to it.

Yet it was obvious that the scope for expansion in sixth form provision was enormous and those who were still fired by ambitions for change, and also shocked at the narrowness and insularity of the experience offered to many sixth form students, were eager to take up the challenge of the Crowther Report and contest the notion that discussion could revert to mundane questions of access and of tinkering with existing arrangements. The fading influence of the Association for Education in Citizenship as a focus for innovative activity was counterbalanced by the founding and burgeoning of the General Studies Association which built its rationale on the existing and admitted deficiencies of the academic curriculum rather than on a call for 'citizenship' education which was intrinsically ambiguous in its implications. If the Crowther Committee did deliberately intend to uphold the traditional character of the sixth form as an educational institution, then it was correct in its instinct that it was the curriculum that presented an essential key to that character and must be defended by all means. Even if the defence the Committee put forward was less than convincing at the time, and in retrospect rather ludicrous, the attempt had to be made. If the curriculum were to change in response to the well known reservations expressed about it, it would almost certainly be in the direction of a form which would tend to blur the distinction between the 'academic' and the 'non-academic' students. And with that, the whole practical and symbolic importance of the institution would be put at risk. The General Studies Association, which grew out of an 'Agreement to Broaden the Curriculum' supported by a number of schools in 1961, provided a rallying point for those who saw it as one of the advantages of curriculum change that it would not only help to solve some of the problems about the curriculum which the Crowther Report had itself identified but would also turn the 'sixth' into a more democratic institution in terms of access and of the sharing of experiences among all students.[4] Eventually, these concerns were embodied in policy initiatives mounted by the Schools Council from 1964 onwards, but the vigour of the debate of the early sixties was never recaptured and the likelihood of substantial curriculum change gradually faded as a further decade passed in which the forces of conservatism grew in confidence.

This period did, however, see some significant innovations affecting the character of the sixth form which Crowther had not foreshadowed. In view of the degree to which its work had taken place under the influence of economists it was strange that these developments, which were essentially economic in origin, had been left out of account. What Crowther set out to justify in its consideration of the sixth form curriculum was a very expensive style of teaching. If the justification of what was to be done lay in notions of the virtues of specialization and intellectual discipleship, then there had to be a liberal provision of teachers who were also very highly qualified and well paid. And, to counter any suggestion that what was being offered was narrow and arbitrary, a wide range of specialist subjects should be available. Furthermore, if the 'moral' character of the sixth was to be preserved, it had to continue to be part of an eleven-to-eighteen

161

secondary school. There is no suggestion in the Report that sixth forms might be separated from schools. The 'County Colleges' which the Report recommended were expressly designed for those who had opted out of the possibility of a sixth form education and were at risk of being corrupted by the outside world ('As he enters the outside world, he finds that much that would have been condemned at school or in the family is tolerated and accepted as natural'[5]). Thus, what Crowther was suggesting was that a very expensive form of education should be expanded in a location where economies of scale would be very difficult to secure. Once again, we are perhaps in the presence of the idea that what suits the leading public schools can be transplanted automatically to the state system regardless of the fact that its whole system of organization and working is radically different. Public schools can run cost effective sixth forms on the traditional pattern because they set out to offer an expensive education. They have favourable staffing ratios and well qualified specialist teachers. They have the whole day in which to arrange contact and private study time, and their sixth forms are large in proportion to the size of the school because the age of transfer is thirteen and entry to the sixth is normal. In the state system, however, even the Grammar Schools found it difficult to run cost effective sixth forms. Often the costs were hidden by driving down the staff-student ratios in the lower schools and resisting at that level the creation of smaller groups for students needing special attention. But, as sixth form numbers grew, the problem, far from becoming more tractable, became more obvious. The extra cost of educating a small elite is either borne gladly or is readily concealable. But, as the elite gets bigger, so does the bill. All of this would have been bad enough, but within a very short time of the publication of the Report the Grammar Schools were in full retreat and being replaced by the 'experimental' comprehensives. This multiplied the number of sixth forms and raised the demand for qualified specialist staff to a level that could not be satisfied.

Even the possibility that sixth forms might become cost effective was removed. In this situation, one of two things had to give way. Either the curriculum of the sixth form had to be modified or the sixth form had to begin to give up its traditional attachment to the secondary school.

Though the two issues of the curriculum of the sixth and where sixth form education should be provided were essentially linked with one another, they were pursued quite separately and in different ways. The difference arose from the particular character of English state education as a 'national system, locally administered'.[6] Whatever the 1944 Act might say about who was responsible for the curriculum of the schools, the curriculum of the sixth form was a 'national issue' because it was examination-based, depending on syllabuses devised by examination boards whose work was nationally co-ordinated and overseen by the DES, first through the Secondary Schools Examination Council, and, after 1964, the Schools Council. Moreover, the entrance qualifications of universities and other institutions of higher education, and of professional bodies and many employers were expressed in terms of the existing GCE O- and A-level system. Nothing could change without some sort of agreement among all the interested parties - though what would constitute a sufficient agreement was never clear - resulting in an official endorsement of some new scheme by the DES either directly or through its backing for a decision of the Schools Council. The matter of how sixth form education should be provided was, however, something that had to be decided on a local basis. Local education authorities were free to submit to the DES schemes for the reorganization of education in their areas of almost any imaginable character. Some might want to concentrate their sixth forms in a small number of schools and have students transferred to them from others which did not provide education after the age of fifteen; others might aim to develop sixth forms in all the secondary schools for which they were responsible - whatever mix of grammar, secondary modern and comprehensive that represented; authorities could propose a variety of ages of transfer so that sixth forms could be housed in eleven-to-eighteen, twelve-to-eighteen, thirteen-to-eighteen or even fourteen-to-eighteen schools. Some even began to think about schemes for separating sixth forms from schools entirely by setting up 'sixth form colleges'. In theory, the DES could have decided that only one form of organization was to be permitted. But it would have been a very impracticable step, given the limited resources available to it, to actually try to control the system and it would also have been ideologically unacceptable as being totally against the notion of the administrative partnership that was supposed to exist between central and local authorities. When government did intervene in 1965 to try to institute a national system of education which was comprehensive in character, it was in order to insist on the principle of comprehensive education, and not in order to impose a common form of organization on all authorities. Circular 10/65, which signalled the government's intention to press reluctant authorities into schemes for change, allowed about half a dozen types of scheme and many variations upon them. Thus a situation was created in which, on one front, that of its place in relation to schools, the character of the sixth form was set upon an apparently inexorable path of change as enrolments continued to rise, and as comprehensive schools passed from 'experimental' status to become part of the wobbly, but still effective 'consensus' on educational policy; however on another front, that of the curriculum, policy was firmly in the hands of the traditionalists who stuck to the position that 'more' meant 'more of the same'. On the one hand contexts were being created in which boundaries could be eroded, while on the other the distance between 'insiders' and 'outsiders' was maintained.

The key influence in sustaining this tension between organizational innovation and a frozen curriculum was that of the universities. At the time Crowther reported, they provided places for about 25,000 students per year out of just over 40,000 who were technically qualified for admission. The fact that not all of these would be seeking entry is balanced by the thought that any estimate of the scarcity of places based on these figures represents an average position and, since entry was decided essentially by departments within universities, many students might face odds well above the average. Thus there was severe and increasing pressure on sixth forms to coach and to 'cram' students for A-levels and for university entrance examinations. At the same time, the shortage of university places acted as a brake on the expansion of traditional sixth forms, though one which was not holding very well. By 1964 an increase of 4,000 in admissions had been outrun by a rise of 14,000 in the number of qualified applicants. In 1963, the Robbins Committee on higher education delivered its report.[7] This was the last of the expansionist reports and in many ways the most significant. It was significant for two reasons. First because in any country which has a fundamental attachment to elite forms of education, the most sensitive decision that can be made is one to increase the availability of higher education. The expansion of secondary education is an important step, and the loosing of bonds on the sixth form or its equivalent, a more important one. But in either case, the university remains as a repository of the ultimate values, where, as T.S. Eliot said, education can be preserved 'within the cloister uncontaminated by the deluge of barbarism outside'. The publication of the Robbins Report was predictably the occasion of a further chorus of dire warnings about 'more meaning worse'. But the second significant thing about Robbins was that it saw clearly that this was not the point. Unlike Crowther, Robbins stated unambiguously that more meant different:

> The present distribution of students between
> different types of honours course is therefore
> unsatisfactory. A higher proportion should be

receiving a broader education for their first
degrees . . . we regard such a change as a
necessary condition for any large expansion of
universities.[8]

Robbins did not, however, grasp the further nettle and apply the
'more means different' argument to the question of staff/student
ratios. On this front it was content to point to reasons why a
comparison with foreign universities was misleading and suggest
that the system should be expanded on the basis of current
assumptions about teaching loads. Once again the expansion
advocated was expansion of a costly model. The drawbacks of this
were not so apparent in a relatively affluent era, but a useful
weapon was left lying around for the elitist lobby when times got
harder.

The Robbins proposals for the founding of new universities,
the expansion of existing ones, and the redesignation as
universities of colleges of advanced technology were accepted by
the government, and by 1970 the annual rate of admission to
courses had increased to over 50,000 students. At the same time
the number of those qualified for entry had passed 75,000, thus
restoring the kind of equilibrium which had existed ten years
earlier. While this rapid growth of the universities through the
1960s took the worst pressures off the sixth forms, a further
initiative also helped. At last a common clearing house for
applications was set up which put an end to the situation in which
each university or even department might set its own entrance
tests and procedures. With the exception of Oxford and
Cambridge, all English universities henceforth worked completely
within a common system organized by the Universities Central
Council on Admissions (UCCA). Thus, the conditions were created
in which curriculum reform was possible, and in the late 1960s a
number of initiatives were taken which might have made it a
reality. The newly formed Schools Council was interested in the
future of the sixth form curriculum and had funds for research

and development work. A number of influential reports, such as Dainton and McCarthy,[9] drew attention to problems: for example, the shortage of science students, which seemed to be related to deficiencies in course provision at the sixth form level. A research project was started to develop a test of academic aptitude to assist in decision-making on university entrance. Interest was aroused in the International Baccalaureate as a possible alternative form of curriculum.[10] But the key to success of all these activities lay with the universities. These were autonomous bodies which were under no direct control by the DES or any other branch of government, in spite of the fact that they were publicly funded. No national rules existed (or exist today) about who is to be admitted to university courses. Each university publishes details of entry qualifications which are, in fact, rules of exclusion. They provide grounds on which universities may refuse applications, but no basis on which a student can claim entry. A study of university admissions procedures carried out in 1970 and 71 showed that this system put specific and detailed pressures on schools both as regards what should be taught in sixth forms and how closely it should be tailored to 'making the grade' in examination syllabuses. Effective decision-making was in the hands of admissions tutors in departments, who in their handling of applications, reflected a strong sense of hierarchy in their evaluation of subjects of the curriculum, preferred traditional to innovative syllabuses, rigidly separated arts and science qualifications and emphasized the achievement of high grades in specialist subjects against all round achievement.[11] These values and preference were reflected in the subjects and levels of performance demanded of applicants, and these in turn set curricular priorities for the schools. The net effect of all this was that it was practically impossible for any movement to take place in the traditional curriculum of the sixth, and that, in turn, meant that a rigid separation was maintained between sixth formers taking A-level courses and those with other ambitions. Reform depended on a decision on the part of the universities to modify their procedures and requirements for entry - something which they were quite entitled to do irrespective of what was being done elsewhere, but which they could not in the normal course of events be made to do.

A number of initiatives might have been taken which could have removed the pressure from schools to segregate groups of students and coach them intensively through highly specialized curricula. One would have been to press further in the direction established by the creation of UCCA and move towards more centralization of decision-making so that less of the process was hidden to schools and at least some students could be admitted to courses on the basis that they were **a priori** 'qualified'. Another would have been to support the work on aptitude testing so that decision criteria would be available that did not depend on performance in examinations based on content-heavy syllabuses at A-level. Again, formulae might have been found whereby equivalences were set up between A-levels and other levels of examination so that, at the discretion of universities, qualification might be earned in a variety of ways. Research showed that such moves would have had the support of many heads of schools with sixth forms.[12] With the major stumbling block of the university admissions question removed, or at least rendered less significant, an atmosphere would have existed in which the policy initiatives of bodies such as the Schools Council might have resulted in a general agreement on a new form and style of curriculum. However, over the period extending roughly from 1965 to 1978 when the issue was being treated in working parties, research, publications and conferences, the universities made no move on the matter of admissions and gave little indication that they saw it as something which was central to arguments about the sixth form content of courses.

In retrospect, it seems to have been an unreasonable belief that the universities might have acted differently. Like the sixth forms, their structures had evolved over a long period in response to an ideology of education which stressed the distinction between 'those who know' and the rest and emphasized the unchanging nature of educational standards and ideals. When Robbins suggested that the Colleges of Advanced Technology should be designated as universities, the Report was merely recognizing a fact of English higher education - that new institutions, if they are successful, gradually reshape themselves to approximate more closely to the stereotype of the old. This tendency is related to ingrained attitudes towards learning and knowledge. If there is a 'best' which is fixed and enduring and if that 'best' is not available to everyone, then it is important that it is marked off in visible ways and its character rendered as consistent as possible. This was true of universities just as it was of sixth forms. The university system, both before and after the Robbins expansion, was based on the idea of equivalence of degrees. Students either successfully completed a course deemed to be of a common standard wherever it was taken, or they were excluded from university degree qualifications altogether. The boundary between those on the inside of the system and those on the outside paralleled that which still existed, though less clearly than before, between 'sixth formers' and the rest, and the now rapidly disappearing one between 'grammar school' students and the rest. In all these cases, 'boundedness' was as intrinsic part of the meaning of the institutional category.

Such an approach to education could be represented as 'fair', in that those who were selected for higher status were guaranteed first class treatment. The new post-Robbins universities were held out as in every way as good as all of those already in existence (with the possible exception of Oxford and Cambridge which still in some ways claimed privileged status), in the same way as much was made of the fact that working class children enrolled in the most selective grammar schools (the 'direct grant' schools) received exactly the same education as their peers from families of high social status. These were examples of the 1960s version of the style of democracy which informed the public schools of the previous century: the extension downwards of privilege coupled with responsibility to those prepared to accept, or make a show of accepting, an upper class view of how society should be organized. On the other hand, it could equally be claimed that the democratic principle is best embodied in institutional categories that avoid the creation of boundaries, either by opening courses to all or by offering a wide spectrum of types of course which shade off into one another without clear demarcation. In either case, the notion of fixed standards has to be given a lower ideological priority. Where an institution is open to all, and all are encouraged as a matter of policy to be enrolled in it, as is the case with the American high school, there is no way of enforcing standards of achievement and no way of securing uniformity of achievement between schools. Where a variety of institutions exists, it is assumed that a prestige hierarchy will establish itself. Yet, if the fixed standard ceases to enjoy the status of a determinant of policy, it is not clear that levels of performance necessarily fall. In systems that operate with strong boundaries, those beyond the bound are likely to be disaffected, pulling down the average level of achievement. 'Standards' are likely to be thought of only in terms of the performance of elite groups.[13]

Soon after the adoption of the Robbins Report, the socialist government of the day gave a clear indication that universities were to continue to see themselves as operating within a bounded system, when the question of the relation of the newly established polytechnics to the universities was resolved by declaring a 'binary' policy. University status was to be confined to institutions under the national University Grants Committee, while the polytechnics became the responsibility of local authorities. They would not follow the universities in becoming degree granting institutions. Their degrees would be awarded through a central body to be known as the Council for National Academic Awards

(CNAA). Thus fortified in the belief that, in spite of expansion, their traditional status was assured, the universities proceeded to increase in size and in numbers, implementing the expensive form of provision in terms of plant and staff-student ratios which Robbins had advocated, but adhering to a pattern of teaching and admissions based on specialist degree courses.

In the crucial years of expansion between 1964 and 1968, while total entries rose by about sixty per cent there was only a marginal rise of some twenty-five per cent in the proportion admitted to non-specialist courses.[14] As regards the process of admitting students, this was centralized sufficiently to ensure that the system worked smoothly and without evident bias or unfairness. But control was left firmly in the hands of departments and little or nothing was done about the Robbins recommendations that there should be more contact and co-operation between schools and universities over student transfer.[15] Pressure on sixth forms therefore remained high, in spite of the increase in availability of higher education. The UCCA's **Seventh Report** showed that in the final clearing of candidates not already placed for entry in 1969, thirty per cent of those with three grade 'C' passes at A-level were unable to gain admission for Geography, thirty-seven per cent for History, thirty-nine per cent in Law and fifty-four per cent in English.[16] While such figures point up very clearly the problems that existed for schools in handling the increased intake to sixth forms, they also indicate why universities felt themselves under no pressure to work for change. They were evidently successful. Except in some science areas, demand continued to run ahead of supply thus inhibiting internal pressures for change. And even where demand was less buoyant, places were sometimes left unfilled in preference to admitting students with low, but still nominally sufficient qualifications.[17] The notion of 'expansion without change', defended as the means of ensuring that 'more did not mean worse', sanctioned an approach to university education of

171

which a contemporary writer remarked: 'It is difficult . . . to see on what basis this system was developed other than that it was clearly to the convenience of university teachers.'[18]

On the general policy front, the universities' attitude to reform was predictably luke-warm. Some academics were vocal enough in their condemnation of the shortcomings of the sixth form curriculum, but they never represented a general feeling, nor, when it came to the point, were their contributions to the production of specific proposals very incisive. Their work was not made any easier by the fact that 'boundary' mentality was imported from the beginning into the deliberations organized by the Schools Council which set up not one but two working parties in 1968 to produce proposals for change - one to concern itself with the curriculum of those intending to enter higher education, and another for the rest. Not only did this pre-empt the central issue about whether, especially in view of the growth of comprehensive secondary education, such distinctions should continue to be made, but it also slowed down the whole review procedure through the need to co-ordinate the work of two groups with different terms of reference. Perhaps because of the inability of those in control of the deliberation to see it as a question of the 'middle ground', the proposals that emerged succeeded in offending the conservatives without enabling the innovators to feel that anything worthwhile was being offered.[19] After the initial burst of enthusiasm generated by two early Schools Council working papers,[20] discussion dragged on in an increasingly limp manner until, long before the final proposals were produced in the late seventies, it was already plain that all conviction had gone out of the exercise. Other initiatives too, such as the academic aptitude test, were allowed to quietly fade away.

Meanwhile, however, the schools had not been standing still. Comprehensive reorganization had gained momentum and by 1970 the grammar schools were well on the way to being ousted as the main providers of sixth form courses. The percentage of 'non-A-level' sixth formers was also climbing fast. The combination of these two phenomena meant that the sixth form as an entity in schools had become very difficult to pin down. Comprehensives, for both ideological and practical reasons, were less likely than grammar schools to keep a firm boundary between sixth formers and the rest. Such schools had been set up on the platform of furthering social equality and also needed as many sixth formers as they could muster in order to form viable teaching groups and qualify for the resources and staffing needed for advanced teaching. In the grammar school the sixteen year old who returned to school to retake O-levels would almost certainly be labelled a 'fifth former'; in the comprehensive he was almost equally likely to be welcomed as an addition to the incipient 'sixth'.[21] Moreover, as, even ahead of the raising of the leaving age in 1973, the enrolment rate of sixteen year-olds increased, some students would stay in school to take the new, lower level, CSE examinations, or follow non-examination courses. The net result of all this was that, after 1969, 'Sixth form' disappears as a category from the DES annual statistics and is replaced by a category of 'older pupils'. The 1970 figures for this showed that, over all types of school, 102,000 A-level students were outnumbered by 160,000 following O-level or CSE courses and that, in addition, a further 16,000 were enrolled in courses not leading to public examinations.

Thus, while on one front the universities were helping to shore up the curricular distinction between the A-level student and the rest, and in this way to maintain the sixth form as a distinctive category, on another front its organizational unity was rapidly being lost as it was being separated from its traditional base in the grammar school. As an institutional category, the sixth form, as it entered the 1970s, was in a problematic state as important features of its categorical status changed due to social and economic forces which were beyond the control of central policy-makers.

NOTES

1   Stevens, Frances, **The Living Tradition: The Social and Educational Assumptions of the Grammar School,** London, Hutchinson, 1960, pp.258-260 (In a chapter entitled 'Democratic Minority').

2   Davies, Harry, **Culture and the Grammar School,** London, Routledge, 1965, pp.1, 2 and 5.

3   Young, Michael, **The Rise of the Meritocracy, 1870-2033: An Essay on Education and Equality,** London, Thames and Hudson, 1958.

4   For an account of the establishment of the General Studies Association, see Davies, 1965 **op.cit.,** Appendix 2.

5   Crowther, p.175.

6   See, for examples, DES, **The Educational System of England and Wales,** Feb., 1977, p.2.

7   Committee on Higher Education, **Higher Education,** Report of the Committee, London, HMSO, Cmnd.2154, 1963.

8   Committee on Higher Education, 1963 **op.cit.,** p,93.

9   Council for Scientific Policy, **Enquiry into the Flow of Candidates in Science and Technology into Higher Education,** London, HMSO, Cmnd. 3541, 1968 (Dainton), and McCarthy, M.C., **The Employment of Highly Specialised Graduates: A Comparative Study in the United Kingdom and the United States of America,** DES, Science Policy Studies No.3, London, HMSO, 1968.

10   Peterson, A.D.C., **International Baccalaureate,** London, Harrap, 1972.

11   Reid, W.A., **The Universities and the Sixth Form Curriculum,** Basingstoke, Macmillan, 1972.

12   Taylor, P.H., et al., **The English Sixth Form,** London, Routledge, 1974, p.136ff.

13 The conclusions of the International Evaluation of Achievement study of performance in Mathematics support this view, (Husen, T. (Ed), **International Study of Achievement in Mathematics,** 2 vols. Almqvist and Wiksell, Stockholm, 1967).

14 Reid, 1972, Note 4 to p.111.

15 Committee on Higher Education, 1963 **op.cit.,** p.232. See also recommendations 4-12, pp.277-8, and compare Crowther, pp.297-8.

16 Reid, 1972, Note 4 to p.83.

17 UCCA, **Seventh Report, 1968/9,** Table 5.

18 Pickering, G., **The Challenge to Education,** Harmondsworth, Penguin, 1969.

19 Reid, W.A. and Holley, B.J., 'The Factor structure of teacher attitudes to sixth form education', **British Journal of Educational Psychology,** 44, 1974, pp.65-73.

20 Schools Council, Working Paper 5: **Sixth Form Curriculum and Examinations,** London, HMSO, 1966, and Working Paper 16: **Some Further Proposals for Sixth Form Work,** London, HMSO, 1967. Papers continued to appear up to 1978, when Working Paper 60: **Examinations at 18+: the N and F Studies** (London, Evans/Methuen) was produced. This embodied the final proposals of the working parties. Consultation on them did not provoke much support and no further action on them was taken.

21 At this time, a majority of grammar schools required at least four O-level passes of students seeking to enter the sixth form, while a majority of comprehensive schools had no stated requirement (Taylor et al., 1974 **op.cit.,** Table 1.4). Funding for secondary schools was weighted towards older students and especially those over sixteen.

As we have seen, from 1970 the DES gave up the attempt to publish annual statistics on 'sixth formers' and substituted a category of 'older pupils'. By that date although the number of grammar schools in England and Wales had declined only slightly, and still stood at just over 1,000, comprehensives had become the second largest group after secondary moderns, while technical schools, never very numerous, had practically disappeared.[1] The extent of the 'comprehensive revolution' was, however less than it seemed. Although in some local authority areas secondary provision had been reorganized in such a way that selection for different types of school was eliminated, there were others where schools designated as comprehensive were in competition with grammar schools and virtually indistinguishable from the more ambitious secondary moderns which had developed post-sixteen courses. The signal difference was that, whereas the secondary moderns had been discouraged from venturing on ground which had traditionally belonged to the grammar schools, the comprehensive label could only be justified if some students attempted 'grammar school' work - and the authorities were actively promoting the efforts of the new schools in this direction. It was not clear, however, that the boundary around the 'sixth' could be held firm in the comprehensive school as it was in the grammar school.

Practical considerations of staffing and organization, as well as ideological motives stemming from the comprehensive ethos, pressed the schools towards an erosion of barriers at the point of entry to the sixth, and this tendency was confirmed by grant regulations which provided far more lavishly for older than younger students, irrespective of what kind of courses they were enrolled in. Schools which felt under an obligation to make available courses which were expensive in staff and equipment had to pay for these amenities by boosting their numbers of post-sixteen students. Research carried out in 1970 showed that in a sample of LEA maintained schools sixty per cent of those with the most selective eleven-plus intake required at least four O-level passes for admission to the sixth form and only fifteen per cent had no stated requirement, while in the least selective group the figures were thirty-five per cent and forty per cent.[2] But, significantly, the term used to describe students who were entering sixth forms with few or no O-level passes was 'new sixth former'. The use of this expression recognized the fact that, as the range of those admitted became broader, it was impossible, because of the inflexible nature of the curriculum, to assimilate everyone within a single category. In a sense, **the** sixth was unchanging and the new situation could be met only by putting alternative and less prestigious versions of the sixth alongside it - in much the same way as the public schools of the nineteenth century had provided 'modern' sides for those who were not up to the work of the classical sixth or who perhaps had good reasons for preferring something different. But what could be provided in the way of new courses was severely constrained by the pressures put upon schools by the requirements of the traditional sixth form curriculum. The new comprehensives had to justify themselves not just by broadening their post-sixteen provision, but also by facing up to the grammar schools on their own ground by cramming students for high levels of performance at A-level. Fifty-five per cent of a sample of head teachers surveyed in 1970 said that their freedom to provide courses for students **not** intending to enter higher education was 'much' or 'very much restricted' by pressures exerted by the universities.[3]

In all of this, the schools got no help from the DES. The central authority made no move either to assist the Schools Council in its deliberations on reform of the curriculum or to restrict the influence of the universities. Admittedly the Council had got off on the wrong foot by its decision to have two working parties, one to make recommendations for the curriculum of 'degree aspirants', and one concerned with sixth formers 'not aiming for degree courses.' This could be seen as a tacit admission that, while bridge building might be undertaken, assimilation was out of the question. But from 1966 onwards the Council produced a string of proposals which might have gone some way towards a solution of the problem.[4] The contribution of the DES, which was represented on or sent observers to all the Council's main committees was to remain silent or, on occasion, make it clear that it would always reserve the option of declaring that a Council decision 'affected policy' and could be overturned however much work and preparation had been put into it. Meantime, the fact that the whole curriculum of the sixth was under review provided the excuse to withhold official recognition from the Certificate of Extended Education (CEE) which was a natural upward growth of the Certificate of Secondary Education (CSE), introduced in 1963 to cater for those students who were not regarded as sufficiently able to be entered for O-level. Thus the schools were left to put whatever bits and pieces they could alongside the regular A-level provision. Very often this turned out to be repeats of O-level or CSE courses already taken with modest success lower down the school. This may have been a satisfactory state of affairs for those who wanted the sixth preserved uncontaminated in spite of comprehensive reorganization, but it was one which contained the seeds of its own downfall. The failure in the post-Crowther period to move towards more flexible curricular patterns, coupled with the broadening of the intake to sixth forms meant that the costs of sixteen-to-nineteen provision escalated rapidly. This provided an economic impetus towards a style of sixth form organization which had, on other grounds, already been implemented in some areas - the sixth form college.

The first serious proposal for a sixth form college had been put forward in Croydon in 1954 and had raised a storm of protest because it struck at one of the basic assumptions of the sixth form ideology - that sixth formers should stand in an authority relationship to younger pupils. This had been central to the original Arnoldian conception and remained an article of faith for many heads and teachers, as well as for a wider public. [5] The sixth form college also implied an extension of the mixed sixth form which many were quick to resist, and carried an implication that the notion of the 'continuous course' from eleven to eighteen was a mere facade, since a break of institution at sixteen was held to be tolerable, if not positively beneficial. All of these widely publicized objections, which made their appearance in letters to the press and statements from teacher associations, related to those moral qualities which had, from the outset, characterized the sixth form. Wearing King, the Croydon Chief Education Officer who instigated the sixth form college scheme supported a view of education centred on the good of the individual in opposition to one which assumed the priority of the moral community: 'To say that sixth formers are a good influence in the school and therefore they ought to remain there whether it is in their interest or not is to deny them a fundamental right, namely to be educated for their own proper benefit'.[6] Moreover, to retain sixth formers in schools where the total enrolment in advanced courses was small was to deny them a fair chance in examinations which brought them into competition with students from the larger grammar schools and from public schools. King gave his estimate of 'the minimum sixth form group to give a fair opportunity in the modern world' as between 400 and 500 and added 'It could well go appreciably higher'.[7] Even Crowther's upper estimate of 2,000 as an appropriate size for an eleven-to-eighteen comprehensive school would hardly be enough to produce such a large sixth - and King, in 1968, was thinking of a sixth form in the traditional academic mould, rather than one which provided other kinds of courses as well. The sixth form surveys of 1970 already mentioned provided some confirmation for his argument. In a sample of 150 schools with sixth forms, sixty-three per cent of those with up to sixty sixth formers placed themselves in a low success category for university entrance, while only four per cent

of schools with 181 or more students in the sixth placed
themselves in the same category. (See Table Four).

TABLE FOUR

Success rates in university entrance by
size of sixth form (%)[8]
(n = 150)

Success rate of applicants Size of sixth	up to 50%	50-70%	over 70%
up to 60	63.2	5.3	31.6
61-120	34.5	31.0	34.5
121 - 180	8.0	56.0	36.0
180 and over	4.3	60.9	34.8

Arguments based on fairness were also advanced by King
in favour of the mixed sixth. Far from seeing girls as a source of
contamination for the pure ideals of the sixth, a perspective
inherent in the character of the boys boarding school sixths of the
nineteenth century and one which, as we have seen, surfaced in
the Crowther Report, he regarded them as an under privileged
group who would benefit from the 'break with the normal public
school tradition which in the end has got to be made'.[9] Finally, he
claimed that the notion of the 'continuous course', of which so
much had been made in the Norwood Report and the post-war
Ministry of Education statements on the grammar school
curriculum, was pure rhetoric: 'The statement, so often glibly
made, that there is no break between fifth and sixth forms, and
that the whole is a single process, is quite untrue . . . In fact, in

a strictly academic sense the break here is probably greater than the break between sixth-form work and university work.'[10]

None of this endeared King to the many heads and teachers who held to a pure ideological position on the sixth: opposition to his scheme was well organized and decisive, though it did **post facto** find support in an unexpected quarter. Geoffrey Crowther contributed a preface to King's 1968 book in which he stated that over the period of the preparation of the **15-18 Report** the sixth form college had become his 'favourite project', and that he was astonished to find that all but one or two of the dozen or so professional educators engaged in the work of the Committee 'closed their minds to its merits'.[11] Crowther endorsed the idea that benefits are to be derived from the larger numbers of students that colleges could bring together and supported King's attack on the 'continuity of curriculum' argument. He concludes in phraseology that contains some hint of frustration, if not bitterness: 'With all these advantages one would have thought that there would have been a willingness at least to experiment with the Sixth Form College. But the teaching profession, for reasons which I fear reflect no credit on it, has succeeded in putting a virtually complete ban on the whole idea.'[12]

Why were the teachers so opposed to the idea of a sixth form college? King seems to think that their motives were fairly mercenary and even cynical. Teachers enjoy taking small groups of sixth formers in classes where they can indulge their academic interests in a congenial atmosphere while at the same time basking in a glow of status and prestige: 'Sixth-formers are to be retained in the school not for their own benefit but to please the staff'.[13] Heads, he thought, were rather good at doing sums and finding out how to increase the resources of their schools and, incidentally, their own salaries: 'I have known of grammar school heads who in public were denouncing my idea of a break after the fifth form, and at the same time were telephoning round neighbouring modern schools to ask if they had any promising candidates for the sixth'.[14] King is accurate in pin-pointing this kind of inconsistency which characterized the teachers' position. He might also have stressed how it extended beyond the teaching profession to the offices of the Ministry of Education. The civil servants, however, were not obliged to parade their inconsistencies because they could exert most influence simply by keeping silent - as they would later when the Schools Council was considering the curriculum of the sixth. (In the case of Croydon, supporters of the plan considered bringing in the Senior Chief Inspector as a consultant, but he 'was so non-committal that it seemed pointless to invite him.' Only later was it discovered that the Minister at the time, Sir David Eccles, had all along been in favour of the scheme.[15])

However, King probably misses the extent to which ideologies function precisely to prevent their supporters becoming aware of inconsistencies in thought and behaviour. If something is adopted as a result of rational argument it is a theory, proposition or hypothesis, not an ideology. Ideologies are absorbed together with supportive rhetorics which provide not logical justifications, but ready made responses - repertoires of statements and sentiments that are triggered by ideas or actions perceived as potentially threatening. It so happened in this case that support for the traditional sixth brought personal convenience and advantage to teachers associated with it: it should also be appreciated that these conveniences and advantages had been planted there, over many decades, by supporters of the ideology. They are better seen as the means whereby teachers were co-opted into being exponents of a conventional rhetoric already passively absorbed than as inducements to take up false positions in argument. The teachers believed what they said - on the whole. They did not see inconsistencies because they were not defending a rationally adopted position; they were impervious to argument because they saw the other side as advancing not arguments, but threats.

But inconsistencies which can be ironed away or overlooked on an intellectual level are less easily ignored when they have significant economic implications. And, precisely because of the problems posed by the persistence of the traditional A-level curriculum, the idea of colleges did have strong economic attractions, whatever the merits of King's social and educational justifications for his advocacy of them. They allowed the scarce resources of books and equipment needed for advanced teaching to be concentrated on one site instead of being scattered over several; and, if the colleges were purpose-built, teaching spaces could be rationalized to allow for a combination of small and large groups which was impossible in most secondary schools. But more compelling from the point of view of local authorities and rate-payers were the economic advantages which related to the major cost of a labour-intensive system of education - staffing. King's analysis of sixth form provision in Croydon in 1954 showed that, of 150 sixth form groups in the Borough, only twelve per cent contained ten or more students while twenty-five per cent consisted of only one.[16] In the less popular subjects, the average group size worked out at less than five. In spite of the later expansion in sixth form numbers, the persistence of the curriculum model endorsed by Crowther meant that economies of scale were slight as long as sixth forms remained as part of the eleven-to-eighteen secondary school. As groups in the more popular subjects grew larger in the grammar schools, this benefit to staffing costs was offset by the introduction of new subjects (Economics, Russian, Modern Maths), the decline of subjects which were dropping out of favour (Greek, Latin), and the arrival of new and under-populated sixth forms in comprehensive schools. Thus, national figures for 1978-9 reveal that just over half the secondary schools with sixth forms failed to enrol more than 100 students in them, and that the average group size for sixth form classes in comprehensive schools was still below ten.[17]

Even the most impervious ideology has difficulty sustaining

itself in the face of figures like these and, from the beginning of the 1970s, the trickle of schemes for sixth form colleges, which had begun in the mid-'60s with Luton and Mexborough, became a flood. They were of all types. Some involved the use of existing buildings and some were set up in new premises. Some concentrated on traditional A-level courses, some aimed at a wider spectrum of students. A few, generally referred to as tertiary colleges, combined sixth form provision with facilities for taking further education courses. By 1972, fourteen colleges had been opened and a further forty-three were planned. At this stage the schemes were confined to areas which had not reorganized their secondary provision and opted for colleges as part of a plan for 'going-comprehensive'. The peak of this phase was reached in 1974, when twenty-five colleges were opened, and by 1977 the total number had passed 100, enrolling over 50,000 students. In most of the authorities concerned, there was resistance to the introduction of the break at age sixteen based on claims that it was being done for 'merely economic' reasons and not on good educational grounds. But these reactions became progressively more muted as the realization grew that comprehensives of the size needed to sustain viable, let alone economic, sixth forms presented their own problems of curriculum and organization for teachers, especially where they could be created only by the use of split sites. Moreover, such large schools were difficult to justify in terms of educational advantage to students. In fact, ideological antipathy towards colleges could hardly fail to be associated with a distaste for large comprehensives since they were just as remote from the traditional image of the 'community of scholars'. As long as the choice had been, or had seemed to be, between the grammar school sixth and the college, it had not been a choice between evils. But by the early seventies there were enough practical examples around for it to be plain what the real alternatives were - colleges as against comprehensives of 1000-2000 students - and some who would have been bitterly opposed to colleges a few years before were now not so sure, especially if, as was often the case, the plan involved forming the college out of an existing grammar school. Others, however, softened their attitudes to comprehensives as it became apparent that these might be the only hope for the preservation of a sixth integrated into the secondary school.

In terms of the character of sixth form education as it was practically exemplified, the period from 1965-75 represented a revolution, in which the colleges were of even greater significance than the comprehensives - though, as we have seen, the one cannot be understood without the other. But the revolution was an even greater one in terms of its general impact on the thinking of the public, the professions and the politicians about sixteen-to-nineteen education. Ideologies are undermined not by theories, but by realities. By the mid-1970s real manifestations of alternative ways of organizing the education of sixth formers were abundant, and significant not just for what they were, but also for what they implied about possible future developments. Sixth forms in comprehensive schools represented a new **species** rather than a new **genus:** some were growing up where no sixth had existed before and, much as the incipient sixths of new grammar schools after 1902, could be seen as evolving towards the archetypal form; others took over an unbroken tradition from an established grammar school sixth. In most cases, rivalry with neighbouring schools ensured that the tendency was to preserve the traditional trappings of captains, prefects and uniforms. Everywhere the comprehensive sixth was an organic part of the whole secondary school. Typically, it was small and of low prestige compared to the sixths of the grammar and public schools and, locked into the traditional and unyielding pattern of the academic curriculum, there was no road it could follow which would take it very far from the path of orthodoxy. The colleges were a different matter altogether. Even where they grew out of the grammar schools and were guided by heads and teachers whose sympathies were more with the old than the new, the possibilities for change were potent.

Shorn of the lower school, college sixth formers became democratized; the symbols of leadership and status lost their meaning. Arguments that dress and conduct must be regulated 'to set an example' to the less mature students became irrelevant. Evolution towards a less hierarchical and more relaxed kind of society was inevitable, especially since all but one of the 100 colleges open by 1977 were mixed. But, with heads and teachers who shared Wearing King's positive vision of what the college could offer to its students, quite bold courses could be steered. The colleges were usually large and without competition in their immediate area. They could set fashion rather than follow it. In the case of Solihull College, for example, which was set up in 1974 in an area where there had been very strong support for the traditional grammar schools, uniform was abolished, students were permitted to be off the premises when they were not scheduled for teaching and important areas of decision-making on policy and finance were handed over to them. The fact that the building was a new one also permitted some innovation in teaching method through the use of tutorial suites and large lecture theatres. Colleges like this moved rapidly and purposefully towards a realization of King's vision:

> This then is the concept: a collegiate institution
> taking pupils who have passed the fifth-form
> stage, at whatever age, and providing for them in
> a more adult atmosphere than is possible in a
> school; not tied to the school day; not using the
> prefectorial and disciplinary methods of a school;
> and taking the pupils through a professionally
> planned syllabus, giving them responsibility not for
> the conduct of their juniors but for their own
> educational advance; with individual time-tables

and the tutorial method as well as lectures and seminars superseding the idea of a class or form.[18]

Beyond that, the colleges posed in a very clear way the question of the relationship between sixth forms and the technical and vocational courses offered in colleges of further education. From the beginning of the sixth form college movement there were those who saw the institution of a break at sixteen as an opportunity to bridge over the division between the 'academic' students and the student looking forward to qualifying for entry to a specific trade. In thinly populated areas there was an extra incentive to look into such possibilites, and as early as 1970, the first tertiary college combining sixth form and FE provision was set up in Exeter. In the following years the idea was copied in other areas, and in some which had originally stuck to a traditional definition of the sixth form student the attraction of the more broadly defined college began to assert itself.

From the mid-seventies, colleges were numerous, popular, and visibly successful. King's claim that, where A-level success was concerned, more was better seemed to be amply borne out. Parents who had been disconcerted by the move away from the conventional apparatus of the grammar school sixth were considerably mollified when they found that the new institutions were delivering academic success even more predictably than the old regime had. And gloomy forecasts that the break of school at sixteen would deter students from staying in full time education were nowhere confirmed in practice. For every student who could not face an unfamiliar sixth, there was at least one more who welcomed the chance of a fresh start in a college where he brought no reputation other than his public examination results. [19]

Thus, a new **genus** was established which shared some characteristics of the old, but was also interestingly different. As far as the basic curriculum was concerned, the colleges, like all other sixth forms, were constrained by the unvarying diet of advanced specialist work enforced just as surely by inaction on the part of the central authority as it would have been if established by decree. To some extent they could experiment with new teaching methods though, since the majority of establishments had inherited existing buildings, the scope for this was limited. Their high levels of enrolment (the average of ninety-seven colleges in 1979-80 was 501[20]) enabled them, if they wished, to go further than most schools could in providing complementary or 'general studies' courses. But most colleges concentrated on the traditional A-level courses, which were wanted on average by about eighty per cent of their clientele, and taught them in the time-honoured way - through factual, transmission teaching which, much as it might be deplored by educational theorists, was not in the least resented by the majority of the students.[21] In their successful teaching of the A-level curriculum, the colleges preserved and embodied Crowther's first three 'marks of a sixth form' - '(A) close link with the university', 'subject-mindedness' and 'independent work'. Solihull College, for example, in 1975-7 enrolled all of its students in A-level courses, achieved pass rates of over eighty per cent in most subjects (against a national average of about seventy per cent), sent about sixty per cent of its leavers on to higher education, and made special efforts to foster private study. This, one might have thought, would have met with near universal approval - from those who were inclined against sixth form colleges as well as those who naturally favoured them. In fact, many people found it worrying. For the first time, the platonic chain of approximations to the ideal sixth form was broken. The conception had been born in the public schools, passed on to the reviving grammar schools and transmitted to the nascent LEA secondary schools. In the mid-sixties this hierarchy still persisted: if you wanted to know what a sixth form **should** be like you looked to the leading independent schools; the grammar schools struggled to follow them, and the comprehensives struggled to draw themselves after the grammar schools. All was in its proper place. Colleges like Solihull challenged the natural order; not only were they bidding to become as academically successful as the independent schools, they were actually attracting students away from them. Boys who would not have contemplated leaving Solihull School for a maintained grammar school were finding in the Sixth Form College a real and preferable alternative to their public school sixth. This was deeply disturbing to anyone with an ideological commitment to the idea of the sixth form. Worse, however, was the colleges' neglect of 'marks' four and five - intellectual discipleship and social responsibility.

In what way, it might be wondered, were the colleges transgressing in terms of 'intellectual discipleship'? Surely, the preservation of the A-level curriculum guaranteed that there would continue to be a close relationship between teacher and taught? The groups were, from the point of view of both economy and good teaching, satisfyingly larger than those found in comprehensive schools which traditionalists attacked for lacking 'the stimulus that comes from competition', but the average size was still only eleven or twelve.[22] Moreover, the colleges were attractive precisely to those teachers who were well qualified in and committed to their subjects. What, then, was the difficulty? Crowther discusses discipleship only in terms of time spent in the sixth - though the Report refers to 'frequent contact between a teacher and a small group of pupils over several years'. But separation of the sixth from the lower school affects the teacher-student relationship in a quite fundamental way. To understand how this comes about, it is necessary to consider the notion of 'sponsorship'.

Sociologists have distinguished two types of elite linked to educational systems: 'sponsored' and 'contest'.[23] Schooling aimed at producing a 'contest' elite sets out to retain as many students as possible in a common system of education up to a final point at which an objective criterion of achievement is applied to determine who is qualified for entry to the elite and who is not. The 'sponsored' elite model depends on the idea that there is no need to operate a common system because elite qualities are identifiable when children are quite young. What is required is a system involving parallel types of schooling and continuous selection. In principle, this kind of education could also make use of objective tests of achievement but, since the difference between the systems is one of philosophy as well as of practice, something else is added to or substituted for examination: a support system for pupils identified as 'elite material'. This ensures that the arbitrary nature of early selection is disguised, and that the system is one of self-fulfilling prophecy rather than trial and error.

These descriptions are of 'ideal types' which nowhere exist; different education systems approximate to them more or less. The traditional sixth form approaches the 'sponsorship' model. This part of its inherent character was strengthened when maintained grammar schools were opened to the more able elementary school students. The system created was a parallel one with sideways transfers from elementary to secondary school. Sponsorship which had begun in the first school was continued by grammar school teachers who encouraged promising children to stay in school to take certificate examinations, and then enter the sixth form, not just to continue full-time education, but to study **their** subjects. After the 1944 Act had finally established the principle that secondary education should be 'end-on' to primary education, the parallel system still continued at the upper end of the secondary stage. Students over sixteen in secondary modern schools were not sixth formers. If they wanted to become sixth formers, they had to be accepted into grammar schools. Within the selective system of secondary education, the significance of the teacher-student relationship lay in its development over time. The continuity of contact from lower school to sixth form was played off against the discontinuity created by the curriculum shift to advanced level work which, as King pointed out, was really far more significant than any claimed curriculum progression from age eleven through to age eighteen.

Viewed in one way, the 'discipleship' of the sixth form marked a weaning away from teacher-dependence and towards self-directed learning; viewed in another, it was a process which ensured that the self-direction occurred within approved limits and that the sixth former saw his status as something collectively established and protected (comparisons could be made with initiation into professions). This, of course, was the vision of sponsorship rather than the reality. Not every sixth form teacher saw his role in this way, or had his teaching organized in a way to make it possible. Often they might have little contact with the lower school. But ideologues do not ask whether what they believe to exist actually does exist; they look for reassurance that nothing in the prevailing circumstances rules out the possibility of it being the case. Where the sixth form college was concerned, it was plain that the teachers **could not** have known their 'disciples' before they entered the sixth; moreover, the lack of any previous contact tending to set up the dependency relationship would inevitably mean that teachers and students would meet on a level of greater equality than would be the case in the school. Thus the duality of status of the sixth former as independent learner **and** pupil, to which so much importance was attached, would be broken down. At root, what was involved here was the same concern as was raised by the colleges' most obvious and serious departure from the conventional 'marks' - social responsibility. In the conventional ideology, this was narrowly defined as the exercise of authority over younger children. Plainly, no argument could be made that social responsibility defined in this way was being exercised by college sixth formers. Indeed, it was an article of faith among their supporters that this was one of the outstanding virtues of colleges - they allowed students to create their own adult society, untrammelled by the need to adjust to and regulate a younger age group.

It is worth pausing at this point to consider why the 'social responsibility' issue should assume such a central significance in the traditionalist arguments against sixth form colleges. The obvious answer is that the separation of the sixth from the lower school produced an institution with a built-in tendency towards openness, equality, flexibility and pragmatism. This movement away from the notion of the sixth as fixed, as linked to differentiation and hierarchy, and as controllable, presented two related and equally distasteful possibilities of development for those attached to the traditional ideology of the sixth. On the one hand, it moved the conception of the sixth away from the small world of the community of scholars and confounded it with a larger world which was to be distrusted - that Great World which Francis Cornford described as 'a distant and rather terrifying region, which it is very necessary to keep in touch with, though it must not be allowed on any account to touch you'.[24] The college promised visions of mass education pandering to the interests of the Great World: interests of lower class students, of ill-informed parents and mercenary employers. It had overtones of the kind of education associated with the United States which had been anathema to Arnold and Norwood. On the other hand, it provided a context within which democratization seemed inevitable. Even the preservation of the A-level curriculum was no guarantee of the security of hierarchy.

Democratization was already taking place both within the academic curriculum and across its boundary. Comprehensive schools operated quite effectively as instruments of exclusion at the level of the academic sixth form; not because they intended to, but because the effort of staffing an open choice specialist curriculum stretched their resources and, unless they were schools which built on an existing grammar tradition, they found it hard to create sixth forms large enough to generate confidence and enthusiasm in the face of a school of over a thousand which was drawn towards different conceptions of education. Sixth formers were often a beleaguered minority pursuing courses which seemed fairly meaningless in terms of the ethos of the schools as a whole. Colleges, on the other hand, even those that claimed titles like 'open' or 'comprehensive', had a firm centre of gravity in A-level work with good specialist teachers and substantial classes. Here the student who would have been 'marginal' in the comprehensive sixth could be readily co-opted into the academic curriculum. Except in some areas where the grammar school tradition had itself been weak, colleges found less problem than the comprehensives with the 'new sixth' former. The public schools had been showing for years that students of modest ability could cope with a curriculum that was supposedly for the academic 'high flyers';[25] grammar schools, with their selective entry had never really had to face up to the problem. Now the colleges were beginning to show that, given the right kind of institution, the maintained sector could generate the kind of expectation and commitment which can expand enrolments even in apparently 'exclusive' courses.

Moreover, entry to the A-level curriculum was cutting across the sponsorship system. With the break at sixteen giving students an opportunity to think seriously about what they wanted to do instead of simply following their teachers' expectations, leavers from grammar schools began to choose vocational courses in further education, and some from secondary moderns preferred to aim at A-level. Over a four year period from its opening, the percentage of entrants to Solihull College coming from ex-selective schools in the Borough fell from seventy-four to fifty-six, while the intake from the ex-secondary modern schools rose from fifteen to thirty per cent.[26] Solihull was an exclusively 'A-level' college, but in others where different kinds of courses were available, democratization occurred across the boundary, even where it was not actively encouraged. With no history of lower

194

school careers shared between students, no experience of the effects of sponsorship or its reverse, or differential relationships with juniors to divide them, students began to shape communities where each was valued for himself and for what he brought to a fellowship of equals. The notion of a level of perfection against which the sixth former was measured in terms of how near he approached it, or how far he fell short of it was being lost. What is more, in the tertiary colleges, the distinction between academic and vocationally oriented students was being eroded. The tradition of 'knowledge as an end in itself' was in danger of being confounded with the baser one of knowledge 'as a means to some cheaply utilitarian end'.[27] Such developments were obviously not welcome to the supporters of the traditional ideology of the sixth. Yet perhaps they do not in themselves go to the heart of the matter. In any sponsorship system, it is boundaries which are of prime importance. From the beginning, the sixth, and the route to the sixth, were marked by ritualized transitions, so we should suspect that the 'break at sixteen' might have a significance which goes beyond what is obvious to the casual observer. This idea is strengthened when we contrast the opposition mounted in some quarters to the idea of the sixth form college with the strong advocacy, from the same quarters, that, two years later, the academic student should enter a university course involving residence away from home - enrolment in a 'home' university being looked on as a poor alternative. What is it that distinguishes the one situation so clearly from the other?

We would suggest that what makes the sixth form special is that it is marked at its beginning by a curricular boundary without an institutional one, and at its end by an institutional boundary which is not curricular. The rhetoric of sixth form ideology emphasizes continuity of curriculum - the sixth as the natural continuation and crown of what has gone before - and discontinuity in the social role of the sixth former - the attainment of a status involving personal responsibility and a

195

changed relationship with teachers. Both claims are misleading. As far as the curriculum is concerned, the A-level student moves from a general curriculum of eight to ten subjects with only marginal choice available (though it may be very significant for the career of the individual) and followed in conventional classes with probably no free time, to a specialist one entailing commitment to three or so subjects studied in a depth and detail that in many countries would be associated with university level work, and based on small group tutoring and extensive private study. But this happens within a familiar environment and in the company of well known teachers and a stable cohort of contemporaries. In his new situation, the student has a different role but is still defined as in a state of dependence because his 'sponsors' emphasize both the novelty of the work, which passes beyond common knowledge, and also the responsibility of the sixth formers towards younger students. The state of being in unfamiliar territory with familiar superiors is calculated to produce command of the environment, but in such a way that it seems to arise from guidance, not initiative. The means of achieving success is experienced as a kind of talisman inherited from others, rather than as a developed capacity of the individual. When the break of institution comes, and the sixth former is sent out into the world, as all neophytes must be, however long their period of tutelage, the rules of success will work, more or less, because the task is a familiar one.[28] And, by the time the break comes, there can be some assurance that those destined for high places will not be easily weaned from the philosophy of education they have imbibed. There can be practically double assurance that this will be the case for the next generation of heads and teachers who, almost without exception, come from the ranks of sixth formers. They are unlikely to return to the place of their initiation in order to dismantle it. And that is what traditionalists most need to feel comfortable about.[29]

Viewed against this background, then, the challenge of the

new **genus** was a very serious one. A fresh institution was being created which bore the name of sixth form and performed the core curricular work of sixth forms, but which, contrary to the character of the long established school sixth forms, had inherent propensities towards universalism and democratization, both in a social and an academic sense. By undermining the initiatory function of the sixth the colleges were threatening that peculiar freedom of which Norwood had been such a strong advocate: 'the boy is taught to choose what he ought to choose and that is the real freedom; not the pseudo-freedom of many-headed uneducated democracy'.[30] It was not surprising that, in the context of a revival of hard-line political conservatism, the colleges were to become, in the early '80s the battle ground **par excellence** of competing visions of sixth form education and, even beyond that, of competing visions of the meaning of British democracy in the nation as a whole.

NOTES

1   See Table Three, p.156.

2   See Reid, W.A., **The Universities and the Sixth Form Curriculum,** Basingstoke, Macmillan, 1972, Table 8.12, p.104.

3   **Ibid.,** Table 27.

4   For an account of the Schools Council's proposals, together with some put forward by other bodies, see Taylor et al., 1974, Appendix A. Also Schools Council Working Paper 60, **Examinations at 18+: the N and F Studies,** London, Evans/Methuen Educational, 1978.

5   An account of the origins of the Croydon scheme, and the reasoning behind it, is given in King, R. Wearing, **The English Sixth-Form College: An Educational Concept,** Oxford, Pergamon Press, 1968. King seems to be unaware

that a proposal very similar to his was put forward in general terms by T.C. Worsley in his book **Barbarians and Philistines**, published in 1940. Worsley used the term 'Junior Universities'. He thought they could include students in 'part-time employment or apprenticeships' thus breaking down the gap between 'culture and vocation'. Like King, he saw them as offering the possibility of integrating the public schools into the maintained sector, but in such a way that they would contribute to an education 'on proper democratic lines' and free of 'that prolongation of adolescence which we have noticed as the bad effect of the present arrangement under which older and younger children live together' (Worsley, p.230ff.).

6   King, 1968, **op.cit.**, p.70.
7   **Ibid.**, p.10.
8   After Reid, 1972 **op.cit.**, Table 8.10, p.103.
9   King, 1968 **op.cit.**, p.15. See also, pp.75-77.
10 **Ibid.**, pp. 77-8.
11 **Ibid.**, p.vii.
12 **Ibid.**, p.viii.
13 **Ibid.**, p.79.
14 **Ibid.**, p.61.
15 **Ibid.**, p.126.
16 **Ibid.**, pp.134-6. King's figures relate to numbers of students taking each subject in each year of the sixth. In some cases these groups would be amalgamated for teaching purposes (though King feels they ought not to be). But he claims that 'Where very small groups appear in the . . . tables, it normally means that that small group is occupying the time of one member of staff for about six periods per week' (p.136).
17 Department of Education and Science, **Education for 16-19 Year Olds**, DES/CLEA, 1980, Table 10. Given the disparity in staying on rates in different parts of the

country, the figures provide an over optimistic picture. An average A-level teaching group size of 6.4 revealed in a survey of a large West Midland Borough is not unusual, nor the finding in the same area that 187 out of 538 groups consisted of three students, or fewer.

18 King, 1968 **op.cit.**, p.69.

19 'There is support from work by HMI and analysis of DES statistics that its (separate post-sixteen provision) establishment tends to increase participation in post-compulsory education' (DES/CLEA, 1980 **op.cit.**, p.30).

20 **Ibid.**, Table 4.

21 This was the finding of our own study of three West Midland colleges through observation, questionnaire surveys and interviews with staff and students, 1975-77 (Reid, W.A. and Filby, J.L., **The Organisation and Curriculum of Three Sixth Form Colleges,** Final Report to the Department of Education and Science, Teaching Research Unit, University of Birmingham, April, 1978, p.66).

22 DES/CLEA, 1980 **op.cit.**, Table 10. 'Competition', or in its earlier form 'emulation', has a long history as a component of English educational ideologies. See, for example, Hamilton, David, 'Adam Smith and the moral economy of the classroom system', **Journal of Curriculum Studies,** 12, 4, 1980, pp.281-298. Nineteenth century educationalists such as William Whewell supported examinations because they were 'emulous'. The phrase 'stimulus of competition' comes from a recent critique of sixth form colleges in which it is identified as the principal, if not the only benefit of an increase in the size of sixth-form groups (Naylor, Fred, **Crisis in the Sixth Form,** London, Centre for Policy Studies, 1981, p.6.).

23 See, for example, Turner, R.H., in Halsey, A.H., Floud, J. and Anderson, C.A., **Education, Economy and Society,** New York, Free Press, 1961. The 'sponsored' model aims at

early selection, a concentration of resources on 'those who can benefit', and stresses **espirit de corps** and intellectual values. The elite presents a unified front, while the masses are trained to regard themselves as unfitted for positions of responsibility. The 'contest' model delays selection as long as possible, and emphasises social adjustment training and the practical benefits of education.

24   Cornford, F.M., **Microcosmographia Academica**, London, Bowes and Bowes, 1978, p.8.

25   On success rates at A-level in public schools, see Kalton, G., **The Public Schools: A Factual Survey**, London, Longmans, 1966. Kalton's data on school leavers for the year 1962-3 showed that boys in independent schools stayed longer and got better A-levels than boys in maintained grammar schools. So much better was the performance in the independent sector that the percentage of boys getting two or more A-levels among those known to have **failed** an eleven-plus examination was very close to that recorded by boys in grammar schools (twenty-seven per cent against thirty-three per cent. Among independent school boys who passed eleven-plus it was sixty-seven per cent. Table 6.22, p.102).

26   Reid and Filby, 1978 **op.cit.**, Statistical Appendix, Table 5.

27   Norwood, Cyril and Hope, Arthur H. (Eds), **The Higher Education of Boys in England**, London, John Murray, 1909, p.300.

28   We say 'more or less' because success depends on the character of the individual coupled with the nature of the university to which he transfers. The experience over some fifteen years of the Educational Counselling Unit in the University of Birmingham shows that many students encounter problems of adjustment when they move from the highly supportive atmosphere of a sixth form, probably a small one, to the rather impersonal context of a

'redbrick' university. But the promoters of the ideology typically focus on an ideal situation in which students transfer from a large sixth of a public school character to Cambridge or Oxford, where the college based tutorial system reflects and extends the culture of the upper secondary school. One is reminded of Mark Pattison's comment of the 1880s that Oxford was becoming a 'super public school'. It is a fact that about ninety-seven per cent of entrants to Oxford and Cambridge not only get degrees, but get them on time.

29   The 1970 surveys indicated that teachers on the whole were opposed to change in the sixth form curriculum, but that sixth form teachers, teachers with higher qualifications and teachers with the least experience of alternative forms of education (comprehensive schools, further education) were more opposed than most, and tended to subscribe to an elitist definition of sixth form education (Taylor, P.H. et al., **The English Sixth Form,** London, Routledge & Kegan Paul, 1974, Ch.3).

30   Norwood, Cyril, **The English Tradition of Education,** London, John Murray, 1929, p.79. Compare Friedrich Engels, 'Freedom is the appreciation of necessity'.

Figure 3 (Source: DES/CLEA, 1980)
(See Chapter 10, note 17)

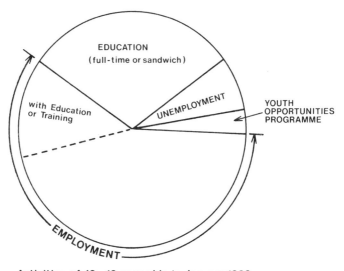

Activities of 16 – 19 year olds in January 1980

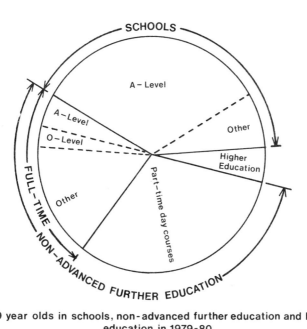

16 – 19 year olds in schools, non-advanced further education and higher education in 1979-80

202

The growth of the sixth form college in the late 1970s was a remarkable phenomenon. By 1980, about 60,000 students were enrolled in colleges, over 12,000 of them in tertiary establishments which combined sixth form and further education curricula. This represented only a fraction of the total number of students in full-time sixteen-to-nineteen education - the A-level group alone now exceeds 300,000[1] - but it was a very significant fraction for a number of reasons. First, because the colleges were very rapidly winning the approval of students, parents and educational researchers; second, because, as had already been suggested, they represented an ideology of sixth form education which was different from, and a potent rival to that projected by the public schools, and third, because there was a strong likelihood that the first wave of colleges - those created by reorganization plans evolved by authorities moving to a comprehensive system - would be followed by a second wave promoted by authorities which had already reorganized, but now saw compelling reasons to give up their initial choice of an eleven-to-eighteen solution.

One of the earliest studies of different types of sixth form provision, that published by Ronald King in 1976,[2] concluded that there was no empirical support for the idea that the move to a college would be unsettling for students: 'These results . . . suggest that contrary to expectation, students, especially boys, may find it easier to settle in to the college organization.'[3] In our own local research we did encounter a minority of students who missed the 'grammar school' atmosphere ('They treat us like adults here . . . but I think we had more respect for the teachers at the grammar'[4]) - as we commented, '(N)ot every student is naturally enthusiastic for freedom and equality' - but the response from most of them to the positive conceptions of the sixth form college put over by principals and staff was an enthusiastic one: 'Friendly atmosphere . . . the teachers here treat you with more respect'; 'They teach you more like adults'; 'There's so much more freedom. I think in a school you're still conscious of all the rules, whereas here there aren't really any'.[5] But this appreciation of the friendly, adult atmosphere of the college was combined with a high priority for academic advancement. In three colleges of very differing character, we found that around eighty per cent of students thought 'getting qualifications for a career or to enter higher education' was 'very important.' No other purpose received anywhere near such universal endorsement. We concluded that 'in the minds of students, opportunities for working, studying the subjects they find interesting and getting qualifications form the most important cluster of aims.'[6] Finally, in 1979, the results of a comprehensive national survey carried out by the National Foundation for Educational Research came to broadly similar conclusions. This investigation, comparing large samples of students in five types of institution (comprehensive schools, grammar schools, sixth-form colleges, tertiary colleges and FE colleges) found that sixth form and tertiary colleges were seen by students as providing a standard in A-level teaching equal to the grammar school sixth, a much better range of optional, non-examination subjects, better common room and private study amenities and more adult attitudes towards students.[7] The NFER team were also able to carry out an analysis of examination results showing that, allowing for the previous exam record of entering students, the colleges achieved results as good as those of grammar school sixth forms. The consensus of these and other research programmes was that, on any criterion, sixth form colleges offered educational provision that was at least as good as anything school sixth forms could provide, and that on some criteria they came out consistently better. Not surprisingly, the NFER researchers concluded that 'many of the doubts and reservations expressed about the effects of a break at sixteen are without foundation' and, more positively, that

(t)he establishment of separate colleges for

students over the school leaving age seems to have much to recommend it. Not only do students prefer them, but the colleges also appear to be developing expertise, perhaps because of their greater resources, in various areas specifically concerning sixteen-to-nineteen, e.g. careers advice and tuition in study skills.[8]

Though the NFER study provided a very thorough and detailed investigation of the strengths and weaknesses of various forms of organisation for sixteen-to-nineteen education, its defect was that it presented them in terms of 'best buy' criteria and missed the extent to which attitudes towards sixth form education, and hence towards empirical measures of its effects, were ideologically conditioned. The earlier investigation carried out by Ronald King was much clearer in this respect. King pointed to the essentially ideological difference between school-based and college-based sixth form education, which he explained in terms of Tonnies' conceptions of **Gemeinschaft** and **Gesellschaft**[9] - roughly translatable as 'community' and 'association'. The school represents a community whose social order 'is based on relationships which are intimate, affective, enduring and involuntary, as between parent and child, and thought to be ends in themselves . . . Its moral custodians are strong and their injunctions well internalized.' Associations, on the other hand have a social order 'based upon voluntary, partial relationships, entered into as a contract for some specific, instrumental purpose', as, for example, in clubs, mutual benefit societies, factories and offices.[10] These are, of course, descriptions of 'ideal types', unlikely to be found in the real world in a pure form. King takes the selective secondary school as representative of the conception of **Gemeinschaft** since, as he points out, 'the idea of community implies consensus' and, the more homogeneous the school, the more it will approximate to the ideal type.[11] The nearest approach to **Gesellschaft** in the spectrum of institutions is found in the further education college. This is likely to enrol a large number of part-time students, to have flexible working hours, and to offer curricula clearly linked to instrumental goals. King places the sixth form college somewhere in the middle. Though it deliberately incorporates some of the features of the further education college, it also tends to stress community values, at least to some extent, and to preserve some characteristics of school life. What King does not do is to take the further step of considering the **Gemeinschaft** function of the traditional sixth form as a 'school within a school'. Nevertheless, he makes out a clear case for believing that the sixth form college is ideologically as well as organizationally significant and that it departs fundamentally from the established form for which the public school functions as a 'high status archetype'.[12] What the later NFER research demonstrated was that the **quasi-Gesellschaft** form of education represented by the colleges had, in a very short time, become strong enough to mount an ideological challenge to the school sixth form in spite of the fact that it lacked a corresponding high status archetype of its own - further education colleges being, within the conventional hierarchy, low status organizations. This challenge arose because the colleges were large, attractive to students, could concentrate specialist resources and project a coherent image and rationale connected with transition to adult status and the acquisition of career qualifications.

For these reasons, colleges were very much in the public eye at the beginning of the 1980s. They were also figuring very strongly in the thinking of chief education officers who were simultaneously subjected to pressures to raise enrolments in sixteen-to-nineteen education and to make their education systems more cost effective. The 1970s had seen a prolonged period of economic stagnation and decline coupled with falling birthrates.

This first of all created a political and social demand that the effects of unemployment, which were differentially severe on school leavers, be alleviated by increasing the enrolment of sixteen-to-nineteen year-olds in some kind of full or part time education. Secondly it made schemes of eleven-to-eighteen comprehensive education, set up on optimistic projections of birthrates, look very unattractive. Many comprehensives, especially those in inner city areas, faced a period of declining demand, rather than the hoped for expansion toward the distant day when their sixth forms would be economically viable. At the same time, teachers found themselves in a contracting industry and less able than they had been in the past to oppose sixth form college schemes with any prospect of success. Given this background it was obvious that the early '80s would see college schemes of various kinds coming forward in such numbers, and affecting such large populations that colleges combining the A-level curriculum with other kinds of academic and, in some instances, vocational courses might rapidly become the normal vehicle of sixth form education. In this way, more students could be enrolled at relatively little extra cost, since concentration of resources would allow considerable economies. Judging by the experience already gained in the first wave of colleges, academic results would improve. Finally, colleges gave considerable flexibility for looking at new possibilities for combining established academic and vocational curricula with the new ones that were likely to come forward in response to the shrinking job market. Once set up they could, if necessary, add on full and part time or sandwich courses by accretion in the way that colleges of further education had done for years - something that the schools would find very difficult: **Gesellschaft** is more adaptable than **Gemeinschaft** as an organizational form.

The educational world waited with interest to see what the Government's reaction would be to the new wave of schemes when they were officially proposed and sent to the DES for approval.

The setting up of colleges in the 1970s had not been a deep political issue. True, labour councils had looked on them with more favour than conservative ones, but colleges had been successfully launched in some of the most right wing authorities in the country - Solihull was a case in point.[13] Where they had been instituted, they were generally regarded as successful. Worries over the adverse effects that the creation of colleges would have on the resulting eleven-to-sixteen comprehensives were not substantiated in any of the major research studies.[14] If problems occurred, these were more likely to be due to failures of planning, where schemes were set up in a hurry or insufficient account was taken of the need for co-ordination between schools, than to inherent problems about lack of resources, staffing or morale. However, the Government which took office in 1979 contained a number of leading figures who were known to be positively in favour of selective education. Moreover, as usual, the position of the DES on the matter of sixth form provision was obscure. It was not certain whether this was due to a genuine openness of mind or to a continued belief in the virtues of a policy of masterly inactivity as a way of maintaining a **status quo** which was looked on with some affection. Some recent hawkish pronouncements on curriculum, reminiscent of the language of the 1904 Regulations lend support to the latter interpretation.[15]

Soon after the 1979 general election, the Council of Local Education Authorities, which was concerned that there should be some official lead on the matter of sixteen-to-nineteen provision, approached the Government to suggest that a joint study group should be set up to look into the question and report back. This initiative received a positive response, and a committee was formed under the chairmanship of Neil Macfarlane, Parliamentary Under-Secretary at the DES 'To review the educational provision made by local authorities for the sixteen-to-nineteen age group in England and Wales, with due regard to factors affecting the demand for this provision and to the impact of related types of

208

provision.'[16] The Committee was to report to the Government and to the Local Authority Associations, but it was not clear from the terms of reference to what extent, if at all, they were expected to make positive recommendations. The only issue on which they were directly invited to pronounce was 'the cost-effectiveness of existing provision'. However, it was obvious that many in the education service, and especially those responsible for the planning of provision for sixteen-to-nineteen year olds at the local level, were anticipating that the Macfarlane Committee would provide at least some guidelines to avoid a situation where expensive and time consuming processes of planning and consultation might be gone through only for schemes to be rejected because they did not meet some hidden governmental criterion.

It seemed that the exercise need not be a protracted one. A considerable amount of published research on sixth form provision already existed and further work had been done by or for the DES itself, by Her Majesty's Inspectors, and within local authority areas. The problem was one of collation and of weighing up evidence on the various facets of the question, of which the economic factor mentioned in the terms of reference was only one. However, well into the Autumn of 1980, as a number of large local authorities, including Manchester and Birmingham, moved towards the formulation of proposals for setting up colleges, no report had appeared. The educational press speculated on why this was so. On November 21st., the **Times Educational Supplement,** apparently on the basis of reliable information, declared that the report was held up because the committee had, in its first draft given too clear a pointer to the superiority of sixth form college systems, and this had given offence to prominent members of the Government, including, it was rumoured, the Prime Minister herself. The TES quoted the wording of the concluding passages of the draft as containing the sentence '. . .in many areas sixth-form or tertiary colleges may be the best solution both educationally and financially.'[17] While not going so far as to advocate separate sixteen-to-nineteen provision as a universal policy, the draft apparently gave it such clear endorsement and quoted such evidence disproving its alleged defects that, had it been published, it would have been very hard for any secretary of state to justify turning down a proposal for colleges in a local area. The Secretary at the time, Mark Carlisle, is thought to have had a favourable attitude towards sixth form and tertiary colleges, but opposition within the Government included prominent and vocal supporters of the grammar school tradition such as Rhodes Boyson, formerly a headmaster and **Black Paper**[18] author.

When the Report finally appeared, just before the end of 1980, it confined itself to setting out a range of facts about the various forms of provision. In its conclusions, the reference to colleges being, perhaps, the best solution 'in many areas' was changed to read 'in some areas': which was really to do no more than recognize the reality which already existed. But favourable comment on colleges was balanced by favourable reference to school-based sixth forms ('We are conscious . . . of . . . the success of many all-through schools, which in some areas may very well exist alongside extensive provision in further education') and to provision through a mix of eleven-to-sixteen and eleven-to-eighteen schools, which also attracted the comment that 'in some areas (this) may be appropriate'.[19] The inclusion of this latter possibility on a level with the others (all are said to be suitable in 'some areas') and with only minimal reference to its likely disadvantages is significant. From the point of view of anyone wanting to preserve the traditional school-based sixth form, the universal eleven-to-eighteen comprehensive is not an attractive solution to back. The average comprehensive sixth is unlikely to be large enough to have much influence on the ethos of the school, which is far more likely to be determined by 'lower ability' junior children. But the comprehensive which, because it draws students from eleven-to-sixteen secondary schools, has a disproportionately large sixth form, is quite a different proposition. Such a school could be very much on the 'grammar' pattern, with students not in the traditional sixth form mould transferring to further education colleges. In some instances schools chosen for this role would in fact be grammar schools or ex-grammar schools which would naturally hold to established styles of organization. And if such schools received their intakes on the basis of the 'free parental choice' already enacted in principle by the 1979 Conservative administration, then they would come to look even more like grammar schools. The Macfarlane Report does make, though without elaboration, the obvious point that 'The residual schools then suffer both from failing to attract a due proportion of the most able pupils, as well as in limitations of staffing that go with both a smaller school and the absence of advanced work'.[20] But, for those who believe in hierarchy this is not, of course, an objection to the idea; it might even be a recommendation.

In the Spring of 1981, two of the largest authorities in the country, Manchester and Birmingham, submitted plans for a complete reorganization of their sixteen-to-nineteen provision, involving the opening of colleges and the removal of all sixth form provision from schools. Both areas were under strong pressure, both for educational and economic reasons, to resolve the problem of small sixth form groups scattered through comprehensive schools with declining intakes. Manchester's figures showed that twenty-five schools in the area averaged only just over sixty A-level subject entries apiece,[21] while Birmingham, in the period from the mid-'60s to 1980, had seen a halving of the birth rate. Within a short time of the proposals being received at the DES, Macfarlane and Carlisle were replaced by Rhodes Boyson and Keith Joseph. Joseph had been instrumental in starting an organization known as the Centre for Policy Studies which in June, 1981 produced a document entitled **Crisis in the Sixth Form.** This, it seems, was intended as a counterblast against any

211

lingering suspicion left by the Macfarlane Report that, in spite of all the qualifications and provisos, colleges were the best option for authorities wanting to reorganize their secondary provision. Under the authorship of Fred Naylor, who had earlier been secretary to the Schools Council's working parties on sixth form curriculum and examinations, it mounted a strong attack on 'sixth-form college euphoria' and lined itself up squarely behind the preservation of sixth forms in school through setting up mixed eleven-to-sixteen and eleven-to-eighteen systems. Attack and defence were based on the traditional arguments in favour of the public school style of sixth form: that colleges gained support only because of economic expediency, that the break at sixteen was 'harmful', that the personal development of children was best assured in schools, and that eleven-to-sixteen schools had 'serious academic disadvantages'. The argument about personal development was made more explicit than is usually the case by linking it to fears about 'permissiveness' and 'vandalism', and, unlike some other commentators, Naylor did make it reasonably clear that what he was really in favour of was the tripartite system of grammar, technical and secondary modern schools as advocated by Norwood.[22] There were clear signs here that, although some of the proposals on the table were from conservative authorities - Surrey, Hampshire and Croydon - a political commitment to the traditional sixth form was being promoted as government policy. This political polarization was strengthened by the Labour Party which was working on its own document on sixteen-to-nineteen provision. Claims that this too was being held up because of a pro-school lobby were denied by Neil Kinnock, Labour spokesman on education.[23] If such a lobby did exist among socialist teachers, it was unable in the end to stop the press for a commitment to tertiary colleges: **The Education and Training of the 16 to 19 Age Group,** produced in November, 1981, came out clearly in favour of the total abolition of the school-based sixth form.

When Keith Joseph replaced Mark Carlisle as Secretary of

State, he inherited the responsibility of pronouncing on the reorganization schemes which had been put forward. His decision would show whether the point had been reached when the contest between alternative ideologies of sixth form education had become a political one which divided the major parties. By mid-November, he was ready to make known his position on the Manchester scheme. It was rejected. In his reply to the Authority, Keith Joseph stated his belief 'that only in very exceptional circumstances can it be right to reduce the age range from eleven-to-eighteen to eleven-to-sixteen of secondary schools of proven quality which continue to demonstrate their success in the provision they make for sixth form education'.[24] Since it would be difficult to find authorities where there were not at least some schools which could be said to be 'demonstrating success' in sixth form provision, this decision appeared to rule out any possibility of schemes from other authorities getting a positive response. The implication of the Secretary of State's decision, which apparently had the Prime Minister's backing, was that authorities which are facing problems because comprehensive schools are unable to build up viable sixth forms should concentrate provision in some schools and leave others as eleven-to-sixteen units - a policy providing, as the **Times Educational Supplement** commented, 'a back door method of recreating grammar schools'.[25] For his part, Keith Joseph declared: 'I don't believe in doctrinaire solutions', and Conservative councillors in Manchester described the decision as 'a victory for common sense'.[26] The Manchester Authority was left to reflect on just how much common sense there was in a decision which rejected two years of careful planning and consultation, resulted in overspending of about £4,000,000 per annum at a time when the Government was imposing drastic cuts in educational budgets, and pressed them to preserve a system of secondary education which was bound to discriminate against those children in most need of help and encouragement.[27]

Subsequent developments have shown very clearly that,

though the issue on which the Conservative Party has chosen to oppose reorganization schemes is that of the 'demonstrably successful' school sixth form, the antagonism to sixth form and tertiary colleges goes much deeper than that. Manchester's immediate response to the rejection was to amend their plan to allow schools actually named by the Secretary of State - three in number - to keep their sixth forms. Conservative councillors voted against the new plan. No doubt both they and the supporters of the revision had their doubts about how long the schools could retain their sixth formers when they were given the option of transferring to a college. And within a month of the rejection of the original scheme, C.B. Cox, Professor of English Literature of the University of Manchester and contributor to the **Black Papers,** had produced a pamphlet, published by the Conservative Political Centre, in which he identified sixth form colleges as 'a particularly dangerous part of the left-wing campaign to control the country's education system'. The colleges he thought, would 'downgrade the status of A-levels and . . . create an egalitarian ethos instead of the environment of a community of scholars'.[28]

These are indications that the Conservative Party had sensed, correctly, given its current ideological stance, that the sixth form has a far greater symbolic importance than the grammar school to which it was conventionally attached. Though hard and bitter battles were fought over the comprehensive secondary school, and attempts made to define the question as simply one of right versus left in the political arena, it was always a more complex issue than that. Broadly speaking, the centre held, if only because some of the most vociferous attacks on the grammar school came from middle class parents whose children were excluded from it. The move towards comprehensive schools, though arousing the opposition of those who thought that central government was wrong to press for so much haste in its implementation, could be seen as a logical extension of the progressive educational consensus which dominated policy-making from the inter-war years. If politicians and administrators had misgivings about it, because their sympathies were overtly or covertly with **Gemeinshaft** and the 'sponsorship model', they could be comforted by the survival of the public schools as a potent living archetype of the style of education they supported. These ensured that the established institutional categories were constantly reinforced in the public mind. What they are faced with now is a new category which generates its own prestige, independently of the public schools; which even attracts students **away** from independent school sixth forms at a time when the government is trying to draft students **into** them through the assisted places scheme;[29] and which, in spite of the continuing hold of the traditional A-level curriculum, proffers an image of realism, maturity and democracy.

This analysis of the reasons why we are seeing an ideological polarization over the sixth form needs to be completed by considering recent government policies towards the universities. These too, like the sixth form colleges came under attack from central government in 1980 and '81. On the face of things, the points at issue seemed to be different ones in the two instances: on the one hand, colleges incurred opposition because conservative opinion was hardening behind a different and more traditional organizational form; on the other, contraction was being pressed upon universities because they were judged to be too expensive in terms of what they offered to the community at a time of economic stringency. Yet, beneath these apparent differences, the issues were, in fact, very similar. In the case of the controversy over sixth form colleges a traditional, but expensive form of organization - the school-based sixth form - was being promoted, though the question was not construed as an economic one: it could not be, because the economic arguments were all on the side of college, and, in any case, the fact of high youth unemployment meant that the government would be forced into a heavy commitment to schemes of education and training for those who had traditionally lost all contact with the system after the age of sixteen. The cost of this would swamp any sums required to keep school sixth forms open for a minority.[30] In the case of the universities too, the meaning of the government's action, was that a traditional and expensive model was preferred to a more cost effective one. Universities might have been told that, without any addition of resources, they had to become more productive; that staff student ratios should move not marginally, but dramatically; that a more flexible use of resources should be achieved by cutting down on specialist courses and introducing more opportunities for students to take general degrees; that more students should be encouraged to be home-based, and that student loans should wholly or partly replace student grants. This would not have saved money in the short run, but neither did the action proposed by the Government which threatened to incur costs arising from contraction, and especially redundancy payments, outweighing the apparent savings. And any argument that the object of the Government's action was to stimulate the universities to focus their efforts on courses seen as 'useful' and 'relevant' in fields of science and technology as against arts and social science was made to look totally ridiculous by the decision to impose the heaviest financial cuts on technological universities such as Aston and Salford which were among the most successful in placing their graduates in commercial and industrial employment. The common theme linking government policies towards upper secondary and higher education is that of support for **Gemeinschaft**, sponsorship models of education which are intrinsically high cost, and whose principal virtue - that they can be offered only to the few - is made more secure precisely by their high-cost status.

The reality of this vision is, of course, problematic. How many students in sixth forms or universities in fact feel that they are part of Professor Cox's 'community of scholars'? How many, even if they feel it, are eager to commit themselves to it? But,

216

as we have pointed out throughout this book, this, for the ideologue of education controlled by a vision of ultimate 'standards', is not the crucial point. The public school headmasters who confronted the Clarendon Commissioners were not put out by demonstrations that most of their pupils left school having learned next to nothing (though they did, prudently, object to having them examined. Dr Balston described this suggestion as an 'interference with the authority and responsibility of the Head Master . . . calculated to produce serious evil'[31]); Norwood's faith in the classics survived unshaken Rouse's 1908 statement that 'of the average boy it cannot be denied that he never understands Latin or Greek, can hardly write a sentence without a mistake, or read a book without a 'crib';[32] the members of the Crowther Committee did not feel the need to look for any evidence of the claims they made about 'intellectual discipleship' and 'subject-mindedness'. All that is required is that some archetype exists that is perceived as lending support to the Platonic vision; and for 150 years that has been supplied by the old public schools and the ancient universities of Oxford and Cambridge. These were the universities which suffered least from budget cuts; they are also the wealthiest.[33]

A final point to note in relation to policies on universities and sixth forms is that they became the focus of central government attention at a very late stage. It could be argued that, faced with the necessity of taking decisive action in 1981, no government could have acted wisely because things had been allowed to drift for too long. Any move to encourage or discourage particular developments, any effort to keep budgets under control was going to involve arbitrary decisions. But why had such a state of affairs developed? The decisions to expand sixth form and university provision had been taken in the early '60s on the publication of the Crowther and Robbins Reports. Why was it that, almost twenty years later, when the number of sixteen-plus students in school had doubled and the numbers entering universities had trebled, little or no progress had been made on questions of what this implied for curricula and forms of organization? Was it simply the result of attitudes inspired by naive 'welfare-statism' which focused attention on budgets, buildings and enrolments to the exclusion of serious consideration of what the money was buying, the buildings housing, or the students learning? Was thinking on the nature and purposes of education so atrophied by a hundred years of insistent rhetoric drawing its inspiration from the intangible that it was incapable of adapting itself to the new situation? Or was there a quiet resolve on the part of key administrators to procrastinate over questions of fundamental change in the hope that 'euphoria', whether over sixth form colleges or new universities, would pass away and the old forms and values could be reinstated?

If this feeling existed among civil servants at the Department of Education and Science, it received a powerful and unexpected boost when, in 1968, the worldwide phenomenon of 'student unrest' expressed itself in a mild form on the university campuses of England. Within only five years of the acceptance of the Robbins recommendations, here was evidence that more meant not just worse, but the creation of a vocal dissident group threatening the political stability of the nation. Without any strong moves on the part of central government, the era of expansion slipped over into one of restraint, even before the economic recessions of the '70s made themselves felt. Maurice Kogan explains:

> hostility . . . towards the universities grew in
> both Whitehall and Westminster. This change of
> relationship was sharpened as universities became
> mass institutions lacking the glamour of the
> prototypal Oxbridge ideal of pre-war, as the
> international movements of unrest hit the
> universities in 1968, and as graduate
> unemployment and economic uncertainties became

stronger . . .[34]

That the relationship between government and universities could degenerate into one describable as 'hostility', and be translated into wrangling over budgets rather than serious discussion of fundamental purposes is ascribed by Crowther-Hunt to 'a Civil Service take-over of an apparently "outside" power centre' - the University Grants Committee. His claim, as a former Minister of State at the DES, is that the UGC was tamed through senior civil servants in the Department assuming control over who should be appointed to it, ensuring that its permanent staff was made up of civil servants on loan from the DES, and not allowing meetings to take place at which they were not personally present.[35] Whether or not this power was used to negate expansionist policies independently of political decisions, the opportunity to use it to this end certainly existed, and any account of why sixth form and university education has developed in the way it has certainly must address itself to the role of the Civil Service, as well as that of Ministers and politicians. It may be that Robbins provided the critical test for how far the Whitehall establishment was prepared to see expansionist policies go, and that its reluctance to countenance 'mass' higher education provided the essential background against which more overtly political forces could later raise a belated standard in defence of the traditional sixth. Had university expansion been allied to a change of role in the direction of a more 'associative' climate and curriculum - a recognition that 'more meant different' - it would be very hard to argue in 1982 that sixth forms should be school-based 'communities of scholars' reared in the **Gemeinschaft** tradition. As it is, sixth form education, which has for so long provided the touchstone against which policies for the whole of secondary education have been judged, is once again at the heart of controversies over the nature and purpose of a national education system in a modern democracy - and this time in a more overtly political way than ever in the past.

The issue of college-based versus school-based sixths, which now divides right and left, links a cluster of value laden areas of educational decision - the role and nature of the comprehensive school, the relation of academic and vocational courses, the future of higher education, the balance of general and specialized curricula - which have been on the agenda for many years and still await serious attention. Resolution of the sixth form question will depend on clarification of the direction that politics is taking in the United Kingdom in the 1980s. Are we seeing the final breakup of the consensus that enabled educational decisions to escape extremes of partisanship through the inter-war and immediate post-war eras? Or is the flight of the major parties to right and left leaving the way open to a more unified centrist position than that which resulted from the uneasy co-existence in the middle ground of Conservative and Socialist parties whose ideological loyalties lay, ultimately, in irreconcilable traditions? This is what will decide whether a democratized sixth can play the role in English upper secondary education that is occupied by the senior high school in the United States, or the Gymnasium in Scandinavia; or whether the belated movement towards democratization represented by the sixth form and tertiary colleges is to provide the occasion for an ideological contest between politicians of the right who aim to check its growth and those of the left who, for equally doctrinaire reasons, may be tempted to see in the colleges an instrument for pursuing grandiose visions of a socialist transformation of society. In neither case would development proceed on the basis of an attempt to consider how an educational tradition can be understood and reinterpreted in order to relate it to the complex social, moral and economic conditions of England in the 1980s; in neither case would the deeper issues of curriculum, so long neglected in favour of arguments over buildings and access to buildings, at last receive the close attention they so urgently deserve.

Postscript

It was announced in February, 1982, that the Secretary of State had approved the revised Manchester plan which retained sixth forms in three comprehensive schools.* A week later, however, he rejected the tertiary college proposals put forward by the Conservative-controlled Croydon Authority.**

* **Guardian,** February 11.
** **Guardian,** February 20.

NOTES

1   Department of Education and Science, **Education for 16-19 Year Olds,** DES/CLEA, 1980, Table 1.

2   King, Ronald, **School and Colleges: Studies of Post-Sixteen Education,** London, Routledge and Kegan Paul, 1976.

3   **Ibid.,** p.79. King found that girls, even more than boys, felt that they were treated more as adults in the context of the college.

4   Reid, W.A. and Filby J.L., **'The Organization and Curriculum of Three Sixth Form Colleges',** Final Report to the Department of Education and Science, Teaching Research Unit, Faculty of Education, University of Birmingham, 1978, p.74.

5   **Ibid.,** pp.65 and 73.

6   Reid, W.A., **'Survey of College Students: Descriptive Statistics - Final Report',** Teaching Research Unit, Faculty of Education, University of Birmingham, 1976, p.9.

7   Dean, Judy, Bradley, Kath, Choppin, Bruce and Vincent,

Denis, **The Sixth Form and its Alternatives,** Windsor, NFER, 1979, Table 6.2. Sample sizes in the various types of education varied from 296 (tertiary colleges) to 563 (sixth form colleges), with an overall total of 2311 students.

8   **Ibid.,** p.324.

9   King, Ronald, 1976 **op.cit.,** p.151.

10   Loc. cit.

11   **Ibid.,** p.154.

12   **Ibid.,** p.165.

13   Reid and Filby, 1978 **op.cit.,** pp.5-15.

14   King, for example, comments of the group of eleven-to-sixteen schools he studied: 'It is clear that this system of short-course comprehensive schools was associated with levels of academic success that compare well nationally, and with high levels of continued education' (King, Ronald, 1976 **op.cit.,** p.87).

15   For example, **A Framework for the School Curriculum** (London, HMSO, 1980). DES discussion papers on the curriculum tended to stress traditional disciplines, basic skills, and so on, while papers emanating from Her Majesty's Inspectors, who are closer to schools, were more likely to talk about general objectives and project a flexible attitude to method and content.

16   DES/CLEA, 1980 **op.cit.,** p.49.

17   **TES,** November 21, 1980.

18   The original 'Black Papers', three in number, were edited by C.B. Cox and A.E. Dyson and appeared in 1969-70. They gathered together a variety of contributions critical of current 'progressive' developments in education, such as the establishment of comprehensive systems of secondary schooling. Two further collections, edited by C.B. Cox and Rhodes Boyson, were published in 1975-77 (**Black Paper,1975: the Fight for Education,** London, Dent and

Black Paper 1977, London, Temple Smith).

19   DES/CLEA, 1980 op. cit., p.36. Naylor claims that 'The Macfarlane Group, because it contained salaried employees from local and central government, very properly refrained from expressing an opinion on the relative merits of different types of sixteen-to-nineteen provision' (Naylor, Fred, Crisis in the Sixth Form, London, Centre for Policy Studies, 1981, p.10). This account is clearly not compatible with the stories of political pressure being brought to bear on the Committee to change the wording of its Report.

20   Ibid., p.30.

21   TES, November 20, 1981.

22   Naylor, 1981 op. cit., p.9.

23   In a letter to the Times Educational Supplement, published in its issue of June 26, 1981.

24   TES, November 20, 1981.

25   Ibid.

26   TES, November 14, 1981.

27   The Macfarlane Report noted that 'Schools which retain sixth forms tend to have more prestige in the eyes of many parents and are apt to be the most popular first choice for pupils at eleven or twelve. The residual schools then suffer both from failing to attract a due proportion of the most able pupils, as well as in limitations of staffing that go with both a smaller school and the absence of advanced work.' (DES/CLEA, 1980 op.cit., p.30). The Manchester schools which had successful sixth forms were principally in middle-class areas of the city.

28   The Guardian, December 15, 1981.

29   Under the headline 'Boyson warning over curbs on sixth-form transfer'. the Times Educational Supplement for January 1, 1982, reported: 'A strong warning to local authorities to stop standing in the way of sixth formers

who want to take up assisted places came in the Commons shortly before the recess from Dr Rhodes Boyson, education junior minister. . . He warned that the local authority power to veto the transfer of sixth formers under the scheme would be withdrawn next year unless there was a significant increase in participation.'

30   Within a month of the rejection of the Manchester reorganisation plan, a Government White paper announced 'a new £1 billion a year Youth Training Scheme, guaranteeing from September, 1983 a full year's foundation training for all those leaving school at the minimum age without jobs' (**TES**, December 18, 1981).

31   **Report** of H.M. Commissioners appointed to inquire into the Revenues and Management of Certain Colleges and Schools, etc., 1864 (Clarendon), Vol.2, p.7.

32   Norwood, Cyril and Hope, Arthur H., **The Higher Education of Boys in England**, London, John Murray, 1909, p.344.

33   In the case of Oxford and Cambridge a good deal of endowment income accrues to the colleges rather than the universities. From the point of view of the student using resources and facilities, the distinction is not an important one.

34   Kogan, Maurice, **Educational Policy-Making: A Study of Interest Groups and Parliament,** London, Allen and Unwin, 1975, p.200.

35   Kellner, Peter and Lord Crowther-Hunt, **The Civil Servants: An Inquiry into Britain's Ruling Class,** Macdonald, London, 1980, p.222.

12 UNDERSTANDING THE PAST AND CHOOSING THE FUTURE

This book has not been written with the idea of providing a definitive history of the sixth form. Had that been the intention, the result would have been very different. What has been attempted is an exercise in using history in order to recover, as usable knowledge, the tradition of sixth forms and sixth form education. If, as we would argue, the development of educational policies is essentially a matter of adapting or redirecting existing forms and categories, then the understanding of traditions is a prerequisite of wise choice. Such an understanding on the one hand illustrates the extent to which traditions arise and are modified because of the existence of unique sets of circumstances, and are therefore always susceptible to revision; on the other hand it also emphasizes that, at any given time, the scope for choice about their future direction is constrained by the same circumstantial conditions. Regrettably, a climate of opinion on sixteen-to-nineteen education is now being created which, in one way or another, offends against such a realistic approach to decision-making. Increasingly, opinions and attitudes are being polarized between an ultra conservative viewpoint which sees no need to understand the tradition because it regards its own ideological interpretation of it as immutable, and a strongly radical one which has no wish to study a tradition which it wants to reject. In a way these positions - that of Sir Keith Joseph and the Centre for Policy Studies and that of the Labour Party's **Education and Training of the 16 to 19 Age Group** - are diametrically opposed; in another they have a lot in common. Both are ideologically based and think in terms of a single ideal solution to the sixteen-to-nineteen question (though the conservative position still has a sufficiently defensive flavour about it to be forced into a certain amount of pragmatism). Both gloss over the fundamental question of how the forms of education come to have meaning and significance for a community. Conservatives assume that what has had meaning in the past will have meaning in the future: that the public will continue to subscribe to an institutional category, the sixth form, offering initiation into a gentlemanly elite and excluding over eighty per cent of the population. Radicals believe, even more optimistically, that universal support will be forthcoming for a totally invented category having no clear relationship to any established tradition.

The work of understanding the past of the sixth form and of examining its potentiality for future development is made difficult by the existence of the conservative ideology which has grown out of the tradition, but which must be distinguished from it. Here, we are using the word 'tradition' to stand for the institutional category of sixth form as it has actually existed and evolved in the minds of various publics over time. By 'ideology', we mean the relatively static set of assumptions which has been used to justify and perpetuate a particular form of the tradition, but which its proponents claim to be synonymous with the tradition. The story of the book has been about the tradition **and** about the ideology. At this point we need to draw together various observations concerning the ideology and put them in a perspective which will help us to see it objectively and judge how appropriate it is as a source of current educational policies. This is an urgent task at a time when it is powerfully influential in government decision-making across a wide spectrum of the educational system, including not only sixth forms and other kinds of post-sixteen provision, but also higher education and the lower secondary school.

The account we have given of the development of sixth forms and of the educational philosophy associated with them shows that they began as a radical innovation linked to fundamental changes in politics and society. For most of the nineteenth century the category evolved both in the sense that educational leaders consciously reinterpreted its form and purposes,

226

and in the sense that the publics for whom it had meaning were extended. However, by the time of the most significant extension of the sixth form as an institutional category, when it was transplanted to the maintained grammar schools after the 1902 Education Act, a fixed ideology had been articulated and this has persisted with little change to the present day. Norwood's 1909 exposition of it in **The Higher Education of Boys in England** is repeated by him almost verbatim twenty years later in **The English Tradition of Education** and enters into the thinking behind the 1944 Education Act through the **Report** produced by the SSEC under his chairmanship. It surfaces again in the **Crowther Report** which set the tone for expansionary policies towards sixth forms in the 1960s and it now appears with little change in **Crisis in the Sixth Form,** a document of the Centre for Policy Studies justifying the rejection of schemes for the setting up of sixth form colleges and announcing itself as the work of an author of 'independence and intellectual vigour'.[1] Salient features of the ideology are: a belief in revealed and immutable truth; the sanctity of leadership and the need for obedience; the importance of maintaining a 'moral aristocracy'; fear and mistrust of non-initiates and justification of privilege through emphasising notions of service and responsibility.

The development of the sixth form ethos in the middle of the nineteenth century made an important contribution to the problem posed by the transformation of England from an agricultural country, locally administered, to an industrial country with centralized bureaucratic structures and rapidly growing overseas investments. The problem was how to expand the governing class beyond the traditional landed aristocracy which was neither numerous enough nor sufficiently inclined towards the routine of administration to manage an expanding and increasingly rationalized polity. In response to the fears of revolution which plagued the early years of the century the class system was becoming more rather than less rigid and direct modification of it was not a realistic possibility. A way had to be found of creating a group which could coexist with the class system without seriously upsetting it. This meant that a criterion of membership had to be adopted which was not related to birth or heredity. One solution might have been to cultivate a group defined by wealth - a commercial elite; another was to form an elite defined by sponsorship and adherence to a moral code - a kind of freemasonry; or an elite compounded of both elements might have emerged. The prejudice of those who had some power of choice in the matter was in favour of a unified elite which would offer a better guarantee of stable government, and against the elevation of entrepreneurs who, on religious and other grounds, were alienated from the landed aristocracy. Therefore the solution which emerged was one which enabled the new rulers to be merged into a freemasonry with the old, though at the price of the relegation of the wealth producing sectors of the nation to second class status. The major instruments for bringing about the transformation were the public school, and particularly the public school sixth form, and the old universities of Oxford and Cambridge. In the context of its time, the solution was brilliantly successful. England weathered, almost unscathed, the revolutionary storms which swept most of Europe; aristocratic leadership was revitalized and resources of just and efficient administration unlocked which assured peace and prosperity not only at home but, by the end of the century, across half the globe. In fact, the work of the nineteenth century leaders in education was too successful; so dazzling were British achievements in the fields of culture, government and economic development that few paused to ask what kind of a price was being paid for them. More commonly, the response of educators was to formalize what they thought to be the bases of a triumphant policy into a fixed and unchallengeable doctrine.

This doctrine can be understood as advocacy of sixth forms and universities as the means of producing a freemasonry uniting the old aristocracy with elements of other classes, and principally of the middle class. The first key ingredient in the doctrine is the idea of a fixed and unchanging truth to which the initiates must subscribe. Public school heads of the earlier period, such as Thomas Arnold, were conscious of living in a time of uncertainty. Politics were confused, the future course of society unpredictable, the Church in turmoil. Arnold's correspondence is full of self-doubt. What was certain was the authority of the individual headmaster. His was a personal authority, personally demonstrated in the schoolroom and the pulpit. By the mid-century, however, the ground was prepared for Matthew Arnold's message of sweetness and light. The future began to seem more assured. With Newman's departure from Oxford in 1845, the religious choice facing clerical headmasters became clear: most would take a 'broad church' view of Gladstone's remark that the materials of 'classical training were . . . the complement of Christianity in its application to the culture of the human being'.[2] As controversy waned, the head's authority gradually became less that of the person and more that of the representative of a 'providentially prepared' curriculum. And it was in the name of that curriculum, or more particularly of the 'truth' that lay behind it, that authority came to be exercised. For Norwood, the head is to be 'a living incarnation of strength and justice' a leader in the search for the 'true ideal'.[3] Present day apologists for the doctrine talk in terms of fixed 'standards' and of unchanging moral values and continue to stress the need for heads to have absolute authority.[4]

If standards and values do not change, and heads and teachers embody them, then it is encumbent on pupils to obey, though the special position of sixth formers gives them the chance to exercise as well as submit to authority. In fact, it is **because** they have submitted to authority that they can aspire to be rulers themselves. This core conception of the ideology is attributed, with doubtful authenticity, to Arnold: 'He had defined and established the fundamental principle of the true English discipline that you must obey loyally in order that you may be fit to rule wisely'.[5] It was more properly a product of the rationalized and Romanized public schools of the high noon of Empire. In all of this, of course, we can recognize strong elements of Platonism. This is not surprising, seeing that **The Republic** was a standard text in the classical curriculum and that Plato's problems - how to establish a stable regime and avoid class conflict, and how to control the potentially destabilizing but nevertheless necessary activities of entrepreneurs - were also those of the nineteenth century gradualist reformers. He too advocated a kind of initiatory collectivism based on fixed ideals and with a strong emphasis on leadership and obedience: 'The greatest principle of all is that nobody . . . should be without a leader'.[6]

Once the idea is established that truth is beyond the reach of discussion because it is fixed and because it is made available, not directly, but through 'those who know'[7], then the ground is laid for a true corporate freemasonry in which individualism is contrary to the prevailing ethos. Here again, we are dealing with a post-Arnoldian phenomenon. In the 1830s the war of attrition against schoolboy anarchy had only just begun. Individualism in dress, manner and conduct was still the norm and though 'breaking of wilfulness' was on the programme it was in the name of a loving God and undertaken in a spirit which had in it a strong admixture of fatalism. What Arnold did contribute to the corporatist doctrine was his mimetic, or imitative theory of education: that categorical membership is achieved not just through book learning, practical experience or display of skill, but through the association of all of these activities with the living presence of an exemplar - the master - who enters into a personal though ritualized relationship with the pupil. This is the idea which is strongly promoted under the name of 'intellectual discipleship' in the Crowther Report of 1959. But the use of the word 'intellectual' diverts attention from its principle role in the ideology which is more properly **social and moral.** Arnold, it will be remembered, put 'religious and moral principles' and 'gentlemanly conduct' ahead of 'intellectual ability' as aims of education. Similarly, we find today that the anti-sixth form college lobby identifies 'personal development' as the area which is 'so crucial that it ought to be the focus of the main debate on the sixteen-to-nineteen provision'. And proper 'personal development' is held to depend on the implementation of mimetic styles of education: 'The great strength of the English sixth form has been its offering of opportunities to its members - under the guidance of adults - to exercise limited authority over, and to assume responsibility for, those in the lower age groups. The assumption of these responsibilities is part of the process of character building traditionally associated with membership of the sixth form.'[8]

Categorical status, in the conventional ideology, has come to be equated with membership of an aristocracy much broader than the old traditional one because it is defined in moral terms and not in terms of hereditary status or ownership of estates. In its widest definition it was understood in Victorian times as consisting of those fit to be called gentlemen. Both gentlemanly qualities and the route to the possession of them were derived from chivalric models. Knightly virtues were virtues associated with corporate life: loyalty, trust, service and self-sacrifice. Chivalric order allowed for gradations of initiation into the fellowship. From the middle of the nineteenth century all who submitted to the discipline of the public school were, by definition, gentlemen. Sixth formers, who submitted not just to the school as an organization, but also to the highest demands of the curriculum, were gentlemen **and** scholars. Teachers, as guardians of the curriculum, were masters of the order. This development depended on the progressive rationalization and routinization of the schools which characterized the latter part of the nineteenth century. As more and more of school life assumed corporate form, greater stress was put on comradeship and brotherhood.

Subordination of the self to the team in organized games was an important part of this process. Norwood states the link clearly in his discussion of 'The Danger from Individualism':[9]

> The life of . . . society cannot be lived, if each member is to be taught that every rule of the game is a matter of individual opinion. . . One might as well try to play a game of cricket in which every boy was free to bat, and not field, or to bowl and not bat. . . There is an inherited system of morality, which represents the experience of the race, the rules which our ancestors have found to govern the game. . .[10]

Individualism, he believes, 'disintegrates a society'. The thought is echoed in the **Centre for Policy Studies** document:

> (The) link between the generations, whether it be expressed in terms of the ties between parents and children or older children and younger children, is essential for the transmission of moral values and the continuous development of society. If these links are broken society will disintegrate.[11]

As the freemasonry of public school, sixth form and university grew in size and significance, and as its links with government and administration were strengthened through the use of examinations as a criterion for entry to civil service and other high level occupations, so fear of challenges to its authority became more urgent and the need for a rhetoric of justification more pressing. When it became clear that the time of State intervention in secondary education could not be indefinitely postponed, there was real anxiety among headmasters that the days of the public school and its associated ideology of education were numbered.[12] Internal unity of the order was by now well assured. Within its own bounds it was democractic. The definition of the gentleman allowed all to be postulants, though, in practice, the need to pay the fees of boarding education ensured that the correlation between gentlemanly status and the possession of a comfortable income was quite strong. While subscription to religious principle was demanded it was not required to be dogmatic, or even wholehearted. And the technical requirement of obedience was quite compatible with the understanding that members, whatever their status, would help each other in their dealings with the outside world, and that, in any case, whatever their rank in the order, **all** were gentlemen. Internal dissension was not the problem: the elite that was being formed was truly consensual. The problem now lay outside. How was the elite status of a minority to be justified in the face of the majority who were excluded?

Part of the answer lay in stressing the technical openness of the order while doing little to remove the real obstacles to entry. Public schools have with great regularity and for a long time promoted schemes to make it easier for state school pupils to enter them or share in the experiences they offer. The scholarship system of entry to the grammar school was progressively developed through the first half of the present century and up to the point where the introduction of widespread comprehensive secondary education made it unnecessary. The direct grant school, until its recent abolition, gave long service as a symbol of the availability to working class children of the highest forms of secondary education.[13] But more important as an instrument of legitimation has been the promotion of the sixth form elite as a 'moral aristocracy'. The elite **had** to rule because they were morally superior and had sole access to the higher reaches of the order and the guardians of the truth. They undertook this rule as a social responsibility and as a service to the community. Privilege was a burden not a pleasure. Those entering on office could say, with John Halifax, Gentleman, 'I believe, with His blessing, that one may "serve the Lord" as well in wealth as in poverty . . . I am not afraid of being a rich man. Nor a great man neither, if I were called to such destiny'.[14] Such virtue was not hidden under a bushel; it was advertised - as it had to be if the rhetoric was to be effective - in speeches and sermons, in books and in the press. It was also made clear that it was not just being displayed as something to be admired in others; like Christianity, with which it was closely associated, it was a message that could be received and adopted by all as an animating principle of their lives. Exemplary literature was widely available in the form of novels and stories of the public schools, and practical initiation into a kind of 'associate' status was available through organizations such as the Scouts.[15] If there were people who would not accept the tenets of the only true doctrine then they were at least misguided and probably of bad character, or even of a rebellious disposition. The antidote to fears that the elite will be undermined resides in stressing the message of moral superiority and labelling those who fail to accept it as stupid or wicked.

This is the only kind of analysis which makes sense of some of the more purple passages of **Crisis in the Sixth Form**. How else can we understand the thought behind a belief that:

> the compulsory break in schooling at 16+, itself a
> break with English tradition, would in time have a
> profound effect on our society. For it would
> interfere with the process by which values are
> transmitted across the generations, a process
> which is necessary for the stability of any
> society?[16]

This may, on the face of things, look like a piece of conventional wisdom until one reflects that this compulsory break, associated with the setting up of sixth form colleges, is going to affect at most twenty per cent of the population, even if implemented as a national policy. Why is the 'break' so significant when over eighty per cent of the population are experiencing it, one way or another, already and will continue to do so (the author finds no problem about the transfer of those who want to enrol in courses in colleges of further education[17])? Perhaps the key consideration is not that a small section of the population would experience a 'break' which is at present absent from their educational careers, but that junior forms will be deprived of the benefits of having sixth formers in their school. This idea is hinted at rather than introduced as an integral part of the argument. The danger of raising it to too high a degree of prominence is that the reader will make too ready a connection with another leading recommendation: that the existence of too many small sixth forms should be remedied by concentrating provision in certain designated comprehensive schools, while the rest cater for the eleven-to-sixteen age group. In that case, presumably, fifty per cent or fewer students would be in schools with sixth forms and, as the author makes clear elsewhere, he supports the 'tripartite' system and therefore would not be unhappy to see that percentage decline to thirty or so.[18]

The only grounds on which the argument maintains some plausibility is that it is not directly about the spiritual welfare of the population as a whole, as one might easily assume, but about preserving the legitimacy of the 'moral aristocracy' which has to maintain its right to dictate to the rest what precepts they should follow. Once the corporatist 'Gemeinschaft' form of education is taken away, a key factor in the production of the moral aristocracy is removed, its self-confidence is undermined, other factions lay claim to portions of the truth and the monopoly of 'sweetness and light' is lost. Along with it will go the right of some to impose their vision of the truth on others. Like Norwood, the author of **Crisis in the Sixth Form** argues against individual freedom which is labelled 'permissiveness'. A denial that sixteen-to-eighteen year olds can be treated as adults is juxtaposed with references to vandalism and delinquency and seven pages of Appendix are devoted to a pastiche of opinions and theories on the collapse of adult authority and the moral degeneracy of society.[19] This is a familiar theme of groups who believe that there is only one true path to salvation and that they are the designated guardians of it. Woodard believed that if the lower middle class were admitted to power 'in any large numbers' then 'corruption and bribery or a far worse mischief must ensue'.[20] Norwood fears 'the power of the mob-orator and the cheap journalist' and rails against time wasting on 'degrading amusements' such as frequenting 'cinema houses'.[21] Davies, in the 1960s, warns that young people with a taste for 'pop records, magazines and films' are 'an easy target for the ingenious advertiser who will allow no scruple to stand in the way of a quick profit'.[22] Anyone who does not subscribe to the tastes and values of the elite is an object of fear and derision. The problem **they** pose is not one of moral inheritance, but of political and social control.

The optimistic version of the ideology considers that the democracy of the freemasonry can ultimately be open to all: that all men must eventually recognize the truth and faction will become a thing of the past. Politics will then be superceded by a consensus of reasonable men who are unhindered in their pursuit of solutions to the world's problems. The realistic version recognizes that the idea of abolishing politics is utopian and the idea of an elite that includes everybody a nonsense. However, the theory that truth must eventually conquer reached a level of quasi-plausibility around the turn of the century and has enjoyed some currency ever since. It was greatly helped by the development of British rule overseas and especially in India. Here it seemed, once the memory of the Mutiny had faded, was living proof that an apolitical government of right thinking men could bring peace and order to the world. The ideal put before schoolboys 'that they should be Christians and gentlemen' was, says Norwood, 'an ideal of uprightness, honour and incorruptability, of the honest governor, the righteous judge, the ruler who should be the father of his people'. And its most notable achievement was 'in India, where it created the most honourable and successful Civil Service of an alien governing power that the world has seen.'[23] In so far as success eluded it, it was because it still had not transcended the limitations of its social class origin. The work of the schools had to be to refine and extend the 'classless class' through active proselytizing: 'education can create a nation that is in truth one'.[24] But even that was not the limit of ambition:

> Before that nation, if it can be brought to birth,
> lies the opportunity of being one of the leaders, if
> not the chief leader . . . in the task of advancing
> with the United States of America and the great
> countries of Europe towards a system which may
> become the United States of the world. . .[25]

This was the kind of spirit that animated the Association for Education in Citizenship and its successor the Council for Education in World Citizenship which were active in the sixth forms of the 1930s, '40s and '50s.

By the 1960s, the euphoria of the winning of the Second World War and the setting up of the United Nations had faded, but enthusiasm for the possibilities of expanding sixth forms and higher education was borne up by equally grandiose, but less morally crusading theories of economic expansion and 'pools of ability'. Now those too are generally regarded as over-optimistic and the realists who have always understood the limits and problems of elites, however consensual they may seem, have become the spokesmen for the traditional ideology. 'Grammar school education for all', announced by Harold Wilson in the 1960s, was translated into comprehensive schools with a selective curriculum, and now even these are seen as too much of a concession to the forces of factionalism and individualism. The focus is turning to preservation of the purity of the elite and emphasis on the need to discipline those outside it. The present Secretary of State for Education has presided over a scheme to cut back resources for higher education which leaves the older universities virtually untouched. This he says will improve 'standards'. He has consistently rejected schemes for establishing sixth form colleges, and has encouraged colleges of education to reject for teacher training students who have not graduated in the traditional academic disciplines.[26] His under-secretary has campaigned against 'permissiveness' and declared that a judgement of the European Court against corporal punishment in schools will impair 'the defence of a disciplined and structured society' and lead to 'anarchy'.[27] With rising unemployment and the decline of the labour market as a disciplining force for those not able to enrol in sixth form courses or higher level vocational courses in further education, a massive programme of job related basic skills courses has been mounted outside the school system. Young's vision of a meritocracy alienated from and eventually overthrown by the less privileged classes looks increasingly plausible. The idea that 'all Englishmen should be gentlemen'[28] has gone the way of 'the United States of the World'. At least the ideology has to present itself in such a form that its true nature cannot be disguised.

But at this point we should remember that it is the ideology and not the tradition that has been the subject of discussion. The choice is not in fact between the conservative doctrine currently on offer and some left wing alternative that would reject most of what the past has to offer and set out in totally uncharted directions. Ever since the sixth form was brought to state schools, and expecially over the last thirty years, the schools, including some of the public schools, have developed the tradition they inherited. They have worked to allow the curriculum to be more flexible, so that membership of the sixth can be based on a broader criteria than success in academic examinations. They have de-emphasized the traditionally masculine aspects of sixth form education, team games and prefectship, in favour of qualities of caring and co-operation. They have encouraged individuality and creativity and looked for ways of making the sixth form a more open and reflective institution. In all of these respects they have been doing what the public schools of the nineteenth century did: they have been consciously adapting the tradition to the political and social realities of an evolving society; working with the publics for whom sixth form education has meaning to reinterpret its form and content; now leading opinion and now following it.

Until recently, it was quite easy to overlook this evolution of the tradition. The schools in which it took place were not those immediately in the public eye, still less in the eye of politicians. The larger independent and direct grant schools were still seen as the repository of what is good in sixth form education. More importantly, the conventional ideology worked to reduce opportunities for innovation. Here, the support it gave to the examination system was crucial. As Meyer has pointed out, the scope for adaptation of institutional categories is greatly reduced when uniform national tests are adopted.[29] When these are coupled to selection processes the brake on evolution is particularly strong.[30] From an early date, sixth forms, though then based in independent schools, became linked into a national system of examining which grew to the point where it became definitive of successful completion of sixth form courses and essential for entry to higher education. Access to higher education was limited and all universities declared to be equal in terms of academic standards. Since then every reform effort directed at the sixth form curriculum has stumbled on the unwillingness of those in authority to make any modification to this system. Within recent times it has to an extent been broken, and by institutions which, at the same time, have been able to present to local and national publics examples of an adapted tradition of sixth form education. These are the sixth form colleges which, over the last decade, have drawn together the many strands of evolution which have for long characterised the work of the maintained schools. In the colleges, changed attitudes to sixteen-to-nineteen education generally have been combined with student numbers which have given their innovations a clear public visibility and have also enabled them to assert their right to determine their own curriculum against the pressure of universities.[31] The rejection by central authorities of all schemes for modifying the public examination system has denied them the possibility of embarking on substantial change, but much has been achieved within the existing constraints. These are the institutions which embody the living tradition of the sixth form, and which are violently opposed by supporters of the conventional ideology. It is critical that, if a choice is to be made, it is in the direction of supporting this line of evolution which is not simply 'expedient' as its critics claim but which is based on a philosophy growing out of the experience of the past while also taking account of social and cultural developments. Support for such a choice will be of consequence not just for sixth forms or for sixteen-to-nineteen education but for the education system as a whole.

As we have shown in previous chapters, the sixth form ideology has at many crucial points determined the whole course of development in state schools. It has done so first of all as a key factor in the approach to education as something which is planned in a downward direction, beginning with 'the best' or 'the elite' and designing curricula and organization on the basis of criteria established at those levels. This is what is really at issue in discussions of 'standards' and 'values' which often draw an unfavourable contrast with the ethos of more democratically based systems such as that of the United States. Norwood says that

> European education which began in Universities
> has always known the meaning of intellectual
> values, for it has begun at the high level, and
> percolated down to the low. American education,
> which has of necessity been based upon the
> primary school, has never had the same standards,

240

for the proper process has been reversed, and the movement has been from the lowest levels upwards.[32]

Such a statement is, of course, just as much social and political as educational. Popper has pointed out that one of the most important effects of fixing standards and using them for selection purposes is to arrest change. This is why an education system of this type appealed so much to Plato - because he was so afraid that his perfect society might evolve into something different; it is also a major reason for its popularity with supporters of the traditional ideology of the sixth form. If 'intellectual standards' were really the issue then a different approach would be needed for

the secret of intellectual excellence is the spirit of criticism; it is intellectual independence.[33] This however . . . leads to difficulties which are insurmountable for any kind of authoritarianism. The authoritarian will in general select those who obey, who believe, who respond to his influence. But in doing so, he is bound to select mediocrities. . . Never can an authority admit that the intellectually courageous, i.e. those who dare to defy his authority, may be the most valuable type.[34]

The impossibility of devising a curriculum for the comprehensive secondary school has hinged on the prevalence in sixth forms and universities of an educational ideology based on exclusion. If they have failed, as some critics maintain, it is because, while they have been permitted to exist organizationally, they have been prevented by the activities of these same critics from ever offering a curriculum which was much more than a tripartite one in disguise. The latest major report on the school curriculum, **Mathematics Counts,** pinpoints the issue:

241

. . . syllabuses now being followed by a majority of pupils in secondary schools have been constructed by using as starting points syllabuses designed for pupils in the top quarter of the range of attainment in mathematics. Syllabuses for pupils of lower attainment have been developed from these by deleting a few topics and reducing the depth of treatment of others; in other words, they have been constructed 'from the top downwards'. We believe that this is a wrong approach and that development should be 'from the bottom upwards' by considering the range of work which is appropriate for the lower-attaining pupils and extending this range as the level of attainment of pupils increases.[35] (emphasis in original).

This 'top down' approach to syllabus-making arises from the implantation of the public school tradition of curriculum thinking into the municipal grammar schools set up after the Education Act of 1902, and can be remedied only when sixth forms are allowed to develop not only organizationally, but also in a curricular sense through a reform of the examination system. The encouragement, as an alternative, of the introduction of vocational and 'skills-based' curricula only serves to emphasize the gulf between those whom the system includes and those whom it excludes: between those who are 'educated' and those who are not.

But policies towards sixth forms have also influenced the education system in a detailed way. Arguments about sixth form numbers have determined thinking about the size and organization of grammar schools, bilateral schools, and now comprehensive schools. Arguments about sixth form curriculum have shaped the curriculum framework for the lower secondary school, especially in terms of option systems. Arguments about the content of sixth form examination syllabuses have influenced teaching styles in lower forms. These aspects of the problem are, of course, interrelated. If we could think differently about the sixth form curriculum, then the basis of the argument about numbers would be changed because enrolments could be higher, and there could be more flexible use of resources. And all of this has to be seen against the background of the long-standing connection between sixth forms and the civil service, beginning with the Trevelyan-Northcote Report of 1854 which 'established the principle of government by men who have received a liberal education'.[36] Many who might have used their influence in the direction of assisting the evolution of the sixth form tradition have prefered to promote, actively or by default, policies based on the narrow version of liberal education which was the means of their own elevation.

The case against the ideology is not, however, to be confused with cases made against the tradition. The public school may be a very bad model on which to base ideas for the shape of post-sixteen education in the country at large, but it is, in terms of its own publics, successful and illustrates the importance of educational planning which pays due regard to questions of what meanings the institutional categories of education can have for the communities which support them. The extent to which categories reflect public meanings determines how far students will feel commitment to them, and no programme of education which fails to generate that commitment can be accounted a success. Therefore we should not invent categories in the hope that support for them will be in some way forthcoming once they exist. The history of the sixth form is one of an evolving category which has always built the new on what already existed in order to maintain the significance of its forms and activities; a significance which has always related to status enhancement rather than skill enhancement. The attempt to generate student commitment by emphasizing currently meaningful skills can succeed only when these are related to an occupation to which the student also has current commitment. Otherwise they lose their connection with future status and with it their potential for having significance for students. Thus, plans to shore up a traditional sixth form liberal education by directing those excluded from it into courses based on personal and vocational skills will almost certainly prove to be an expensive miscalculation.[37] But equally misguided would be efforts to remove the notion of liberal education from the post-sixteen curriculum altogether. What is needed is a reinterpretation of liberal education which construes it in terms of inclusion, of critical teaching and of the politics of evolution, rather than of exclusion, of authoritarian teaching and belief in fixed standards and a fixed social order.

Since Matthew Arnold, English writers on liberal education have been obsessed by the 'sweetness and light' ideology. In so far as ideas on liberal education have informed the development of the comprehensive secondary school curriculum, they have been derived from educational philosophers such as Hirst who have worked in this tradition. For Hirst, the content of a liberal curriculum is fixed and is understood in terms of the application of disciplinary frames of knowledge to objective data: 'A liberal education in the pursuit of knowledge is . . . seeking the development of the mind according to what is quite external to it, the structure and pattern of reality.'[38] Belief in a fixed external reality fits well with notions of standards, of testable knowledge, of selection and qualification. There is little room for doubt, criticism or evolution, except within well defined limits. It also fits well with a division of the world into 'the men who know and the men who don't know' which, as Norwood said, was a 'distinction which Plato drew long ago'.[39] Democracy then becomes a matter of the individual being

> prepared to accept the view of the expert, in
> matters which he does not know, and cannot

know, and to give the view of an expert,
impartially and according to truth, in matters
where he has the knowledge, and is called upon to
impart it.[40]

Here knowledge, defined in some objective sense, is the criterion
of the right to participate and possession of knowledge a function
of educational status.

Another view of liberal education would hold that
knowledge is never so certain or enduring as this prescription
makes out and would emphasize the need for widespread possession
of the arts needed for contributing to deliberation on uncertain
questions of public policy. It would uphold the position of the
Harvard Committee Report on General Education which Hirst
criticized for basing its conclusions more upon appeals to desirable
qualities of mind than to fundamental forms of knowledge, and for
ignoring 'the belief that in metaphysics man has knowledge of
ultimate reality'.[41] It would look to those very qualities of mind
as an insurance against the failures of leadership and government
which Jefferson saw as inevitable, and would see the linkage
between educational categories and future status in terms of
opportunities for and responsibility in the exercise of wise
citizenship, rather than in the creation of the moral or technical
aristocracies which perform the function of 'virtual representation'
in a Burkean conception of democracy.[42] To this end, such a
conception of liberal education would be prepared to tolerate
imperfections - to find room in the world of education for Sancho
Panza as well as Don Quixote; to this end it would foster
educational institutions which were not neat and tidy, but allowed
for flexibility and ambiguity. The American High School plays its
part in the creation of elites but, as Ringer suggests, its
'amorphous structure disguises realities of stratification'.[43] The
disguise is not simply a matter of concealment; organizations
which are less visibly structured tend to promote higher levels of
student participation. And visible structuring is, of course, closely

related to the existence of central control over curriculum through public examinations: 'centralized systems tend to have tighter controls over instruction and learning, and probably obtain less participation and total learning.'[44] This is the complaint of the authors of **Mathematics Counts.**

Ultimately, the choices we make about sixth form education are choices about what form we would like democracy to take. Should it be one which leaves effective power in the hands of an elite marked off from the rest of society by a curriculum based on principles of exclusion? Or should it be one which sets a high value on the incorporation of as many of the population as possible into shared conceptions of democratic citizenship? Whenever in the past decisions have had to be made about the reform of education, these have tended, in England, to take the form of decisions about control and availability and not reappraisals of the style and function of the curriculum. Especially, this was true of the extension of grant-aided secondary education after the 1902 Act and of the setting up of systems of comprehensive education in the 1960s and 1970s. Now, decisions about sixteen-to-nineteen education are being taken in a similar manner. The academic A-level curriculum is being preserved, and parallel forms are being created alongside it, in the shape of lower grade academic courses, vocational training programmes and work experience schemes to offer low status education to those seen as 'less able'. 'Real success' is still to be the preserve of the few. The 'sixth' is to be protected rather than adapted. The focus is still to be on the notion of immutable 'standards'. We are not making an argument that there should be no differentiation of curricula or of institution; that all should be treated exactly alike. What we are suggesting is that, when policies for sixteen-to-nineteen education are discussed, we should be clear that the issues are not simply 'educational'. Any resolution of the tension between a press to design education from the top down or an aspiration to plan from the bottom up has clear political implications. We consider that the time is long overdue when such resolutions should be made in favour of incorporation rather than exclusion and when we should weigh the success of our policies in terms of the learning and the commitment of the majority rather than the academic advancement of the few. To do this, we have to create curricular structures which are less clearly differentiated, to make nationally monitored standards less of a priority and allow institutions more freedom to determine, for their own localities, what the appropriate standards of achievement should be. Such new conceptions, built around the still potent image of the sixth form, would enable us to offer to students educational experiences in tune with the ideals of an open, democratic society, without sacrificing our commitment to the ideals of a liberal education or abandoning traditions which have given meaning to the educational experiences of many generations of sixth formers.

NOTES

1   Naylor, Fred, **Crisis in the Sixth Form**, London, Centre for Policy Studies, 1981, title page.

2   **Report** of H.M. Commissioners appointed to inquire into the Revenues and Management of Certain Colleges and Schools, etc., 3 vols., 1864, Vol.2, p.281.

3   Norwood, Cyril and Hope, Arthur H. (Eds), **The Higher Education of Boys in England**, London, John Murray, 1909, p.302.

4   See, for example, Naylor, 1981 **op. cit.**

5   Norwood, Cyril, **The English Tradition of Education**, London, John Murray, 1929, p.65. The idea is Platonic. See Popper, K.R., **The Open Society and its Enemies**, 2 vols., London, Routledge, 4th. Edn., 1962, Vol. 1, Note 22,

p.268.

6   Popper, 1962 **op. cit.,** p.7.

7   Norwood, 1929 **op. cit.,** p.90.

8   Naylor, 1981 **op. cit.,** p.17.

9   The title of chapter 15 in Norwood, 1929 **op. cit.**

10   **Ibid.,** pp.227-8.

11   Naylor, 1981 **op. cit.,** p.35.

12   Fears of state intervention dated from at least as early as the setting up of the Taunton Commission. The Headmasters Conference was founded in response to this in 1869. By the turn of the century, some independent school heads thought that the passing of an act allowing the use of public money to support secondary education would lead to the extinction of their schools.

13   Many, though not all direct grant schools maintained the curriculum and organization of the public schools. Since direct grant status ceased, a large number have become independent.

14   Mulock D.M., (Mrs. Craik), **John Halifax, Gentleman,** London, Dent, Everyman's Library, 1906, p.302. As a symbol of the openness of the gentleman class, John Halifax's status is doubtful. He was an orphan, but had a bible which belonged to his father inscribed 'Guy Halifax, Gentleman'.

15   Behind movements such as the Scouts and the Church Lads Brigade lay a millenarian belief that all levels of society could unite behind the cult of the gentleman. See Girouard, Mark, **The Return to Camelot: Chivalry and the English Gentleman,** New Haven, Yale University Press, 1981, Ch.16.

16   Naylor, 1981 **op. cit.,** p.18.

17   **Ibid.,** p.23.

18   'If successful tripartite systems . . . had been allowed to develop, . . . the crisis we are now facing could have been

avoided' (**Ibid.,** p.9). The shocking results of the break at sixteen are illustrated by reference to the American senior high school (**Ibid.,** p.19.). This ignores the fact that almost a quarter of US high schools combine junior and senior grades. The number of students experiencing the break is not, in fact, very different from that produced by a 'tripartite' system (National Center for Education Statistics, **Digest of Education Statistics** 1980, US Government Printing Office, Washington, D.C., p.62).

19   **Ibid.,** pp.29-35.

20   Heeney, Brian, **Mission to the Middle Classes: The Woodard Schools, 1848-1891,** London, SPCK, 1969, p.127.

21   Norwood, 1929 **op. cit.,** pp. 310-11.

22   Davies, Harry, **Culture and the Grammar School,** London, Routledge, 1965, p.14.

23   Norwood, 1929 **op. cit.,** pp.111-12.

24   **Ibid.,** p.6.

25   **Ibid.,** pp.6-7.

26   **Daily Telegraph,** December 8, 1981.

27   **Daily Telegraph,** February 27, 1982.

28   'A great Oxford teacher . . . some few years ago concluded (his) . . . address . . . with a wish and a prayer, conceived in the spirit of Moses' aspiration that all the Lord's people should be prophets. It was that . . . all English citizens . . . should be gentlemen.' (**Report** of a Conference on Secondary Education in England convened by the Vice-Chancellor of the University of Oxford, Oct. 10 and 11, 1893, Oxford, Clarendon Press, p.81.)

29   Meyer, John W., 'Levels of the educational system and schooling effects' in Bidwell, C.E. and Windham, D.M. (Eds), **The Analysis of Educational Productivity,** Vol.2, **Issues in Macroanalysis,** Cambridge, Mass., Ballinger, 1980, p.52.

30   **Ibid.,** p.55.

31   For an account of the pressures exerted on the sixth form curriculum by university demands, see Reid, W.A., **The Universities and the Sixth Form Curriculum,** Basingstoke, Macmillan, 1972.

32   Norwood, 1929 **op. cit.,** p.330.

33   Popper, 1962 **op. cit.,** Vol.1, p.134.

34   **Ibid.,** pp.134-5.

35   Report of the Committee of Inquiry into the Teaching of Mathematics in Schools under the Chairmanship of Dr. W.H. Cockroft, **Mathematics Counts,** London, HMSO, 1982, p.133.

36   Kitson Clark, G., **The Making of Victorian England,** London, Methuen, 1962, p.266.

37   See Meyer, 1980 **op. cit.,** pp.30 and 39.

38   Hirst, P.H., 'Liberal education and the nature of knowledge' in Archambault, R.D. (Ed), **Philosophical Analysis and Education,** London, Routledge, 1965, p.116.

39   Norwood, 1929 **op. cit.,** p.90.

40   **Ibid.,** p.276.

41   Hirst, 1965 **op. cit.,** p.117.

42   For a further discussion, see Reid, William A., 'Democracy, perfectability, and the battle of the books', **Curriculum Inquiry,** 10, 3, 1980, pp. 249-263, and compare Popper, 1962 **op. cit.,** Vol.1, chapter 10.

43   Ringer, Fritz K., **Education and Society in Modern Europe,** Bloomington, Indiana University Press, 1979, p.258.

44   Meyer, 1980 **op. cit.,** p.52.

STATISTICAL APPENDIX

Growth of Sixth Forms

'Sixth form' as a category appears in Ministry of Education/DES annual statistical reports only between 1957 and 1969. Both before and after that date, students enrolments are reported by age and not by status. Inferences have to be made about how many students at various ages might have been in sixth forms. Complications arise not just from the fact that some older students might have been in other forms, but also from the practice of some schools, especially Direct Grant Schools, of 'accelerating' students into the sixth form at age fourteen or fifteen. In the early years after the introduction of the 1904 Regulations the relevant figure is that for students in 'forms above those taking the approved course', which is certainly close to the definition of 'sixth form'. Some central statistics report figures for independent as well as maintained schools, but most do not and, to arrive at a total for sixth form enrolments, an adjustment has to be made. Around 1904, the independent schools would have contributed about fifty per cent of sixth form numbers. By the mid-fifties this had declined to around twenty per cent and the figure is now nearer ten per cent though the independent sector still accounts for over twenty per cent of sixth formers taking three or more A-levels.[1]

Before 1904 no regular statistics were published and estimates of enrolments have to be made from reports such as Clarendon, Taunton and Bryce. These give figures for individual schools or areas from which it is possible to derive national statistics, though not with a high degree of accuracy.

Figure Four shows a graph based on the available sources illustrating the pattern of growth in sixth forms over the 100 year period from 1870 to 1970. It uses absolute numbers and takes no account of the varying size of age cohorts. There is no dramatic

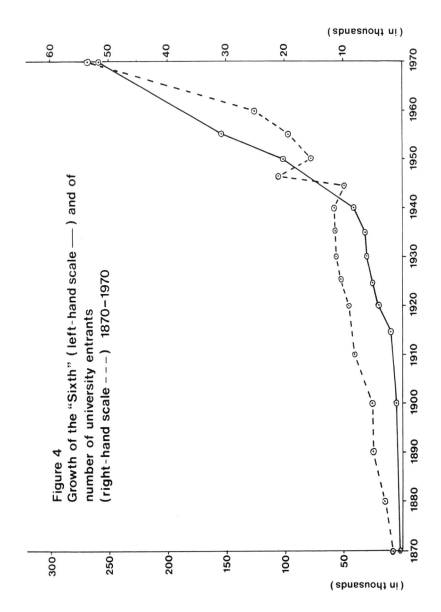

Figure 4
Growth of the "Sixth" (left-hand scale ——) and of
number of university entrants
(right-hand scale – – –) 1870–1970

(in thousands)

(in thousands)

rise in enrolments after the 1902 Act because, initially, most of the maintained secondary schools were existing establishments which changed their status. Growth after the First World War levelled off in the 1930s but that associated with the Second continued to the end of the 1960s. Had the graph been extended, the 1970s would have appeared as another period of slow growth.

Growth of the Universities

Membership in the sixth form has popularly been associated with entry to the universities, and Figure Four also plots figures for this. Again no account is taken of age cohort size. Recent statistics on university entrance are available in published reports of the University Grants Committee. As in the case of sixth forms, statistics for years prior to the collection of national data have to be obtained by combining those for individual insitutions. This has been done for the period 1861 to 1931 by Roy Lowe, and Figure Four draws upon his work.[2]

The Clarendon figures for 1861 indicate that about one leaver in three from the 'nine' entered a university. It is difficult to evaluate what this meant for sixth forms, since it was not uncommon at the time for public school boys to proceed to a university without entering the sixth. Between 1870 and 1890, due largely to the arrival of the 'red brick' universities, higher education expanded faster than sixth forms, and the correlation between sixth form and university became particularly strong. Between the wars these trends were reversed, and it would seem that through the 1930s sixth form leavers from maintained schools were more likely to enter employment than higher education. Public schools, however, continued to maintain a close connection with the universities and to provide more than half their entrants. In the post-war period expansion of the universities, though rapid, failed to restore the balance which had existed in the 1890-1914 era. Claims of a close relationship between membership in sixth forms and university entrance are true only if they refer to

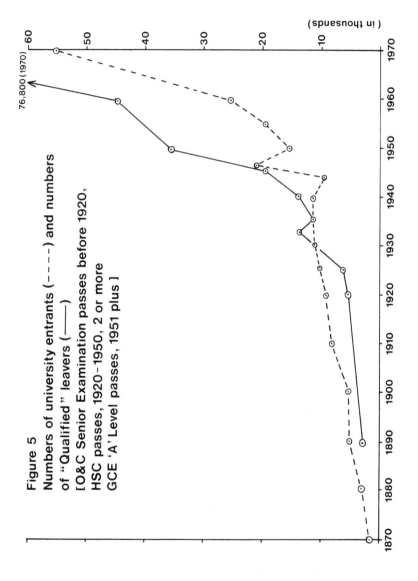

Figure 5
Numbers of university entrants (– – – –) and numbers
of "Qualified" leavers (———)
[O&C Senior Examination passes before 1920,
HSC passes, 1920–1950, 2 or more
GCE 'A' Level passes, 1951 plus]

(in thousands)

76,800 (1970)

254

independent schools. It is not clear that such a relationship has ever existed in the maintained sector. It should be noted that, even today, the independent schools provide around fifty per cent of entrants to Oxford and Cambridge.[3]

Examination Passes

Figure Five plots numbers of university entrants against numbers of leavers 'qualified' in terms of public examination results. Qualification, in the English system of entry to universities, does not imply right to a place. On the other hand, before the Second War actual entry requirements were both flexible and highly variable. Universities often conducted their own entry tests. Hence, we find that, until 1930, the number of university entrants exceeded that of the group conventionally defined as 'qualified'. In other words, the period of correlation between membership in the sixth and entry to a university was also one when few hurdles were placed in the way of applicants. Since 1930, the number of 'qualified' applicants has risen in step with the growth in sixth forms and has stayed ahead of the available places. By 1960 the 'qualified' exceeded the entrants by over sixty per cent. In 1970, expansion of the universities had reduced to about forty-five per cent.

Involvement of the total population in sixth form education

So far the question of sixth form enrolment has been dealt with in terms of absolute numbers. Such a perspective leaves an impression of steady expansion with periods of very rapid growth, especially between 1950 and 1970. When we consider the figures in terms of percentage enrolment in the age cohort a very different picture emerges, as is shown in Figure Six. Here the statistic used is the percentage of the seventeen year-old age cohort in full-time education. This is highly correlated with the growth of sixth forms over the period in question, and enables a direct comparison to be made with data for the American High School.[4]

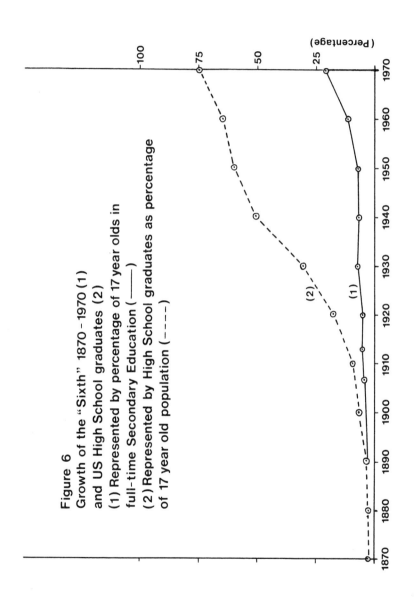

Figure 6
Growth of the "Sixth" 1870 - 1970 (1)
and US High School graduates (2)
(1) Represented by percentage of 17 year olds in
full-time Secondary Education (———)
(2) Represented by High School graduates as percentage
of 17 year old population (– – – –)

The High School and the sixth form were both, until the 1890s engaged essentially in college preparatory work. In the early 1900s the curriculum of the high school was reformed and it began to attract a wider section of the population. Over the period 1920-1940 when there was slow growth in sixth forms the high school more than doubled its enrolment of seventeen year-olds, and by 1950 it was the norm for them to be in school. High school graduation of seventeen year-olds reached seventy-five per cent in 1970, at which point it has levelled off. At that time the corresponding enrolment in England was just under twenty per cent.

NOTES

1   This statistic is given in Rae, John, **The Public School Revolution: Britain's Independent Schools, 1964-1979,** London, Faber and Faber, 1981, p.17.

2   Lowe, Roy, 'The expansion of higher education in England' in Jarausch, K.H. (Ed.), **The Transformation of Higher Learning 1860-1930,** Stuttgart, Klett-Cotta, 1982.

3   Rae, **loc. cit.**

4   Data given in Dreeben, R., 'American schooling: patterns and processes of stability and change', in Barber, B. and Inkeles, A. (Eds.), **Stability and Social Change,** Boston, Little Brown, 1971, Table 1.

NAME INDEX

Hughes, Thomas, 23, 40, 41, 42, 43, 46.
Husen, T., 175.
Hutchins, Robert M., 7, 14.

Inkeles, Alex, 14, 118, 257.

Jarausch, K.H., 257.
Jefferson, Thomas, 6, 14, 245.
Jencks, Christopher, 15.
Joseph, Keith, 211, 212-213, 225.

Kalton, G., 200.
Kellner, Peter, 224.
King, Ronald, 203, 205-206, 221, 222.
King, R. Wearing, 180-184, 187, 188, 191, 197, 198, 199.
Kingsley, Charles, 148.
Kinnock, Neil, 212.
Kipling, Rudyard, 43, 81, 86, 105.
Kitson Clark G., 64, 83, 85, 86, 250.
Kogan, Maurice, 218, 224.

Lacey, Colin, 107, 117.
Lee, James Prince, 59, 75, 85, 129, 147.
Lowe, Roy, 103, 105, 158, 253, 257.

Macfarlane, Neil, 208, 211.
Mack, E.C., 78.
Maine, Henry, 47.
Mangan, J.A., 15, 85, 86.
Meyer, John, W., 10, 11, 15, 239, 249, 250.
Meyer, Marshall W., 15.
Mill, J.S., 47-48, 54-55, 56, 64.
Morant, Robert, 91-92, 95, 103, 109, 127.
Morris, Max, 134.

Mulock, D.M., 248.
Musgrove, Frank, 29, 43.

Naylor, Fred, 199, 212, 223, 247, 248.
Newbolt, Henry, 156.
Newsome, David, 20, 39, 40, 53, 65, 66, 85, 86, 105, 135.
Norwood, Cyril, 94-101, 103, 104, 116, 117, 119, 122, 123,
       127-128, 131, 134, 149, 151, 156, 159, 193, 197, 200,
       201, 212, 217, 224, 227, 229, 232, 236, 240, 244-245,
       247, 248, 249, 250.

Orwell, George, 38, 42, 43, 49, 65, 86, 116, 160.
Orwell, Sonia, 65, 86.

Passeron, J-C., 15.
Pattison, Mark, 76, 201.
Peterson, A.D.C., 41, 155, 174.
Pickering, George, 175.
Plato, 31, 96, 97, 105, 230, 241, 244, 247.
Pollock, B., 129.
Popper, K.R., 241, 247, 248, 250.
Pugin, A.W.N., 60.

Rae, John, 257.
Reader, W.J., 86.
Reid, W.A., 174, 175, 197, 198, 199, 200, 221, 250.
Renan, Ernest, 29, 42, 129.
Richards, Frank, 79, 82, 86.
Ringer, Fritz K., 9, 14, 245, 250.

Schon, Donald A., 45, 46, 64.
Seaborne, Malcolm, 15, 39, 65, 103, 105, 158.
Shannon, Richard, 65.
Skrine, J.H., 156.

Smith, H. Llewellyn, 68, 85, 86.

Smith, M., 86.

Smith, Peter, 64.

Spencer, Herbert, 29, 42.

Stanley, A.P., 19, 40, 42, 66.

Stevens, Francis, 159, 160, 174.

Summerfield, Geoffrey, 64.

Swift, Jonathan, 30-31.

Talmon, J.L., 64.

Tawney, R.H., 118.

Taylor, P.H., 155, 174, 197, 201.

Temple, Frederick, 76.

Thring, Edward, 24, 41, 76.

Tocqueville, Alexis de, 29, 42.

Tonnies, F., 205.

Turner, R.H., 199.

Vachell, H.A., 81, 134.

Wankowski, J.A., 155.

Wellington, Duke of, 57.

Whitmarsh, G., 118.

Willis, Paul, 82, 86.

Wilson, Harold, 237.

Windham, D.M., 15, 249.

Woodard, Nathaniel, 58-59, 63, 66, 67, 91, 236.

Worsley, T.C., 27, 41, 75, 76, 83, 85, 86, 116, 134, 140, 154, 197-198.

Young, Michael, 160, 174, 238.

Eton College, 13, 22, 52, 53, 60, 61.

Examinations, Public, 3, 72-73, 83, 102, 112, 122, 142, 163,
       180, 188, 191, 199, 204, 239, 242, 246;
       for army, 25, 72, 112;
       for civil service, 25, 72, 112, 232.

Exeter Tertiary College, 188.

Faculty Theory of Education, 93, 110.

France, 9, 150;
       Revolution of **1789**, 18, 29, 45.

Further Education, see Colleges of Further Education.

Games, 3, 14, 15, 20, 38, 73-74, 76-77, 96, 97, 102, 116,
       232, 238.

Gem, 38, 79.

Gemeinschaft, 205-206, 215, 216, 219, 235.

General Certificate of Education (GCE), 131, 132, 163;
       A-level, 131, 146, 153-154, 163, 165, 168, 173, 178, 188,
       189, 200, 202, 251;
       O-level, 131, 132, 133, 163, 173, 178, 179, 202.

General Studies Association, 160-161.

Gentlemen/Gentry, 12, 13, 17, 21, 22, 24, 26-27, 35, 61, 64,
       83, 226, 231, 233, 236, 238, 248, 249.

Germany, 9, 150.

Gesellschaft, 205-206.

Girls, as sixth formers, 89, 102, 112, 113, 116, 153-154,
       155, 181, 221.

Governing Bodies, 53, 93-95, 104.

Greek (as school subject), 24, 75, 101, 217;
       as part of sixth form curriculum, 4, 184.

Haileybury, 102.

Halifax, John 233-234.

Harrow (School), 13, 22, 61, 70, 74, 94, 122.

Harvard Report, see Reports.

Headmasters, 52, 59-60, 62-63, 75-76, 82, 84, 91, 93-94, 95-96, 217, 229, 232;

    power of, 23, 95, 130, 147, 229;

    relationship to sixth form, 3, 22-23, 151.

Headteachers, 104, 114, 125, 141-142, 178, 182, 196.

High Schools (in USA), 102, 118, 170, 220, 245, 249, 255-257.

The Hill, 81.

History (as school subject), 55, 93;

    in sixth form curriculum, 4, 62, 112, 146, 154.

Ideologies, 183, 186, 192, 236;

    of chivalry, 51, 153;

    of comprehensive education, 173, 177;

    ethnocentric, 116;

    of grammar school, 125, 127, 141, 142, 237, 239, 240;

    of intellectual discipleship, 230-231;

    of political parties, 214, 215, 220, 225;

    of public schools in 19th. century, 94, 112, 123, 125, 129, 134;

    of sixth form, 179, 182, 193, 195, 200, 203, 226, 227, 229, 231;

    of sweetness and light, 145, 169, 217, 227, 241.

Independent Work (See also Private Study), 146, 147, 151, 189.

India (See also Civil Service), 72, 81, 82, 236-237.

Industrial Revolution, 18, 26, 45.

Institutional Categories, 8, 11, 17, 59, 132, 170, 225, 239, 243;

    definition of, 10;

    public school as category, 17, 39, 51, 59, 78, 109, 215;

    sixth form as category, 11, 14, 22, 39, 51, 101, 126, 169, 173, 215, 226, 227, 231.

International Baccalaureate, 167.

Labour (Socialist) Party, 121, 212, 220, 225;
>Report on Secondary Education (**1922**), 107-110, 115, 118, 125.

Latin (as school subject), 24, 69, 93, 123, 133, 184, 217;
>in sixth form curriculum, 4, 154.

Leadership, 21, 34, 36, 187, 227, 229, 230, 245.

Liberal Education, 7, 55, 95, 113, 116, 123, 150, 243, 244-245, 247.

Local Education Authorities (see also Birmingham, Croydon, London, Manchester), 89, 92, 93, 94, 96, 104, 127, 163, 164, 170, 177, 203, 209, 223-224.

London, growth of in 19th. century, 45;
>school board, 68, 92;

>survey of secondary education in (**1890**), 69-70;

>university, see Universities.

Luton Sixth Form College, 184.

Magazines for Boys, 78-80, 102.

Magnet, 38, 79, 80, 82.

Manchester, local education authority, 209, 211, 213, 214, 221, 223;
>school board, 68;

>university, see Universities.

Manliness, 76, 86, 97, 102.

Marlborough College, 57, 62, 66, 79, 94.

Mathematics, (as school subject), 28, 175;
>Cockroft Report on (**1982**), 241-242, 246;

>in sixth form curriculum, 4, 62.

Merchant Taylors', 13.

Mexborough Sixth Form College, 184.

Middle Class, 12-14, 17, 26-27, 29, 31, 33, 34, 45, 47-49, 51, 53, 54, 56, 58-59, 62, 63, 66, 68-69, 70, 71, 84, 91, 113, 115, 129, 137-138, 154, 214, 223, 229, 236.

Mimetic Theory of Learning, 22, 147, 151, 230-231.

Stalky, 82, 98.

Stalky and Co., 81, 82.

Standards, 31, 72, 148, 170, 217, 229, 238, 240, 241, 244,
246, 247.

Subject-Mindedness (See also Specialization), 146, 151, 153,
155, 189, 217.

Sweetness and Light (See also Ideology), 30-31, 32, 35, 49,
55, 96, 127, 129, 140, 145, 153, 229, 235, 244.

Taunton Commission, 13, 28, 29, 103, 248;
scheme for the reorganization of secondary education, 58,
67-68.

Teachers, 19, 48, 73, 84, 114, 124, 125, 142, 182, 183, 190,
191, 192, 196, 201, 203, 207, 212, 230, 231.

Teaching Methods (See also Faculty Theory of Education, Mimetic
Theory of Learning), 61, 70, 71, 147, 155-156, 165,
167, 187, 189, 243, 244.

Tom Brown's Schooldays (See also Brown, Tom), 23, 77,
78-79.

Tripartite System of Secondary Education, 121, 212, 235, 241,
248-249.

Unemployment, 202, 207, 215, 219, 238.

Uniform, 20, 38, 74, 103, 186, 187, 230;
worn for games, 74.

United States of America (See also High Schools), 5, 9, 11,
14, 29-30, 46, 81, 129, 142, 150, 193, 237, 240;
Revolution of 1776, 18, 45.

Universities Central Council on Admissions (UCCA), 166, 168, 171.

Universities, 30, 84, 101, 108, 111, 112, 145-147, 165-172,
189, 195, 200, 215-216, 217, 219, 232, 238, 240, 250;
Birmingham, 112, 200;
Cambridge, 48, 62, 72, 112, 166, 169, 200, 201, 217, 218,
224, 228, 255;